SO YOU WANT TO GO BACK TO SCHOOL

Facing the Realities of Reentry

SO YOU WANT TO GO BACK TO SCHOOL

Facing the Realities of Reentry

Elinor Lenz
University Extension
University of California, Los Angeles

Marjorie Hansen Shaevitz
University Extension
University of California, San Diego

McGraw-Hill Book Company

New York St. Louis San Francisco Auckland Bogotá Düsseldorf
Johannesburg London Madrid Mexico Montreal New Delhi Panama
Paris São Paulo Singapore Sydney Tokyo Toronto

Photographic Credits

University of California, San Diego	facing page 1
Herb Taylor/EPA Newsphoto	p. 26
University of California, San Diego	p. 52
University of California, San Diego	p. 78
Eugene Luttenberg	p. 110
James Ruebsamen/Evening Outlook	p. 130
University of California, San Diego	p. 152
University of California, San Diego	p. 170
Al Green Studio	p. 196
University of California, San Diego	p. 214

SO YOU WANT TO GO BACK TO SCHOOL
Facing the Realities of Reentry

Copyright © 1977 by McGraw-Hill, Inc. All rights reserved.
Printed in the United States of America. No part of this publication
may be reproduced, stored in a retrieval system, or transmitted, in any
form or by any means, electronic, mechanical, photocopying, recording, or
otherwise, without the prior written permission of the publisher.

1234567890 DODO 783210987

This book was set in Times Roman by Monotype Composition Company, Inc.
The editors were Robert G. Manley and Phyllis T. Dulan; the designer was
Joseph Gillians; the production supervisor was Robert C. Pedersen.
The drawings were done by J & R Services, Inc.
R. R. Donnelley & Sons Company was printer and binder.

Library of Congress Cataloging in Publication Data

Lenz, Elinor.
  So you want to go back to school.

  Includes index.
  1. College student orientation—Handbooks, manuals, etc. 2. Continuing education—United States. I. Shaevitz, Marjorie Hansen, joint author. II. Title.
LB2343.3.L46   378.1'98   77-2877
ISBN 0-07-037178-4

Contents

Acknowledgments   vii

Introduction   ix

Chapter
1 Why Are You Returning to School?   1
2 What Can You Expect?   27
3 The School of Your Choice   53
4 Getting Past the Gatekeepers   79
5 Resources to Help You along the Way   111
6 Myths about Maturity   131
7 New and Former Relationships   153
8 How to Study and Make the Grades   171
9 Avoiding the Traps and Traumas   197
10 Making It Happen   215

Appendix
A Financing Your College Education   223
B College Terminology   231
C Regional Associations and Professional Agencies   238

Index   243

Acknowledgments

Because so many people have contributed to this book, it would take another book to do justice to their generosity, their enthusiasm for this project, and their willingness to share their thoughts and experiences. Our colleagues at University of California, Los Angeles Extension and University of California, San Diego Extension, particularly Martin N. Chamberlain, deserve a special vote of thanks for their support and for providing insights, information, and other valuable resources.

Acknowledgments are due to: the Rand Corporation for Figure 2 from their report, *An Evaluation of Policy Related Research on Programs for Mid-Life Career Redirection, Vol. II—Major Findings,* by A. H. Pascal, et al.; the Public Information Office, University Extension, University of California, San Diego, for many of the photographs that appear in this book; Educational Testing Service, *About the SAT,* College Entrance Examination Board, New York; CLEP General and Subject Examinations; College Entrance Examination Board, New York; Volume 7, Number 7, *Change* Magazine, NBW Tower, New Rochelle, New York; *Daedalus,* Journal of the American Academy of Arts and Sciences, Boston, Mass., Spring 1976, *Adulthood;* University of Chicago Press, *The Awareness of Middle Age,* by Bernice Neugarten.

Our thanks also to Susan Orlofsky for her editorial assistance and to Debbie Wilson and Sydney Andrews for typing.

Our appreciation to the above and our gratitude to those stalwart supporters who stood by throughout it all, offering aid, comfort, and valuable criticism—our husbands, Leo Lenz and Morton Shaevitz.

Elinor Lenz
Marjorie Hansen Shaevitz

Introduction

It is time that we had uncommon schools, that we did not leave off our education when we begin to be men and women. Thoreau, Walden.

Once upon a time, education was a clearly marked territory with recognizable boundaries and identifiable inhabitants known as "students." You entered at a certain age, and you left at a certain age, your passage from start to finish took anywhere from twelve to sixteen years, depending on whether your destination was a high school diploma or an A.B. degree. (If you wanted to travel further to a professional degree, you tacked on another three or four years.)

As you moved from level to level, you were always in the company of your peers. It was a land of eternal youth, except for teachers and administrators, a world sealed off from anyone much past the age of twenty-two. And when you reached the terminus, a fixed point called "graduation," you were handed a piece of paper called a "diploma," which was, in effect, your exit visa. Your schooling was now complete, and you were finished with education forever.

That's the way it was, not very long ago. But something has been happening in recent years, something that is changing our ideas, not only about education, but also about the needs, aspirations, and potential of people past the first flush of youth. We are beginning to realize that education is too valuable and pleasurable to be cornered by one segment of the population or confined to one brief period in an individual life. The idea of education as a lockstep progression with a fixed upper limit is giving way to such concepts as "continuing education," "lifelong learning," and the "learning society." There is a growing realization that education is a continuing process, as dynamic and ongoing as life itself. To learn is to grow and to be fully human.

And there is even more to it than that. We live in a highly developed technological society which places special demands and pressures upon its members. Change occurs with such rapidity that a year ago may seem as remote as the last century. Social movements—black power, civil rights, women's liberation—sweep over us like tidal waves, leaving their mark on our consciousness as well as on our laws and institutions. It is not only future shock but also present disorientation that afflicts us. When familiar values, institutions, and technologies are constantly being revised or replaced, it becomes a problem to feel at home in one's world. Obsolescence, personal and technological, is the twentieth-century Sword of Damocles, the threat that hangs over all of us.

But if change carries a threat, it also offers a promise and a challenge. And it is this promise and this challenge that are bringing so many people back to school who thought they had left their education behind them forever. They are coming back in ever-increasing numbers—to four-year colleges and universities, community colleges, extension divisions, and adult schools, wherever they can find courses and programs to meet their needs. They are studying part time, full time, in the evening, during the day, by correspondence, through newspapers, and by means of radio and television. A leading adult educator, Cyril Houle, sees adult and part-time students as the "new majority." In higher education, the percentage of adult students, those beyond the usual eighteen- to twenty-two-year age range, is the fastest-growing segment, making up 48 percent of the total enrollment. In the State University of New York, 35,000 students out of the 400,000 enrolled are over the age of thirty-five; almost three-quarters of them are women.

That there are more women than men in the new majority is a natural outgrowth of changing attitudes toward sex roles and the emerging social and economic realities of our time. The search for new opportunities, new careers, and new sources of intellectual stimulation has propelled women toward college campuses to pick up their education where they left off at the time of their marriage. Many of these women, now divorced or widowed with children to support or with husbands nearing retirement, are motivated by sheer economic necessity.

Similar motivations are bringing a steadily increasing number of men back to school as they discover that it is possible—and, at times, a matter of survival—to change life styles in midstream. In fact, what we are witnessing may be one of the most important developments in the history of modern education. And it is a movement which is gaining momentum around the world. In a recent meeting held in Stockholm, the education minister of twenty-one European countries endorsed an extensive program for international cooperation to promote "lifelong learning opportunities."

The return of adult students to educational institutions designed for the young will certainly have a profound and far-reaching impact upon these institutions. Margaret Mead has said that we are entering a new era, in which the traditional educational process will be reversed: Instead of the younger generation learning from their elders, the older generation will learn from the young. Mead calls this "prefigurative learning" and regards it as an inevitable development in a society which has broken continuity with the past and cannot form a coherent image of the future.

But as adults reenter the educational system, it is very likely that the teacher-learner relationship will come into balance. Education is a social process, and as the generations mingle and interact, the various age groups will be able to learn from one another. Among the fringe benefits, we can expect a narrowing of generation gaps and a weakening of age stereotypes.

This book, then, is dedicated to all of you who are planning to go back to school and would like it to be a rich and rewarding experience. The chapters that follow are designed to acquaint you with the realities and equip you with the information you need for a successful educational reentry. With some preparation and a clear sense of what awaits you, returning to school can be one of the most exhilarating adventures of your life.

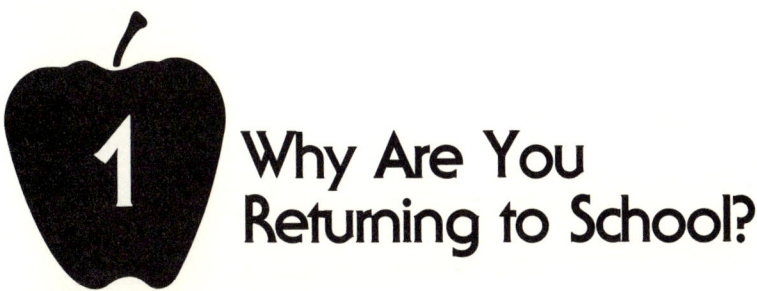

Why Are You Returning to School?

I really feel that all people at all times should have access to educational opportunities. Men, women, young people, old people, and anyone else who wishes to learn or make a commitment to want to learn should have the opportunity. All modes of communication should be used, and all segments of life and living problems should be offered. Iowa housewife.

The Returning Student: A Group Portrait

You've been thinking about it for several weeks or several years, or it just popped into your head the day before yesterday. "Why not?" you ask yourself. "Why shouldn't I do it?" Suddenly, it all seems so clear, so absolutely right. Your memory takes you through a series of flashbacks: There you are walking across a college campus, a book or two tucked under your arm, on your way to a class. And there you are again—in class, totally absorbed, as the professor brilliantly dissects the nineteenth-century novel or takes you through the intricacies of intermediate calculus. Click: You are now in a seminar, engaged in lively intellectual jousting with the professor and the other students.

Those were the days when your mind was being stretched in all directions and there were no limits to your plans and prospects. Your view of the future included not only a college education but also graduate school; or you might go on to professional training—law, medicine, engineering, architecture. Time would tell. Somewhere at the end of this preparation time, the real world would begin; you would move into a job or profession that would be both personally fulfilling and financially rewarding. Along the way, there would be marriage and a family.

And then certain things happened. You dropped out of college, probably in your freshman year (the highest dropout rate, 40 percent, occurs among freshmen) for reasons that made perfectly good sense at the time. There was a chance for a job, which meant that you could buy your own car and become financially independent without waiting all those years till graduation. Or maybe you weren't really ready for college after all. It was tougher than you'd thought; you hadn't yet developed the necessary self-discipline, and there were too many pressures and no visible support systems. Besides, you could always go back someday.

Or—if you are a woman—you may have left because you and your boyfriend decided to marry and you would need a job to cover expenses while he continued his education. According to the conventional wisdom of the time, it was *his* career that mattered; he would provide the financial base for your future together. And, of course, you could always go back someday.

There are any number of variations on this basic theme. Maybe you went on to graduation, grabbed your baccalaureate degree, and ran—toward that beckoning world with all of its tempting options and opportunities beyond the halls of ivy. You had such great expectations. You were sure your education would last forever, an investment guaranteeing lifetime dividends. And yet you realize now that much of what you studied and stashed away in your memory bank not only is irrelevant in today's world but also has been discredited by subsequent research.

Anyway, here you are, with a job and a family or both—or neither—and a gnawing sense of restlessness and dissatisfaction with the way things have been going for you. You feel as though life is passing you by, leaving you with not very much to show for the accumulated years. A phrase that keeps recurring in your thoughts is "If only...." "If only I had a college degree...." "If only I'd gone to law school...." "If only I'd taken a teaching credential or learned how to program computers...." "If only I were working at something I care about...."

At this point in your thinking, you begin to wonder: Why not? Why not go back to school and this time make it really count? After all, you're older and wiser now, and you know what you want. Why not make this the beginning of a new and different life? And then you ask yourself: Can I do it? Have I got what it takes? Is it realistic to suppose that, at my age, after being away from school for so many years, I can study and cram for exams and compete with people who are five, ten, twenty, or more years younger than I am?

But the question is not: Can you do it? We know the answer to that, if only because so many others in a similar situation have been and are doing it. The question is: How will you do it? How will you go about making your reentry into the educational system a successful one? As one woman who returned to college at the age of forty-five expressed it: "I was determined not to be a middle-aged dropout, but there were times when I came very close."

So this time you are going to profit by your previous school experience and by all the information available to ensure that your return will be an investment that really pays off. But before you decide to join the 7 million people over the age of twenty-five who are in college now (a figure expected to jump to 11 million by 1980), let's have a look at what's behind this burgeoning back-to-school trend. What sort of people are reentering the educational system?[1] From a recent study, we can put together a group portrait of these "returnees" which looks like this: Almost half are between the ages of thirty-one and fifty. Men make up 41 percent, and women 58 percent. Twenty-three percent are single, 63 percent are married, and the rest are separated, widowed, or divorced. Most have a family income ranging from $9,000 to $25,000. Fifty percent completed college, 20 percent have M.A. degrees, and the rest have some high school background, a high school diploma, or one to three years of college. Apparently, there is no such thing as a "typical" returnee; people going back to school come from all age and income groups and from an assortment of backgrounds.

As a group, they differ in several respects from younger students. A survey conducted by the Educational Testing Service comparing community college students in the eighteen- to twenty-one-year and twenty-two- to twenty-nine-year age ranges with those over thirty revealed that older students are less likely to experience academic problems. (Only one in six students over thirty reported academic difficulty, compared with one in three in the eighteen- to twenty-one-year-old group.) Older students have more clearly defined goals than younger students. Other data from the survey indicate that older students tend to find their courses more satisfying and to spend more time studying and preparing.[2]

As for their educational interests, adults want to study, in order of preference:[3]

1 Vocational skills—architecture, business administration, computer science, education, law, salesmanship

2 Hobbies and recreation—crafts, fine arts, travel

3   Home and family life—child development, home repair, cooking

4   Personal development—the occult, personal psychology, physical fitness, public speaking, investments

5   General education—public affairs, religion, agriculture and farming

PSYCHOLOGICAL REASONS FOR RETURNING
The Midlife Identity Crisis

The motivations of returning adults are as varied as their interests, but generally they fall under two headings: psychological and economic, with, in many cases, considerable overlap between the two. The psychological area has been strengthened during the past decade by a growing appreciation of human potential. Reacting against the mounting bureaucratization and impersonalization of society, encounter movements and various forms of "groupism" have attempted to put people in touch with one another and with their own buried selves. Followers of Abraham Maslow, a psychologist at Brandeis and a leader of the humanistic psychology movement, promulgated his concept of "self-actualization," which refers to the highest level of growth that an individual is capable of achieving.

Psychological motivations are especially potent among women who are reaching their forties and seeing their children leave home; the realization that in serving their families they have been denying their own needs and interests has produced a sense of lost identity, of the need to recover control over the direction of their lives. A questionnaire given to a group of women applying for reentry to a college in New York asked them to state their reasons for returning to school. Their answers suggest the psychological needs of women in the "middle-motherhood" or "post-motherhood" period, when the demands upon their time and energy are sharply reduced.

The women queried said such things as: "I wanted to grow up and find my own identity." "I need constructive interests outside the home." "I desire self-fulfilment." "I'm feeling stagnant and want a meaningful career." "I need to find myself as a person."[4]

A woman who returned to college in her mid-fifties describes her experience as follows:

> My decision to return to school after fifty coincided with my youngest child's departure for college. This brought me smack up against that critical time: the postmotherhood phase. I had watched any number of women like myself during the fifties and sixties—healthy, energetic, devoted to home and family —come aground on this rocky shoal. We were pre-women's lib vintage; as we tended to the needs of our growing families, we were unaware that our

husbands, nursing ulcers in their advertising or stockbroking offices, were oppressing us.

We had dutifully attended PTA meetings, collected money for the Red Cross, and baked cookies for church suppers. We had cooked, nursed, comforted, pleaded, cajoled, and coped. Now suddenly we were drifting aimlessly. Our husbands, at the peak of their careers, were absorbed by concerns beyond the range of our interests and experience. Our children, who had been the center and purpose of our lives, were moving off into worlds of their own which was strange and baffling to us. What were we supposed to do? The options seemed awfully limited: golf, bridge, endless orgies of redecorating the house, or wallowing in boredom and self-pity. I took another route—to the admissions office of the nearest university.

Another woman nearing forty whose husband's work took him away from home for long periods of time and whose youngest son had just graduated from high school recalls her "moment of truth," when she decided to do something about what she felt was the increasing emptiness and pointlessness of her daily existence. "Just to get myself up in the morning, I'd promise to do one constructive thing. One day it boiled down to painting the domino set and then I knew I'd had it." The family had saved enough money to send the younger son to college, but when he refused to go, "I thought: why force him to go when I have the motivation? Spend the money on me, I told my husband, who was thunderstruck...."[5]

Although at first glance the two cases cited above seem very similar, closer inspection reveals significant differences which are highly instructive. The first woman, in looking at her options, saw a series of activities that would ordinarily have filled her leisure time—golf, bridge, redecorating the house. These time-fillers she saw as time-killers, and she knew they would bring her little satisfaction. "When I married, I thought that was it," she says. "I enjoyed being a housewife and loved taking care of the children. I never looked ahead or worried about what I would do with myself." But motherhood turned out to be a temporary job, and marriage a domestic arrangement rather than a career. But: "I don't think I want a career. I don't really know what I want to do. I just want to do something on my own, achieve something all by myself. I just don't want to go on feeling like a nonperson." Returning to school provided her with an alternative to boredom, a way of using her leisure time which she hoped would be fulfilling and constructive. With no specific career goal in mind, she chose a liberal arts college and a broad humanities curriculum with a major in English literature.

For our second woman, there were additional factors entering into her back-to-school decision. "My parents sent my two brothers to college but felt it would be a waste of money for me since I, of course, would marry and raise a family. They couldn't imagine any other life for me.

They used to say the only degree I needed was an M.R.S." But her first marriage ended in divorce, and she soon discovered that, with only a high school education, she wasn't qualified for anything except factory work or routine clerical jobs—"and I hated both." But there were other kinds of work she did enjoy: "building and designing things from cabinets to clothes—throwing away my mistakes as I went along." Deciding to study architecture, she enrolled at a community college.

In both cases, the motivating question was: Who am I? However, for the second woman, that question was closely intertwined with: What do I do? In a society like ours, in which one's occupation is a principal element in determining personal identity, it is not surprising that many women feel that the domestic role reduces them to nonpersonhood. Lacking the tangible rewards that are present in other forms of endeavor—grades, honors, promotions, salary raises—"occupation housewife" fails to provide the sense of personal identity that a growing number of women are seeking.

But it is not only women who are experiencing a midlife identity crisis. The number of men past the age of thirty-five who are returning to school testifies to the fact that this is a trend affecting both sexes. For men, midlife change usually means a switch in careers, but there are also retirees who are seeking ways to use their newfound leisure. Many men who return to college are escaping from jobs that they see as dead ends. "I sympathize with women who feel trapped at home," one of these returnees commented, "but how about men who are trapped in stifling and frustrating jobs?"

In some of these cases, women have gone into the job market in order to give their husbands a chance to explore alternatives through a return to college. "It's hard to put in words why a person goes to college at this stage of his life," said a forty-year-old father of four who was pursuing a bachelor's degree while his wife and he worked at part-time jobs. "It's not that I was bored; I was looking for new challenges."

The Need to Know

Another compelling psychological reason for returning to school is the rapid change and growing complexity of contemporary life, which produce a sense of dislocation, both personal and professional. The postwar knowledge explosion, together with the rise of mass communication and computer technology, has altered the world beyond recognition for those whose school years are a decade or more behind them. In the professions, retraining has become a matter of professional survival. In state after state, laws are being passed requiring doctors, lawyers, engineers, pharmacists, dentists, and others to retrain in their professions. It has long been accepted practice for teachers to continue their studies in order to advance in their careers.

But the need to upgrade one's information and knowledge is equally pressing in the course of everyday living. The media bombard us with messages urging us to do this, buy that, support our candidate, make our vote count. There is hardly a question or issue—health care, education, transportation—that does not demand our attention since almost all such issues affect our lives in fundamental and far-reaching ways. To be an effective citizen today requires not only a knowledge of the workings of government and politics but also some understanding of waste management, the use of open lands, school financing, urban planning, and energy utilization.

For many returnees, this need to keep up, to know what's going on, is a strong enough reason for returning to school. "I found myself going stale" is a comment that turns up again and again in surveys of returning students. "It was becoming difficult for me to carry on a conversation with my husband or my college-age children," said a forty-year-old woman who was starting her freshman year as a political science major. "For years, I hadn't read anything but newspaper headlines or written anything but grocery lists. My family is interested in politics, but most of their discussions are way over my head."

This fear of being out of touch, though common to both sexes, appears more frequently among women who, like the one quoted above, have been involved exclusively in domestic concerns since leaving school. Running a house and raising a family can become all-consuming, shutting out other interests. Also, recent trends in family life—suburban living; the decline of the extended family with its ready supply of baby-sitting relatives; and the intense concentration on child development together with the lack of adequate child care facilities—have accentuated women's isolation and dependency. Returning to school reflects a need to supplement family ties and interests with other kinds of associations based on personal interests.

But the need to know goes beyond such specific goals. It is a primary human need and one which cannot be defined in terms of age, sex, background, or personal ambition. Cyril Houle has identified a group of adult students whom he characterizes as "learning-oriented"—those who possess the "inquiring mind" and, agreeing with Socrates that the unexamined life is not worth living, seek knowledge for its own sake. These people are usually avid readers and have been from childhood; they join groups and organizations for the educational benefits to be derived from membership. They select the more thoughtful programs on television and radio, and whether they are choosing jobs or planning vacations, they are influenced by the potential for expanding their intellectual horizons. For the learning-oriented, education is a constant activity, an integral part of their lives; in returning to school, they are pursuing in a structured and disciplined way what they have been doing all along to gratify their appetite for knowledge.

As an example of a learning-oriented person, Houle cites a thirty-eight-year-old father of four who is a skilled laborer in an automobile assembly plant. "I started using the library early. Had to roller-skate twenty blocks there and back.... I'd read at night. I'd have the book under my bed. I was raised right behind the elevated tracks. Sometimes the screech of the trains would wake me up. I'd read until I couldn't fight off sleep any more. Then I'd wake up at dawn and reach under the bed and get the book and read again. I always went everywhere with a book, always, my whole life."[6]

Given the stimulus and nourishment it requires and is always seeking, the inquiring mind can continue to be active and productive throughout a long lifetime. Going back to school is one way to provide the necessary stimulus and nourishment.

Searching for the Past

There is a group of returning students who are engaged in a quest for what Marcel Proust called *temps perdu,* or "lost time." Some of them never went to college and feel that they lost out on an important aspect of their growth. They have a sense of deprivation, a feeling that they have not had a "normal" youth. Others went to college for a year or two or even graduated, but feel that, for one reason or another, it wasn't a satisfying experience. A forty-nine-year-old widow who is now attending graduate school at a Midwestern university and living in campus housing says:

> I went to college in New York City, and I had a good education, I can't deny that. But I was living at home and traveling to school on the subway, and there wasn't any campus life or even a campus for that matter, and I had to work nights and Saturdays for spending money.
>
> I remember hating every minute of it and taking the maximum number of credits so that I could graduate sooner and put it all behind me ... forever, I thought. I don't know why I stuck it out, except that my mother had this thing about all of us being college graduates, and every time one of us threatened to quit, she'd become hysterical. Why have I come back at this time of my life? I guess I'm trying to recover something, the experience of going to college without time or money pressures and living on a campus and being part of a college community.

This desire to be part of a community is another motivating force in the back-to-school movement that grows out of a basic human need. The need to belong is as universal and profound as the need to know. Human beings are social animals, as Aristotle noted in his *Politics,* and contemporary life does not ordinarily offer much in the way of satisfying social ties, particularly in large urban areas, and for people who have grown up in small towns. College counselors are coming across a significant number of returnees who find in a college setting—and even more so in a large university, with its cultural amenities and self-contained environment—a community to which they can attach themselves. The university's ability to provide a core and establish social and cultural interconnections extends beyond its walls. "The campus becomes a center for cultural life; it has a ready-made audience in its students and faculty and it has the physical facilities. Persons attracted by the performing and the visual arts and the lectures come to live around the campus. . . . As the downtown area in some cities decays, the campus takes its place as the cultural center of the community."[7]

Interestingly, this aspect of higher education has also been responsible for the emergence of a new group of "permanent" or "professional" students who, by extending their doctoral and postdoctoral work and eking out their financial support through grants and teaching assistantships, are able to stay on indefinitely in the university "community."

There are also those midlife returnees who are caught up in a kind of nostalgia for their lost youth. Returning to school is for them a way of shedding the years. They find the company of the young bracing, and in the ambience of a youth culture they feel as though they can experience once again the sensation of living through the springtime years. For these people, the college campus offers a pathway back to the past rather than forward to the future.

THE ECONOMIC IMPETUS
Seeking the Golden Key

Psychological motivations, such as those we've been discussing, are potent enough to account for a sizable number of the people who return to school in their middle and later years. But there is also an increasing number of returnees who are motivated principally by the bread-and-butter need to improve their financial situation.

Among these are recently divorced women, particularly those with growing children to support. Present-day alimony arrangements are intended to provide women with the opportunity to become employable; divorced women today cannot always expect to receive alimony indefinitely, and in many cases, even while it lasts, it is not enough to cover the needs of a growing family. So the divorced woman is a prime candidate for training that will equip her within a reasonable time for gainful employment.

Economic pressures are providing a similar motivating force for older people, even those beyond the customary retirement age. Inflation has wrought havoc with many an individual's retirement plans; as a result, organizations such as the American Association of Retired Persons (AARP) have been working on projects to help their members become employable. There are social crystal-ball gazers who have begun predicting that older people will have to work, for one thing, because the level of social security benefits will not increase and probably at some point will have to be cut back.

According to these soothsayers, the demography of our population over the next fifteen to twenty years, with a continuing decline in the birthrate and an extension of the average life span, will mean that fewer young people will be supporting more and more nonworking elderly. Since such a situation, so goes this line of analysis, would soon become intolerable, older people will have to return to the job market. "They will be encouraged to work. There is no question, too, that restrictions on earnings by recipients of social security will be lifted. They will have to be lifted; the economic system simply cannot permit them to go on."[8]

Blacks, Hispanic people, and other minorities who have been returning to school in ever-growing numbers are also looking to education as a means of social and economic betterment. Having been denied educational opportunities for so long, they are counting on higher learning to provide an economic lever that will lift them into the mainstream of American life. For these and others whose overriding motivation for returning to school is economic, the essential question is: Can education improve my earning ability?

LEARNING EQUALS EARNING . . . OR DOES IT?

The direct relationship between education and earning ability has been an article of faith in America ever since the industrialization of the country. With the signing of the Morrill Act by Lincoln in 1862, higher education was no longer to be the exclusive preserve of an elite class; instead, colleges and universities were to open the doors of opportunity to all "qualified comers."

Nevertheless, until the first half of this century, the qualified comers represented a small percentage of the population; during that time, education provided the most reliable route to higher earnings and improved occupational status, and the American higher educational system supplied society with most of its skilled specialists and white-collar workers. In the 1950s and 1960s, the job market for college graduates reached its peak. The insatiable demand for college graduates and the rewards that were attached to a college degree attracted a growing number of young people to colleges and universities and encouraged them to extend their education to graduate school and professional training. The GI Bill brought an influx of veterans. It was the time of higher education's greatest expansion, a golden age that seemed destined to go on forever.

But by the early 1970s, the market for college graduates went into a sharp decline, and for the first time in history the relative earnings of the college-educated dropped drastically, as you can see in Figure 1 on page 12. From 1969 to 1975, according to a study of male graduates' real starting salaries, made by the College Placement Council, those with social science or humanities degrees experienced a decrease of 23 percent; for mathematics majors the decrease was 20 percent, and for beginning electrical engineers with doctorates it was 17 percent. Since comparable declines in real rates of pay have not been experienced by other jobholders, some experts are suggesting that this situation represents a sharp break with the past and forecasts emerging economic realities.[9]

The federal government's response to this trend has been to encourage career or vocational education in order to draw students away from academic courses toward the acquisition of specific job skills. The decline in liberal arts enrollments and the upsurge in vocational training would seem to indicate that the government's campaign has had some success. But a look at the evidence raises some doubts and questions. A survey prepared for the National Institute of Education, one of the federal agencies which have been backing the career-education approach, yields the following data:

> Eight out of every ten graduates of professional- and technical-level postsecondary vocational programs did not get the jobs they trained for.
>
> Eight out of ten graduates of lower-level vocational programs got the jobs they trained for; however, with the exception of secretaries, they barely earned the federal minimum wage of $1.90 per hour.
>
> Women who trained for accounting jobs all became clerical workers instead and earned 23 percent less than men in the same job classification. Women who trained to become computer programmers also wound up as clerical workers and earned 16 percent less than men in the same job classifications.[10]

A major finding of the survey was that students who train for jobs at vocational schools, whether public or private, stand a poorer chance of getting jobs than graduates of four-year colleges and universities. And they earn less money. For example, graduates of public or private vocational schools were paid starting salaries of $131 per week as accountants, while graduates of four-year colleges in the same year were paid $204 to perform the same work. The director of the study, Welford Wilms, of the University of California at Berkeley, calls this "educational inflation": People

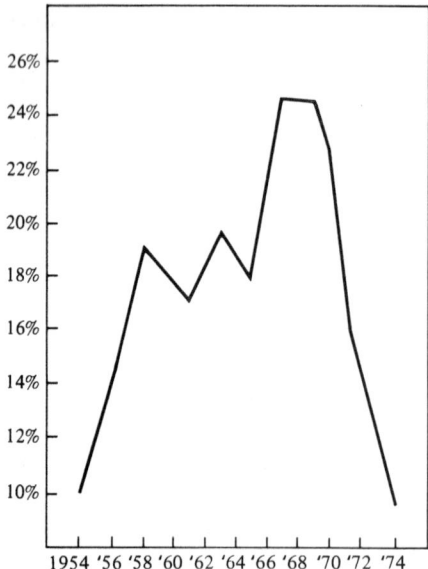

Figure 1 Starting salary advantages over average wage and salary earnings. (From Change magazine.)

need more formal schooling simply to maintain their relative social and economic position. Or, as the Red Queen says in *Through the Looking Glass,* "Now, here, you see, it takes all the running you can do, to keep in the same place. If you want to get somewhere else, you must run at least twice as fast as that!"

What does all this mean to those of you who are returning to school primarily for economic reasons? What are the facts about the relationship between learning and earning? Does a college degree "pay off" in financial terms?

From a look at the current employment picture, it is apparent that the college degree, while no longer the golden key to high-status, high-paying careers, is still an important credential for a wide range of occupations. Despite the decline in real starting salaries noted earlier, present estimates are that, over a working lifetime, the college graduate will earn 30 to 50 percent more than the high school graduate. Further, the training in disciplined thinking that a college education affords, aside from its personal benefits, is invaluable in any number of jobs and professions.

If you are returning to school for the purpose of expanding your career potential, be sure that your career objective is on target. You are, after all, preparing to invest a considerable amount of time, energy, and money at a stage of your life when you cannot afford to misdirect your efforts. It's all very well to make a false start (or even two or three) while you're still in your twenties—that's the time for shopping around, trying this, discarding that—but how about a woman in her forties who puts five precious years into acquiring a teaching credential only to discover that teaching jobs have dried up?

Unfortunately, there are no guarantees against wrong choices at any age. But there are ways to minimize the possibility of error and to enhance the prospects for goal achievement. You can start by having an encounter session—with yourself. Examine your career motivation carefully, subjecting it to the same kind of penetrating analysis it would receive from a career counselor. (The "Career Analysis Worksheet" at the end of this chapter can help you do this.) Now you can begin to analyze your job objective from the standpoint of how well it reflects your interests, aptitudes, skills, and life style.

Here you have an advantage over the younger student preparing for college. Having acquired some self-knowledge in the course of your life experience, you are less likely to be led astray by wishful fantasizing. You will probably not automatically assume, for example, that the compliments you received on your speech in behalf of a candidate for your local school board assure you of a brilliant career in politics or that your penchant for photography, backed up by several albums of superb color shots of your tour through Europe, guarantees success as a commercial photographer. By now you have accumulated enough practical wisdom to ensure yourself against such snares and delusions.

The Midlife Career Change

Also, you probably have a firmer notion now of what your priorities are than you had during your first incarnation as a student. An altered set of priorities often accounts for that phenomenon which is becoming more visible all the time—the midlife career change.

A successful company president whose work required constant traveling decided to quit and train for a new occupation even though his top-management job represented the fulfillment of his early ambitions. His reason? "I decided that my job was not all there is to life. When you're in management, your day never really ends. And traveling so much meant I was losing touch with my wife and children. I found that what I wanted most of all was to be part of a family again." At present, he is studying for a career in urban planning, "something that will give me a chance to work with people and make some sort of contribution that can be measured in other ways than with the dollar."

Adults who, like this former top-level executive, return to school in midlife for the purpose of changing careers are responding to a strong current in the American consciousness which carries with it the conviction that life is open-ended and can always be started anew. The early settlers, the pioneers pushing back the frontier, and the immigrants fleeing poverty and persecution never doubted that they could wipe out the past and build a new life for themselves in the virgin land. Since this country had never had a rigid class system, it was assumed that Americans could move easily from one life style to another. The dream of upward mobility has always been as American as apple pie.

But the dream has not always matched the reality. For a substantial portion of the population, mobility of any kind has been unattainable as a result of poverty, traditional sex roles, race prejudice, or inadequate education. During the upheavals of the sixties, these barriers to a freer and fuller life came under heavy attack, as youth, blacks, women, and others began to protest conditions which they believed were denying them their stake in the American dream.

One result of these developments has been an increase in the number of people who are willing to break loose from their moorings and make changes in midlife or even later. As a trend, it has become sufficiently significant to attract the attention of social scientists, psychologists, and educators. From their studies and observations, we find that people who make midlife changes are usually motivated by deeply felt needs and resentments which are the natural outgrowth of several forces: an increasing dissatisfaction with the rigid, authoritarian work situations in which many people find themselves; growing disillusionment with the highly competitive, "rat-race" occupations which have become synonymous with success; a resentment toward the publicly subsidized educational benefits which have so long been a prerogative of the young; and a developing sense that education and work have become too isolated from each other.

A study of midlife career change revealed a pattern of redirection. (See Figure 2 on page 15.) The starting point is some kind of current work or occupation, either a paying job or unpaid work in the home or in volunteer agencies. Something happens to precipitate the shift in a new direction. The housewife's children leave home, and she finds herself with no outlet for her energies and talents. The miner or aerospace engineer loses his job. An office worker gradually becomes so dissatisfied with the work situation that he or she decides to do something about it. Personal tensions develop between supervisor and employee. These are fairly straightforward instances of cause and effect. However, a midlife identity crisis may symptomatize "a more drastic and traumatic kind of decision, often impelled by divorce, widowhood, psychological change, illness and the like."[11]

Social scientists who have been studying midlife career change, view it as a natural by-product of affluence, reflecting the ability of technically advanced societies to release people from the lockstep of traditional job preparation and the lock-in of lifetime employment which is unsatisfying. Why, they ask, should people be frozen into occupations which they have outgrown or which have never offered personal rewards? A midlife career

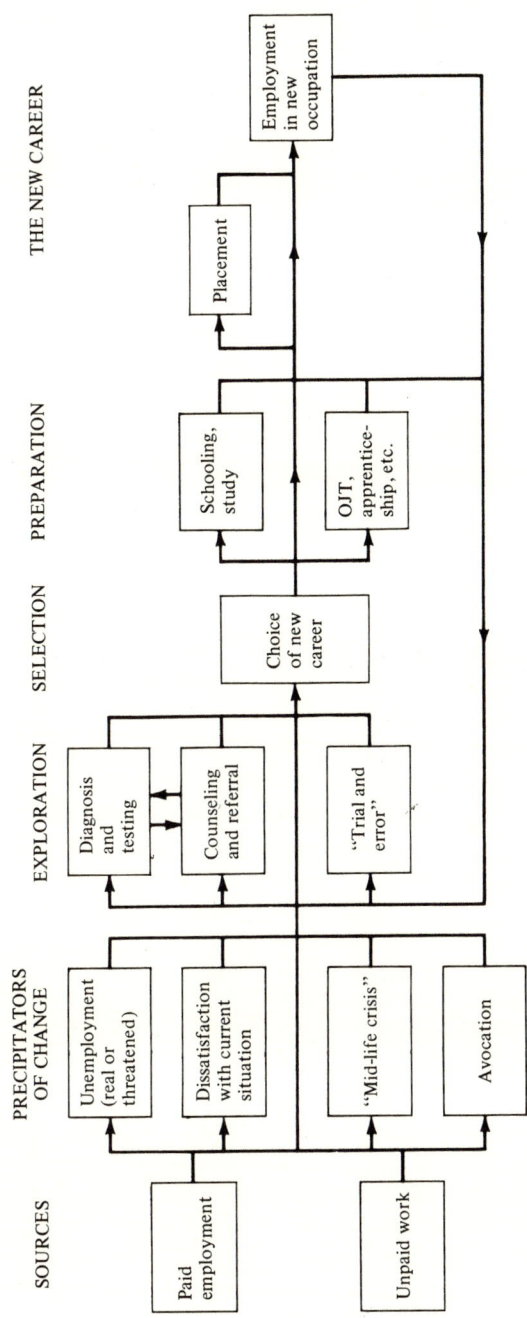

Figure 2 The process of midlife career redirection

WHY ARE YOU RETURNING TO SCHOOL? 15

change is further justified, say the proponents, by the fact that people tend to choose their occupations for limited or capricious reasons—to be influenced by the jobs held by parents and friends, the formal and informal training opportunities in the community, or the job opportunities available at the time, for example. Forces outside the individual's conscious control often seem to be the determining factors in the choice of a lifework. Choosing a second, or even a third, career in maturity offers a means of bringing one's occupational choice in line with personal growth and aspirations.

The social benefits of midlife change, proponents argue, include a vision of a more flexible, adaptive society in which the individual would allocate his or her time among several life phases. To support this trend, it has been proposed that policies be adopted which would encourage:

Paid educational sabbaticals and leaves of absence

The restructuring of educational opportunities in favor of adults, with the necessary financial rearrangements

More flexible career patterns, especially with regard to apprenticeship and part-time work

Your Career Analysis

As you think about the job objective that is sending you back to school, pay particular attention to your listing of Values in the "Career Analysis Worksheet." Does the job you are planning to train for conform with these priorities? Do you know enough about the job to make such a judgment? If you have any doubts, consult a career counselor, search out people who are doing this kind of work, and write for information to the relevant trade or professional association (see the listings in Appendix A). The time spent in research at this stage of your planning will save you from expensive trial and error later on. Once you have a clear idea of the sort of demands your chosen career will make upon your life, you can move toward a decision that has a better chance of holding up in the years ahead.

Also ask yourself whether this career choice reflects your true, tested, innermost drives and interests. Are you responding to external cues, to forces beyond your conscious control, like those suggested above—those family and social pressures which can be so persuasive but which have no relation to you as an individual? Are you rejecting an otherwise attractive option because, depending on your gender, you believe it's "no job for a woman" or "not the right sort of job for a man"? If you were in school during the fifties and sixties, it was no doubt difficult for you to avoid being influenced by this type of stereotypical thinking. If you are a woman, you were probably subjected to cultural conditioning at school and at home that might have induced in you what Radcliffe's President Matina Horner characterized as the feminine "fear of success." Studies of women university students during the late fifties and early sixties showed how this manifested itself: Most of those who had chosen the sciences during their freshman year later switched to what they regarded as more "feminine" fields: nursing, social work, teaching, and home economics. The career motivation of girls has consistently shown a sharp decline beginning in high school.

If you are a man, you were also under pressure to choose a lifework that was appropriately "masculine." If, for example, you had been interested in interior decorating, elementary school teaching, dancing, or writing poetry, wouldn't fear of ridicule have kept you from pursuing such an interest?

Once again, your maturity is in your favor. Since you are now in better touch with yourself, you are less likely to be deflected from your true course by arbitrary sex-role concepts. And the temper of the times, with its more sophisticated sexual attitudes and affirmative action employment policies, reinforces your greater freedom of career choice.

Combating the Ogre of Obsolescence

Once you've made your choice, how can you have any assurance that, when your training is completed, you will find the kind of employment for which you are now preparing? The fact is that in a society as dynamic as ours, choosing a career always involves a calculated risk. Even such professions as teaching and engineering, once considered surefire employment bets, have turned out to be highly susceptible to the vagaries of social change.

Although trying to outguess the future is chancy business, a sharp look at current trends and prognoses should provide you with some guidelines. Occupations that are at present rated "excellent" to "reasonably good" include accountant, actuary, programmer, systems analyst, dentist, dental hygienist, occupational therapist, optometrist, pharmacist, physician, veterinarian, military serviceman or servicewoman, music therapist, social worker, technical writer, and paraprofessional, especially in law and medicine.

Those with a "fair" to "grim" rating include journalist, photographer, advertising copywriter, city manager, lawyer, market researcher, librarian, teacher, mathematician, anthropologist, political scientist, and interior designer.[12]

That your chosen line of work is not among the high scorers does not mean that you should promptly abandon your career objective. If your choice is in accord with the four fundamental criteria—interests, aptitude, skills, and life style that are your very own—your most sensible course is to go ahead and plan to be among the best and the brightest in the field. Even in employment areas of diminishing returns, there is usually room for people with outstanding ability and training.

At the same time, consider a fail-safe tactic, which might be described as the "backup career plan." It works like this: If you have decided on a science or engineering major, you would also take as many language courses as you could fit into your schedule, with the idea of qualifying, if necessary, as a translator of scientific materials. Alternatively, you might select some writing courses with an eye toward the field of technical writing. Or suppose your heart is set on teaching high school mathematics. You would take as many accounting courses as possible so that, in a pinch, you could move into the expanding field of accountancy. The following table shows how this might work in regard to some currently popular occupational choices.

TABLE OF RELATED OCCUPATIONS

If Your Job Choice Is:	Your Related Occupation Might Be:
Mathematics teacher	Accountant Banking executive Actuary
Advertising copywriter	Editor Public relations executive Technical writer
Laboratory technician	Medical supplies salesperson Editor of science books
Librarian	Publisher's representative Researcher
Economist	Financial analyst Mortgage and loan director
Elementary school teacher	Day care center director Children's TV production assistant
Travel agent	Traffic control director Shipping executive
Lawyer	Labor arbitraitor Insurance underwriter

But, you may wonder, is it possible to develop marketable skills in more than one field? Suppose your interests and abilities are concentrated in one specific area—in other words, you're a natural-born specialist. In that case, you will probably concentrate your studies on your specialty and count on offsetting the greater risks by the higher degree of expertise, dedication and training you will bring to your work.

In the normal order of things, however, the natural-born specialist is relatively rare. There may be an individual here and there whose genetic code is such that he or she was destined from the moment of birth to be a bond investment manager or a chemical construction projects administrator, and nothing else. But most men and women are a composite of many talents and abilities, some of which, like unused muscle tissue, atrophy through disuse. A backup career plan is a useful ploy for avoiding a too narrow channeling of your abilities and, at the same time, providing job insurance over the long range.

The Prime Time of Your Life

Before you are completely satisfied that your career objective is on the track, two other questions should enter into your appraisal: What kind of educational background does it call for? How much time can you invest in educational preparation? An interview with a counselor at the school you plan to attend will help you estimate the time necessary to achieve your goal.

Depending upon your career choice, you may be required to invest anywhere from two years at a community college to seven years or more of full-time study if your ultimate goal is a Ph.D. or a professional degree in a field such as medicine, law, or architecture. If you're planning to study part time while working or caring for your family, the time span will be extended according to the number of courses you are able to carry. (Some graduate programs and professional schools do not admit part-time students; better check into this and factor it into your calculations.)

As a student, you will find yourself measuring time in large blocks—either semesters, which run for twenty-six weeks, or thirteen-week trimesters (in some institutions these are called "quarters"), depending upon the system being followed at the school of your choice. Within these large time divisions, "units" or "credits" will mark off the amount of time you spend in lectures, seminars, laboratory studies, and other academic exercises. (A unit or credit represents one semester hour per week or two-thirds of an hour on the trimester plan.)

Since it is these measurements, rather than calendar time, which determine how long it will take you to reach your goal, you have some flexibility in designing your course of study. Most educational institutions impose minimum and maximum limitations on the number of course units you can carry in a semester or trimester, but within these limits you can juggle your time to suit your own purposes. A summer session can speed up your schedule, and subsequent chapters will discuss several shortcuts and time-savers that can also be of help.

A cautionary note: Keep at least one alternative handy in case future unplanned-for developments in your life make it impossible for you to stick to your original schedule. For example, let's suppose that you have always wanted to be a lawyer; you were sidetracked years ago, but now you're in a position to go back and pick up where you left off. You have enough college credits to qualify for entrance as a junior; this means that you must spend two years earning your B.A. and three years earning your J.D., after which you must pass the bar examinations to be admitted to practice.

But along the way, your situation changes, and you find you no longer have the necessary resources of time and money to reach your objective. A sensible goal switch would lead you to a paralegal certificate, which would cut at least 2½ years from your schedule. While working as a paralegal, you can consider going on to law school when the circumstances are more favorable, studying part time in the evenings.

For people resuming their education in midlife, time is a critical dimension. This is your prime time, and you want to use it to your fullest advantage. A clear understanding of your reasons for returning is your first line of defense against the misuse of your time. Until you have sorted out your motivations and know exactly why you are returning to school, you are not adequately equipped either to choose the educational institution that's right for you or to decide what you will be doing there once you're enrolled.

If you're eager to get started on your reeducation but still are not sure what you want to do or be when you "grow up," you can always gain some time by delaying your choice of major—in most four-year institutions, you are not required to "declare a major" until your junior year. This gives you a chance to shop around while fulfilling the breadth or enrichment requirements—that is, those courses which, in addition to your major field, are required for a degree. But somewhere along the way, even if you are not career-oriented, it will become necessary to settle on a goal or direction to guide you in selecting your courses. From here on, the responsibility for your education will be your own, as you design and shape your studies to your individual needs. Recognizing those needs is the first, and most important, step on the path toward a successful reentry.

CAREER ANALYSIS WORKSHEET

By what future time is it necessary or desirable for you to decide on a career goal? (two weeks? two months? six months? one year?) *2 months*

Educational Background
1   What is the last educational grade you finished or degree you earned? (Indicate name of school, date, approximate grade average, and major.)

12th grade   Moon Senior High School

2   What other courses or training have you taken since you last went to school?

all infantry related training courses.

3   Which courses did you enjoy the most? Which did you enjoy the least?

airborne school
armorer's school

Work and Volunteer Background
1   What are your current work or volunteer commitments? (Indicate name of employer and job titles.)

— carpentry work —
(Gorso Construction)

2   What other job or volunteer experiences have you had (beginning with most recent)? (Indicate employer and job titles.)

Carpentry work (Gorso, Pa.)
Laborer work (Cifers, Tenn.)

WHY ARE YOU RETURNING TO SCHOOL? **21**

3 Which of the above did you like the most? Why? *The laborer work / you did a full days work and got respect*
4 Which of the above did you like the least? Why? *The carpentry work would be alright but I'll be gopher for too glong*

PERSONALITY Describe your personality. (For example, are you conscientious, irresponsible, cheerful, moody, etc.?)
1 sensitive
2 cheerful
3 ambitious
4 impulsive
5 ignorant of many things
6 mild and meek
7 at times downright
8 ready to tell the
9 would were to go
10 wide range of swear words

SKILLS and ABILITIES What can you do now? What could you do if you had some additional education or training?
1 I can do anything
2 I want to do !!!
3
4 dig a pretty good
5 ditch !!
6 Work well with kids
7 can make any man laugh
8 it comes natural !!!
9
10 Think I have talent has a writer

INTERESTS What interests you? "What turns you on"?
1 I love to write !!!
2 people
3 travel
4 variety
5 baseball
6 Tennis
7 Sports
8 Liberal arts
9 music
10 night life

VALUES What are your basic values? What or who is important to you?
1 my family
2 a sense of worth
3 respect for others
4 live and let live
5 order
6 staying relaxed
7 brothers and sisters
8 my pride
9 those who need my help
10 God

DESCRIBE THE KINDS OF ENVIRONMENTS YOU WOULD FEEL GOOD WORKING IN (indoors–outdoors; large office–small office; education–business; modern–old; organized–chaotic; few people–many people, etc.).
1 outdoors
2 Sports arenas
3 nightclubs
4 small office
5 traveling in
6 car to different areas
7 The city
8 The beach
9 up in the mountains
10
11
12 I like healthy environment !

22 SO YOU WANT TO GO BACK TO SCHOOL

DESCRIBE THE KINDS OF PEOPLE YOU WOULD LIKE TO WORK WITH (very old–middle-aged–young; individuals–groups; sick–well; educated–not so well educated; poor–rich; men–women; adults–children; supervisees–supervisors, etc.).

1. people full of life
2. concerned caring people
3.
4. academic
5. crazy people
6.
7. basically doing my own
8. thing [with] a critique
9.
10. of finished product!
11.
12.

DESCRIBE THE COMPONENT PARTS OF AN IDEAL JOB (environment, people, type of work, time, pay).

1. salary for finished work!
2.
3. my own time
4. exciting environment
5.
6. photography — free lance
7. writing for a newspaper
8.
9. on the spot reporting
10. involved in profession
11. sports.
12.

WHAT DO YOU DO BEST (work with children, work in the home, job duties, volunteer activities, hobbies, sports)?

1. baseball
2. tennis
3. most sports
4.
5. getting along with people
6. eat
7. working with children
8. discussions
9. arguing with the
10. people who are assholes!

WHAT JOBS OR CAREER FIELDS ARE RELATED to your strengths? Sports & organizing

Samples:
  Gardening—nurseries, teaching, plant care
  Cooking—private catering, restaurants, teaching cooking
  (Sports)—coaching, lessons, recreational therapy
  (Organizing)—administrative work, research, executive assistant

WHAT ISSUES, PEOPLE, OR PROBLEMS ARE KEEPING YOU FROM DOING WHAT YOU WANT TO DO NOW?

1 *money*
2 *getting an education*
3 *need wheels — automobile*
4 *need to get on track*
5 *bad habit of procrastination*
6 *getting up the nerve!*
7 *not dead set on any one thing*
8 *→ But I am almost there*

REFERENCES

1 We are referring to regularly matriculated students, working toward a degree either full time or part time. Students are classified as enrolled in college full time if they are taking twelve hours of classes or more during an average school week, and part time if they are taking fewer hours.

2 *Findings,* vol. 2, no. 1, 1975, Educational Testing Service, Princeton, N.J.

3 Carnegie Commission on Nontraditional Study, 1973.

4 Judith Berman Brandenburg, "The Needs of Women Returning to School," *Personnel and Guidance Journal,* September 1974.

5 "Recycling Lives," *Ms.* magazine, August 1973.

6 Cyril Houle, *The Inquiring Mind,* The University of Wisconsin Press, Madison, 1971.

7 *The Uses of the University,* Harper & Row, Publishers, Incorporated, New York, 1963.

8 Irving Kristol, "The Emerging Context of Continuing Higher Education," unedited transcription of taped recording, speech at conference commemorating the fortieth anniversary of the NYU School of Continuing Education, April 2–3, 1975.

9 Richard Freeman and Herbert J. Hollomon, "The Declining Value of College Going," *Change* magazine, September 1975.

10 Study by the Center for Research and Development in Higher Education at the University of California at Berkeley, 1974.

11 Anthony H. Pascal, "An Evaluation of Policy Related Research on Programs for Mid-Life Career Redirection," report prepared for the National Science Foundation, Rand Corporation, Santa Monica, Calif.,

February 1975. In this report, "midlife" is located in the years between thirty and fifty-five. "By their late twenties, most people have completed their conventional education, whether it be formal professional schooling or on-the-job learning. By 30, the vast majority have settled into lines of work they consider their permanent occupations. By 35, they have had a fair sample of the consequences of their career choices, and probably have a good idea of what the next thirty years will offer in terms of advancement, satisfaction, challenge, prestige and so forth. The late thirties are also the period when many housewives consider entering or reentering the labor force as their children enter school and other household responsibilities diminish."

12 *The Graduate,* Approach 13–30 Corporation, Knoxville, Tenn., 1975.

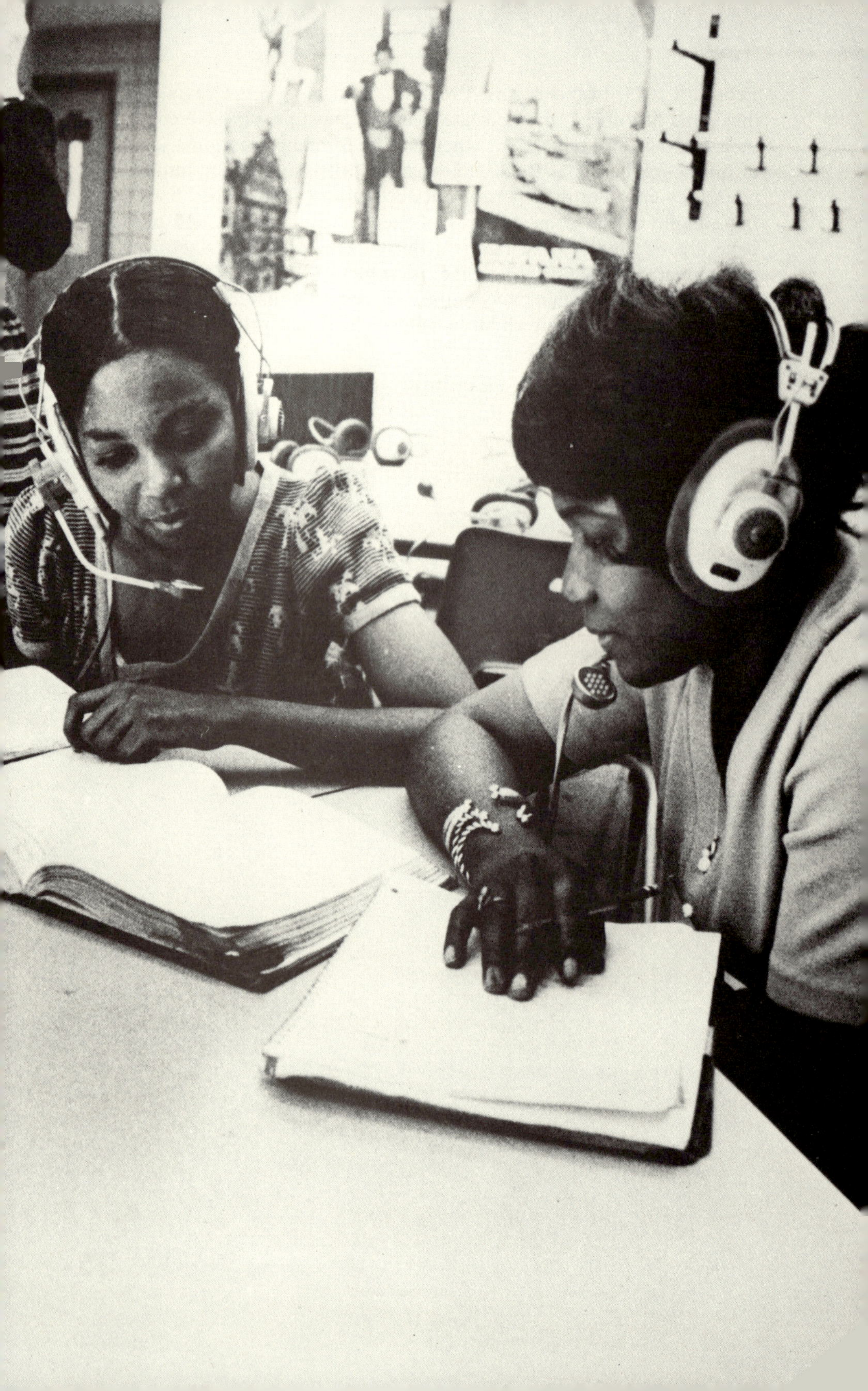

2 What Can You Expect?

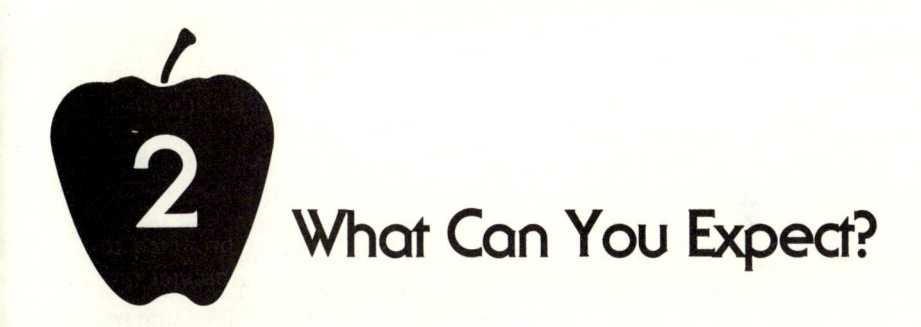

Returning students must be prepared to cope with the institution. John C. Ries, Vice Chancellor, UCLA

The Reality Gap

The college campus occupies a special place in the American scheme of things. The four years that are customarily allocated to the pursuit of the B.A. degree represent a break in time between childhood dependency and the assumption of adult responsibilities. We expect these precious four years to yield a rich lode of personal and social benefits: to define and strengthen cultural values; to encourage rigorous and disciplined thinking; to provide training for jobs and professions; to foster social contacts, perhaps leading to marriage; and as some critics would have it, to "warehouse" young people who would otherwise add to the unemployment rolls.

Further, as William Marvel, a prominent educator, has said, we expect our institutions of higher learning to:

> . . . teach students and the teachers of students; through research, to add to the pool of knowledge and understanding in all fields—liberal, scientific, professional and technical; to stimulate educational progress and reform in the schools; to contribute manpower and skills to the solution of almost any social problem; to assist the people, the school systems, and the universities of other countries—in a word, to provide leadership not only for education and the so-called knowledge industries, but for society at large.[1]

These expectations are frequently intertwined with memories of one's college years, which are recalled as a time of personal discovery and exploration, of peaceful contemplation and intellectual growth.

If you attended a small liberal arts college in a rural or small-town setting, you may remember a placid ambience in which the pursuit of learning was combined with a round of zestful extracurricular activities. Or maybe that's the way you think it should have been if your alma mater didn't conform to this idealized image or if you never got to college at all. And now that you're planning to return, you're looking forward to school —to the kind of learning experience you remember fondly, if not with total accuracy, or to the one you think you missed out on.

One of the major problems of returning students, particularly if they have been away from school for a decade or more, is the gap between their expectations and the reality of the current college scene. It is a problem that can be difficult to deal with since it is rooted in the way we perceive the world. "Consider your normal consciousness," suggests psychologist Robert Ornstein, "and reflect for a moment on its contents: you will probably find it a mixture of thoughts, fantasies, ideas and sensations of the external world." Ornstein goes on to argue that this mixture cannot serve as a mirror of external reality. "We hallucinate, imagine, distort."[2] By applying the corrective of daily experience, we can often gain a clearer view of the world around us. But returning students are not usually able to apply such corrective experience to the world or higher education. They have been absorbed by interests and activities which are for the most part remote from campus life. Attending an occasional concert, film, or lecture at a friendly neighborhood campus is very different from being a regularly enrolled student there. And aside from such headline-making events as the student protest movements of the late sixties, there is little news or information filtering through the media about the day-to-day lives of college students.

So it is not too surprising that midlife returnees often bring with them a "mixture of thoughts, fantasies, ideas and sensations" that are "out of sync" with today's college scene, nor is it surprising that some of them experience at the outset a sensation resembling culture shock. In a few extreme cases, this condition may be severe enough to discourage the returning student from going on. But there are ways to cushion the shock and smooth the transition from your present life to the one that awaits you at the campus of your choice. Let's begin by taking a look at the changing college scene.

The Educational Supermarket

The latter half of the sixties was the great watershed in higher education, a time when colleges and universities were facing the most serious challenges in their history. The year 1968–1969 saw massive demonstrations on campuses across the country. During the spring of 1969, student disruptions occurred on eighty-three separate campuses from City College of New York to San Francisco State. On a single day in April 1969, students were occupying buildings on seventeen American campuses.[3]

Since education at all levels is a reflection of the larger society, the changes that have affected so many institutions, values, attitudes, and modes of behavior since that turbulent time have made a lasting impression upon colleges and universities. Returning students whose education took place in the fifties or earlier are usually unprepared for the kind of changes that have been occurring in the world of higher education.

What are the facts about the changing college scene that the returning student should be aware of? The following news item, which appeared in *The Daily Bruin,* UCLA's student newspaper, is highly revealing:

> Students hoping to drop or add classes at the computer this week have been disappointed by long delays and the usual computer foul-ups. Although the chaos which accompanied last fall's large influx of freshmen has not been as evident this quarter, waiting times have been just as long, if not longer. Monday and Tuesday the waiting time for the computer ranged from one to almost three hours.
>
> Computer operators attributed the long waits to the reduced size of the staff operating the computer terminals. Last quarter there were up to 18 terminal operators while this week there were only eight or nine at any given time. As a result, the average number of students handled each hour by the computer has declined from about 300 last quarter to 200 this week, staff members said.
>
> Most students in line appeared to view the long wait stoically. "It's just something you have to get used to," commented a junior. A sophomore added, "This is one of the disadvantages of coming to a big school, but the advantages make up for it. I just bring a book along and find a seat." . . .
>
> Several students offered their own solutions to the problem of the long lines. The most common suggestion was to hire more terminal operators. One student, however, suggested having the theater arts or music departments give performances while the student waited.

The sheer size of today's postsecondary educational institutions, which produces the kind of situation described in the news story, comes as a jolt to many midlife returnees. Although the growth of many colleges and universities is now leveling off, the rapid expansion that took place in the fifties and sixties has produced campuses with city-size enrollments. Their functions and services have also vastly increased and ramified as they have attempted to respond to stepped-up demands and pressures from the larger society.

It is these large, complex institutions that are receiving most of the returning adults. Although private colleges, such as Sarah Lawrence and Radcliffe, offer excellent special programs for housewives wishing to return to college—"resuming women," as they are called—the large, publicly supported institutions, community colleges, state colleges, and universities are the choice of the majority of returnees for such practical reasons as cost, accessibility, and variety of offerings.

These huge complexes are as far removed from the small liberal arts college as a supermarket is from the corner grocery store. Clark Kerr offers a graphic picture of the University of California, of which he was formerly president:

> ... a total employment of over 40,000 people, more than IBM and in a far greater variety of endeavors; operations in over a hundred locations, counting campuses, experiment stations, agricultural and urban extension centers, and projects abroad involving more than fifty countries; nearly 10,000 courses in its catalogs; some form of contact with nearly every industry, nearly every level of government, nearly every person in its region. . . .
>
> It is the world's largest purveyor of white mice. It will soon have the world's largest primate colony. It will soon also have 100,000 students—30,000 of them at the graduate level; yet much less than one-third of its expenditures are directly related to teaching. It already has nearly 200,000 students in extension courses—including one out of every three lawyers and one out of every six doctors in the state.[4]

The University of Wisconsin at Madison, with its 49,000 students, has a population equal to that of Beloit, Londonderry, or Beverly Hills. It has its own radio and television stations, its own nuclear reactor, a building in which nearly every conceivable environmental condition can be simulated, a 50-Mev fixed-field alternating gradient synchroton, a collection of more than 1,700 United Artist Corporation movies made between 1919 and 1951, and a mastodon skeleton.

Institutions like these "multiversities" can be bewildering to the entering student, whether he or she is an eighteen-year-old with a newly minted high school diploma or a returnee whose sheepskin is turning yellow at the edges. Older students may find themselves at a greater disadvantage since they have not had the preparation usually provided to high school seniors, such as counseling, visits to nearby campuses, and, in some cases, advanced placement in college classes during the senior year. Housewives who have not had the experience of working in large organizations tend to suffer most of all from a sense of acute disorientation.

A thirty-five-year-old mother of three who had been dreaming for years of returning to college describes what it was like during the first few weeks after registration:

> I discovered that higher education, particularly at a large urban university, consisted primarily of standing in lines, filling out innumerable forms, and tracking down a parking place for one's car. I stumbled around in a daze of confusion, doing almost everything wrong. As a result of having failed to follow through the procedures required by the parking office, I missed several days of classes. I attended a lecture course with over 500 students in which my seat was so far back I could barely see the professor or the blackboard. It took me a week before I realized I was in the wrong class.

The bureaucratization, impersonality, and fragmentation that this woman was experiencing are inescapable by-products of the giantism that has overtaken institutions of higher learning. The bureaucratic procedures alone appear to be endless. From the moment you make your application for entrance, you are caught up in what appears to be a relentless regimen of paperwork. The application blank itself will probably run for several pages and will demand information that seems to you exceedingly irrelevant or remote: all the schools you attended since eighth grade and their addresses (impossible to remember), your mother's maiden name, your father's occupation (but not your husband's or your wife's or the names of your children), your athletic achievements (vacuuming the carpets does not count), and your source of financial support. Obviously, college application blanks were not designed for anyone over thirty. Your application will also require that you provide other papers which, with some variations from one institution to another and depending upon whether you are applying for undergraduate or graduate school, will include transcripts from high school and each college you attended, letters of recommendation, and entrance examination test scores. You may also be required to write an essay about yourself—your interests, concerns, expectations, and goals.

As you go along, there will be forms to fill out for the parking office, the library, and the student health service (which may require that you undergo a full-fledged physical examination); for financial aid; for permission to change your major or to drop or add a course; for transferring credits; for the use of special facilities such as the language lab; for a teaching assistantship; and for your regular registration each trimester or semester, at which time you will be presented with a thick set of computerized cards that are not to be "folded, spindled, or mutilated." On all these documents, you will be asked to record your student number, which may run to five or six figures, making you feel like a machine part in an endless assembly line.

This feeling will be intensified when you attend your first class and find yourself in a large lecture hall which is filled to capacity. Hundreds of students surround you, their notebooks open and their ball-points at the ready. At or near the appointed time, the professor enters; places his notes on the lectern; makes a few announcements about required reading, exam schedules, and other housekeeping matters; and then launches into his lecture. Hundreds of pens go into action, scribbling away into the open notebooks. Here and there a tape recorder is activated. The lecture ends, and the professor calls for questions. A few hands are raised. Your head is teeming with questions, but you realize there will not be enough time. Already, the students are gathering up their possessions; the bell rings, and it is time to move on to the next class.

This "massification" of higher learning touches almost every aspect of the experience. Examinations become multiple-choice tests to conform with computer technology. The competition for space, books, facilities, courses, and professors' time becomes sharper as a larger number of students vie for available resources. In order to be assured of a place in some of the more popular required courses, students may resort to the expedient of camping out the night before registration in front of the building in which the registration process will take place.

But though the large urban campus is confusing to returning students and though it is not an environment in which one can easily establish one's identity, it offers, like the supermarket versus the corner grocery store, a wide range of choices. The catalog of the University of Wisconsin contains 3,500 courses, with a choice of over 150 majors. This means that you can pick and choose freely from a feast of educational offerings, and though you can still receive credit for classical Greek and English literature, you can also be credited for renovating old houses, designing low-emission prototype automobiles, or investing in the stock market. The impersonal, anonymous character of the institution may have some negative effects, but it also has some positive ones: It assures you privacy in which to pursue your interests in your own way. It also offers you access to a wealth of resources and facilities: specialized libraries, learning-skills centers, travel programs, women's studies centers, job placement services, financial-aid programs, housing assistance, and many others.

Some returning students find that this freedom and autonomy present them, as freedom of choice has a way of doing, with additional dilemmas. But as we'll see later in Chapter 5, "Resources to Help You along the Way," experienced counselors and others are available to assist you with your choices without impairing your autonomy.

There are also some encouraging signs in higher education of efforts to cope with the problem of bigness. The University of the Pacific and the Santa Cruz branch of the University of California have distributed their students among cluster colleges with, in the case of the Santa Cruz campus, no more than 1,000 students in each. Oakland Community College has developed a new type of institution in which formal course work is minimized and instruction is individualized through the use of study booths, tape recorders, filmstrip machines, and programmed textbooks. A few campuses have established freshman seminars which are taught by senior faculty members for a limited number of students.

In any case, as you move along, you'll find that your own world within the educational supermarket begins shrinking, until soon it has been reduced to a size and scale that you are comfortable with. Even the most multi of the multiversities—the University of Michigan or the University of Wisconsin, for example—contain, within their great size and conglomeration of activities, "miniworlds" of academic disciplines and departments; within these miniworlds you will have ample opportunity, certainly by the time you settle on your major, to carve out your own learning space.

The Curriculum and How It Grows

As a returning student, you will be impressed not only by the quantity of courses available but also by the new kinds of subjects being offered. The changing curriculum is, more than any other aspect of higher education, a mirror image of the changes that have been taking place on and off campuses during the recent past. A visitor from outer space who wanted to know what has been happening in this country during the past two decades could hardly do better than to study the catalogs of leading colleges covering that period. If your college experience goes back fifteen or twenty years, you will surely remember the standard fare featuring American and European history, social sciences, English literature, math, Latin, a modern language (usually French or German), science, and physical education. As you advanced from freshman status, these would be broken up into specialized units to be studied in greater depth: the nineteenth-century English novel, United States local government, trigonometry, biology, chemistry, physics, anthropology, and so forth.

From where we are now, it looks like a narrow and ethnocentric curriculum. The emphasis throughout was on the Western European tradition. The great events, inventions, discoveries, and works of art that made up the typical course of study were the heritage primarily of Western civilization. It was entirely possible at that time to graduate from a well-regarded college or university without knowing any literatures written in languages other than English or without having any notion of where Luwanda might be or of how it could possibly have any relation to life in America (This ignorance of, or indifference to, cultures beyond the boundaries of the West cost us dearly in Vietnam, where we discovered that our highly educated "experts," all graduates of prestigious universities, were ill-equipped to deal with a peasant people whose religion, politics, and history originated in a part of the world unfamiliar to us.)

During the mid-1960s, as American foreign policy began taking on worldwide dimensions, the colleges and universities followed suit by committing themselves to various kinds of international programs. Under these programs substantial numbers of foreign students were admitted to American universities, giving the campuses a more cosmopolitan flavor, and United States students were sent abroad to participate in developmental projects. It was a time when the Peace Corps was opening up opportunities for service in third-world countries. It was also a time when the repercussions from Sputnik were continuing to influence the curricular priorities in favor of scientific and technical studies.

The civil rights movement, the women's movement, and the increasing visibility and audibility of subgroups—these social ingredients have been stirred into the curriculum stew. Women's studies, Afro-American studies, Chicano studies, Asian Studies, and Indian studies—all are here and accounted for. As a result, the old college catalog you may remember from your school days has taken on a sophisticated new personality. Through its once staid pages parade such offerings as Indian Civilization, Cybernetics, Oriental Languages, Advanced Feminist Theory, The Black Family, Creative Problem Solving, Psychobiology, Environmental Quality and Health, Russian Area Studies, Ecosystems, Biostatics, Consumer Economics, Indo-European Studies, and The Psychology of Sex Differences.

The possibilities for mind expansion seem to be unlimited, if somewhat overwhelming. The distance between then and now, as measured by this curricular leap, recalls what Upton Sinclair said of his own experience with higher education:

> I look back now and see myself as I was and I shudder—not merely for myself, but for all other products of the educational machine. I think of the things I didn't know, and of the pains and perils to which my ignorance exposed me! I knew nothing about hygiene and health; everything of that sort I had to learn by painful error. I knew nothing about women; I had met only three or four besides my mother, and had no idea how to deal with them. I knew as much about sex as the ancient religious ascetics, but nothing of modern discoveries or theories on the subject.
>
> More significant, I knew nothing about modern literature in any language. . . . I knew nothing about modern history; so far as my mind was concerned, the world had come to an end with the Franco-Prussian War, and nothing had happened since. . . .[5]

This is not the kind of complaint that is likely to be voiced by today's university student. Together with the proliferation of knowledge in all areas, other forces have been at work in the yeasty expansion of the curriculum: the increasing involvement of the federal government in higher education and the rise of "grantsmanship"; the demand by students for a more student-centered, career-oriented approach to curriculum planning; the rise of experimental centers offering courses in any subject that can attract a requisite number of students, with teachers recruited from nonfaculty ranks; learning resource centers for developing new courses and methods of instruction (the key word for these ventures is usually "innovative"); and the multidisciplinary approach, which integrates the resources of several disciplines.

The Era of the Government Grant

Of these developments the one with the greatest and most far-reaching influence on the size, shape, and content of the curriculum has been federal government support of a wide range of research and other activities. Just as the land-grant university launched a new age in American higher education, the federal-grant university has ushered in another new era which has profoundly altered postsecondary institutions—private as well as public schools, two-year colleges as well as multiversities, and extension divisions as well as the regular campus. The cohabitation of the government and higher education, which began in World War II when major universities were enlisted in the national defense, received further impetus from Russian scientific achievements both before and after Sputnik. Since then, the infusion of government funds into higher education at ever-increasing levels has spawned programs and projects in virtually every discipline and department.

The most noticeable effect on the curriculum has been a tipping of the scales in favor of the sciences and technical studies, which have mushroomed, while the liberal arts and humanities have declined. With most of the funds flowing toward scientific research, fields such as philosophy and literature have been pushed into the background. "That stuff is for those who can't hack the math," is the way one student put it. The humanities have been further weakened by the career-centered interests of today's students; while students of mathematics and the natural sciences are trained to become practicing biochemists, physicists, computer analysts, and laboratory technicians, those with a humanities degree are not similarly equipped to "use" their education in a practical, income-producing way.

Since so many returning students are career-motivated, it is not surprising that more of them are gravitating toward the scientific-technological studies. The trend that was observed among female students in the fifties and sixties, which saw them turning away from the sciences toward the "more feminine" subject areas, is showing signs of reversal. Both younger and older women students are increasingly choosing science majors and are moving rapidly into such fields as public health, physical therapy, medical technology (90 percent of all medical technologists are women), computer programming, and engineering.

A 1975 survey of entering freshmen conducted by the American Council on Education shows that one woman in six (16.9 percent) is planning a career in a traditionally "masculine" field such as business, engineering, law, or medicine. All this is a healthy indication that women are using the curriculum to hoist themselves into a productive role in our scientific-technological society. No longer are they being automatically "tracked" into the arts and humanities to prepare them for a homebound future. But there is also a danger here which, as a returning student, you should be aware of: the risk of taking too narrow a path toward your goal. Two hundred years ago John Adams wrote to his wife, Abigail, that he had to study politics and war so that his children would be free to study mathematics, commerce, agriculture, etc., so that their children would be free to study painting, poetry, music, etc. Our second President saw the arts and humanities as an upward progression in human development.

In the course of an individual's development, the arts and humanities are a vital source of enrichment and enjoyment, a reservoir from which to draw during the later retirement years. It may be that those breadth courses which seem like an unnecessary diversion from the "serious business" of your major and which you plan to put behind you as quickly as possible should be given the benefit of your best thinking. The rewards of such courses may not be as immediate or tangible as those of your career-directed studies, but they may be deeper and longer-lasting.

From the standpoint of curriculum size and diversity, today's college student is in an enviable situation. But for the student returning in midlife, who must carefully budget time and energy, this embarrassment of riches can add to the hazards and complications of working out a course of study. How are you supposed to make up your mind when so many glittering choices are dangled before you? Once you've satisfied the breadth requirements, how can you apportion those precious "electives" over such a wide range of subject areas? Besides, what is one to make of all those "innovative" and "experimental" courses? Are they, perhaps, a bit too avant-garde for someone whose tastes and values are rooted in the pre-sixties?

If confronting a college catalog and trying to choose one subject while rejecting another induces in you a feeling of vertigo, remember that you are not alone. A few other points to remember: Some of the so-called new courses are variations on old-timers with updated titles and descriptive copy. (Writers of college catalogs are not immune to the influence of Madison Avenue.) The Social and Political Milieu in the Early Republic may be the standard American History from 1750 to 1800.

In responding to the demand for more student-centered courses, curriculum planners occasionally find it difficult to filter out the faddish and trendy. This is particularly true of privately supported colleges, extension divisions, and other self-supporting institutions which feel compelled to keep an eye on the educational "market" when designing their curricula. Returning students, particularly those with a strong vocational objective, are advised to keep a safe distance from courses that appear to be hastily contrived to capture a transitory interest or concern.

Your own "gestalt" or frame of reference will help you to put together, out of the multiplicity of courses, a coherent program that is meaningful to you. In some institutions, entering students are assisted in this by being offered a core subject area around which they can group their courses. A few examples follow:

> Major Human Concerns, focusing especially on questions such as freedom versus control, heredity and environment, and contemporary views of the inner man and woman.

> Contemporary America's Dilemmas, with emphasis upon the social, political, and economic forces that have made the United States what it is today.

> The Ecology of Cities, analyzing the forces that shape urban environments and cultures. Los Angeles, Athens, Rome, Boston, Tokyo, and Calcutta will each be studied in historical perspective.

Taking a systematic approach to choosing your major will help you bring order out of the mind-boggling diversity that is spread before you. Here is how one student applied what she had learned in a course on problem solving to the choice of her major: She had started out as a premed student but wasn't completely happy with her choice. She knew she wanted to work with people rather than with things. From there she went on to consider what was most important in her life in terms of academic desires and what she most wanted to avoid. Next, she gave each choice points on a scale between 1 and 10 in terms of relative importance. After totaling up her points, she became a linguistics major.

There are some ways in which "shopping" in the educational supermarket resembles shopping in your neighborhood Food Giant. Your "budget" is the number of units you need for your degree. The breadth or required courses are the staples, which must go into your "basket" first. The remaining units are to be allocated among the meat-and-potato subjects in your major and among the electives, which add sauce and spice to the diet. As in other kinds of shopping, a good rule to follow is: Beware of impulse buying.

Reentering students bring a number of significant challenges to the curriculum area. Adult learners want education that they can relate to their daily lives—education that will help them attain the renewal, identity, and earning power that most of them are seeking. Since they are more aware than younger students of the rapidity with which knowledge, considered strictly in terms of content, obsolesces, they are more concerned with the "how" of learning than with the "what." In this respect, they are tuned in to a trend which is being predicted for higher education: As a result of the rapid increase in the rate of knowledge, more attention will be paid to the management and interpretation of knowledge. Storage, retrieval, and dissemination of information will become as important as production of facts and theories. By the 1980s, as some futurists see it, the skills most needed for survival will be those of communication. The demand for a more humanistic education, for ways to use leisure time to promote personal growth, will become more insistent as the life span extends and there are more retirees among us. The coming years should see adaptations in the curriculum which are a direct response to the growing number of midlife students in postsecondary institutions.

Instructional Methods

What changes should you expect in teaching methods? If what you recall from your previous schooling is lectures, a little discussion, and a lot of exams—the old soak-it-up and pour-it-out routine—well, there have been a few changes but not enough to make you feel as though you're on another planet. The instructional methods you encounter will be determined largely by the kind of institution you decide to attend. The difference between the community college and the four-year state college, on the one hand, and the university, on the other, is essentially the difference between the vocationally oriented and the research-oriented institution. At the community and state college, you will find that the teaching methods are generally of a pragmatic, nuts-and-bolts type. Just as the curriculum offers a wider variety of vocational courses, the instructional style leans toward helping students apply their learning in some practical manner. Students at community colleges "indicate feelings of progress in learning how to get along with people, in learning job-related skills, and in developing a satisfactory philosophy of life."[6]

Since among its many other functions the community college also serves as a pathway to the four-year college and university, there is a strong emphasis on basic skills, such as reading, writing, and math. The fact that, in recent years, more students entering colleges have been deficient in these skills has prompted four-year colleges and even the prestigious universities to make provision for upgrading student learning skills. We can expect this effort to be stepped up as a result of a recent U.S. Office of Education study which found that "approximately one of five Americans is incompetent or functions with difficulty and . . . about half the adult population is merely functional and not at all proficient in necessary skills and knowledge."[7]

The tempo of instruction is another feature that distinguishes the community and state college from the university. Students at the university are more achievement-oriented, and the sharp competition for placement in graduate school contributes to a pressure-cooker atmosphere. This is intensified even further in those universities—such as Stanford, the University of Minnesota, and the nine University of California campuses—which are on the quarter or trimester system.

The division of the academic year into 3 ten-week periods is intended to provide a more efficient, more economical utilization of time, faculty, and facilities. Whether these benefits actually result from the trimester plan is unclear; evidence and arguments are offered on both sides. But if you prefer to do your studying at a slower, more relaxed tempo, the trimester is not for you.

It's Not All in the Books

Because so many students are career-oriented and are demanding education that is "relevant," several campuses have been developing "experiential" or "cooperative" education, which incorporates practical fieldwork into an academic framework that the college or university will accept for credit. These programs are alive and well in the vocationally oriented community and state colleges; they are making their way more slowly in the research-centered universities. The following are some examples of how experiential learning works:

> A student who wants to teach the retarded enrolls in a field study program at a state hospital.
>
> A young woman set on a career in publishing serves as an intern at a publishing house, learning the basics of the business.
>
> A dance major with a flair for choreography volunteers to work at a boys' home helping young residents plan programs.
>
> A student planning a career in government signs up for an eight-week stint in Washington as an aide to a congressman.
>
> A senior studying psychology volunteers at a community center and finds out that a career in social work isn't what he wants after all.

A dean who has been administering one of these programs comments, "Not all learning comes from books, and today's college students find more meaning in their regular studies after taking one of our experiential courses. A classroom course in personality theories will suddenly start to make sense when the student is in daily contact with former mental patients."

It is hard to think of a better way for the returning student to sharpen up skills and acquire practical experience in the shortest possible time than through experiential learning. Even if the activity doesn't carry credit, it can be worth pursuing as long as it fits in with your goal.

Personalized Instruction

As in the curriculum content area, there have been some modest efforts in recent years to individualize the way students are taught. Of these, independent study is the method that is most likely to cross your path, and so even if you are somewhat leery of nontraditional learning techniques, this one is worth your attention. In fact, "independent study" or "individual study," as it's sometimes called, is not as free-form as the name suggests. In this approach undergraduates can design and plan a course for themselves, but only with the permission and ongoing supervision of a sponsoring faculty member. Also, most departments place a restriction on the number of independent study programs a student can pursue for credit.

Independent study offers you the opportunity to study a topic in depth or complete a special field project that doesn't fit into any established course. It offers you more freedom and responsibility than you may think you're ready for, which is why some returnees, particularly during the early stages, when they are trying to get their bearings, tend to veer toward the traditional method. But independent study is an excellent way for you as a reentering student to take the plunge into higher education and gain experience in working on your own. What better way for you to develop the inner security that is so essential to your success as a student?

A new form of independent study that is being cautiously introduced in a few colleges and universities is known as the Personalized Instruction System (PSI). Developed by a behavioral psychologist, Fred S. Keller, PSI is a no-fault, no-fail method in which the course work is divided up into small sequential units, permitting the student to proceed at his or her own pace. When you have mastered one unit, you move on to the next, and there are frequent tests to help you gauge your progress. Lectures are minimized, and a proctor or teaching assistant is available to help you all along the way. The use of a programmed text, a teaching machine, or some sort of computer aid is one of the features of this method, though, as the designer states, this is not "to be equated with the course itself."[8] The following advantages of PSI are cited: It provides positive reinforcement for the student, makes it possible to study at one's own pace even in large classes, and promotes personal interaction between students through the student-proctor relationship.

Teaching and Learning with Technology

The increasing use of technology in the teaching-learning process is something else that is unfamiliar and at times disturbing to reentering students. Depending upon your age, you might not be able to recall from your school days the use of any technical equipment more advanced than the occasional classroom film or slides. And although as an adult living in the "technetronic age" you can hardly avoid being dependent upon various kinds of complex technical equipment in your home, in your work, and in every aspect of your life, you may still be unprepared for the widespread application of technology in higher education, ranging all the way from the cassette tape recorder, used by students as a substitute for note taking, to the 18-billion-volt atom smasher under construction by two megacampuses, the University of California and Stanford University.

Again, this depends upon whether we are talking about community colleges, four-year colleges, or universities. At all these institutions computers, media, language labs, and other technologies will be available to some extent. But it is in the large public university, with its heavy infusion of federal funds, that the use of sophisticated technical equipment pervades large areas of the teaching-learning experience. The following offers a view of how technology is being used by various departments of a major university:

Libraries	Audio dial retrieval system—reel to reel. Spoken-language library (plays poetry, speeches, some folk and pop music, and a few foreign-language audio tapes). Dial access for students; thirty can listen to one tape at a time. Twenty-four listening stations.
Communications archive	Library of audio tapes of campus speakers. Listening facilities; also video tape and dubbing setup.
Language laboratories	Study carrels.

Music audio facility	Approximately 3,000 LPs and 3,000 tapes of classical music. Own record players and tape recorders; accomodates forty students.
Education department	Video tape library (approximately ninety tapes). Film library (approximately 200 films) taping of educational programs for internal use. Has Sony video tape recorders; does still photography and slides; is equipped for black-and-white and color film production. For teacher curriculum development.
	Production facility—multimedia modules in teacher education; video tapes and audio tapes; filmstrips; TV control room; VTR with synchronized generator; film projectors, tape recorders, etc. State depository for textbooks. Audio-visual collection, multimedia kits, etc.
Art department	Video tape lab is used by art students to gain experience in the use of the medium. Equipment: approximately six ½-inch VTRs (Concord); two portable cameras; three studio-size cameras; six ¼-inch portable VTRs; three ½-inch portable Concords; Sony; Concord 1-inch; library of student productions available to other departments.
Psychology department	Video installations to record patient cases (VTR Sony 1-inch and ½-inch).
Chemistry department	TV cameras and monitors, mainly to enable students to watch chemical experiments closely; recording equipment. Some tapes are kept by professors for use in classroom; a few are stored.
Zoology department	Two Sony EV 200 cameras (one to fit on microscope); three student laboratories to give lab practicum videotaped demonstrations; small library; TV monitors in professors' rooms to

	observe animal behavior via video system on roof. Department also owns projectors, overhead projectors, tape recorders, etc., for internal use.
Graduate school of management	Video tape recording and playback facilities.
Journalism department	Tape recorders.
School of law	Video tape recorder, camera, classroom material.
School of architecture and urban planning	Films, mostly on urban planning, done by students.
Engineering department	Learning resource center with taped engineering courses.
Film archives	Collection of feature films.
National television library	Collection of television materials.
Instructional media library	Loan/rental of over 2,000 films to campus departments; research. Previews.

From Gutenberg to McLuhan

As the above listing indicates, communication technology is becoming a tool to be reckoned with in higher education. And here again, if your formal education ended before the sixties, the increasing use of films, slides, and television in the learning process will contrast with your earlier experience. The new visual era in education was ushered in by Marshall McLuhan in the early 1960s, when he made his much-quoted statement, "The medium is the message." McLuhan, a professor at the University of Toronto, has become the apostle of the new learning in which information is received through nonlinear images and in which the "what" and the "how" of learning are merged. As a technical breakthrough, audio-visual technology can be compared with the advance of the book over the scroll. Compared with the parchment scroll, the book had the advantages of durability and convenience, and by the time Christianity was beginning to spread over Europe, books were becoming established as the new medium of learning. Of course, it was not until Gutenberg invented his printing press in the middle of the fifteenth century that books began to be disseminated beyond a very small educated elite.

Audio-visual communications technology has a potential for education that is only beginning to be realized. According to a 1974 report on the role of media in education:

> By the time a person reaches age 18, he/she has watched 25,000 hours of television and, as a result of exposure to these media, important behavioral, attitudinal and cognitive changes occur. Which of these changes can be properly referred to as "educational" depends, of course, on the definition of education one uses. But it seems probable that more people became familiar with the Forsytes via television than through reading Galsworthy when taking courses in English Literature; that more have learned something of marine biology through watching Jacques Cousteau than through university breadth courses in the subject; that more became sensitive to the effects of prejudice through watching "The Eye of the Storm" than through sociology or psychology courses; that more came to understand the connected sweep of the development of western civilization through watching Kenneth Clark than through reading, say, Arnold Toynbee.[9]

The growing reliance on media as a channel of information and entertainment has been cited as the principal culprit responsible for the drastic downslide of reading and writing skills among large numbers of adults and children. This decline in verbal ability, which is causing so much consternation in educational circles, has led to an upsurge in remedial education, one of the few teaching fields that is growing (another is bilingual education for those with non-English-speaking backgrounds who wish to continue their education).

There are ardent McLuhanites who claim that the concern about verbal skills is overblown since we are moving into a new electronic age in which the printed text will be replaced in time by electromagnetic technology. As they envision it, human experience will no longer present itself in verbal symbols marching in linear progression across a page; the new learning will take place through "fields" or "simultaneous interaction," which will bring about a new spontaneity and awaken other senses aside from the reading eye.

Audio-visual enthusiasts point to studies which have attempted to answer the question: How well do people learn through the visual media? In one famous experiment conducted in 1956 by the University of Toronto and the Canadian Broadcasting Corporation, a special lecture entitled "Thinking through Language" was prepared; this topic was chosen because it was considered to be both difficult and stimulating. The students were divided into four groups on the basis of their academic performance, and each group was placed in a separate room. One group heard the lecture as delivered, a second heard it on radio, a third saw it on television, and a fourth read it in printed form. At the conclusion the students took a half-hour examination consisting of multiple-choice questions of fact and one essay question. They were allowed plenty of time, and so speed was not a factor. The mean scores on the test were as follows:

Television	77.2
Radio	69.2
Reading	65.1
Lecture	64.9

In a retest eight months later, it was found that those who had learned more had also retained more.[10]

Subsequent experiments and studies have cast doubt on this early one, and the debate rages on, producing on some campuses a "great divide," with Gutenbergians on one side and McLuhanites on the other. As in most polarized arguments, the truth—or, in this case, the reality—lies somewhere in between. There is little chance in the foreseeable future that visual media will replace the book as the book once replaced the scroll. Learning through visual media is a very different experience from learning through the printed word, and both have their place in the educational scheme of things.

Films, slides, and television convey their messages instantaneously, with individual symbols or "frames" flashing by at the speed of twenty-four per second. There is little time for reflecting or for reviewing facts or concepts. For this reason, most of the films and television programs produced for educational purposes are accompanied by study guides complete with bibliographies. The printed word is absorbed at a slower rate (even if you are a speed reader); there is time to turn back the pages and reread and rethink.

Also, audio-visual media are designed for a collective or group experience; an instructor shows a film or video tape to a group of students who see the same images at the same time under the same conditions. But a book is assigned to individuals who, since books can be picked up and put down without benefit of projectors or monitors, will read it at different times under varying conditions. Reading is essentially a solitary experience in which whatever happens takes place between writer and reader.

There are, in addition, several reasons why instructional media are not likely to grow as rapidly in the immediate future as they have in recent years. One deterrent is faculty resistance, which is based largely on the fear that professors may be replaced by machines—or, at least, that their functions and authority will be diminished; this resistance will probably stiffen in view of the tight employment situation in higher education.

There is also the cost factor; audio-visual equipment and materials are very expensive, and with educational budgets being slashed, few campuses will be in a position to invest in high-priced technology.

What all this means to you in your return to school is that media will probably play a larger role in your learning experience than you had anticipated, particularly if you are in a scientific or technical field. But books will continue to figure prominently in your educational program. In many areas of study, particularly in the liberal arts and the social sciences, you will be spending more time in the library than before a television set, and your research will be drawn from books, documents, laboratories, and fieldwork rather than films.

Mechanical Aids: How Helpful?

The portable cassette tape recorder can be an asset in many of your activities; it can be used for recording lectures, meetings, musical events, poetry readings, and seminars and for building an "oral history" collection of taped statements by people who are important to your field of interest. Your own imagination and resourcefulness will lead you to any number of learning uses for this versatile piece of equipment. But, as with most mechanical aids, you are advised to use your recorder judiciously. It is not, at least for most students, recommended as a substitute for note taking. The process of taking notes is an active one, requiring a high degree of attention and selectivity. Relying on taping does not bring these faculties into play, and furthermore it saddles you with the tedious and time-consuming job of transcribing the tape later on.

The photocopying machine is another indispensable helper, and as you reproduce term papers, parts of books documents, and other materials, you will wonder how students ever managed to make their way through school without it. If you're planning to study a foreign language, the language lab, available on many campuses, will make it possible for you to train your ear and improve your conversational ability at your own pace and in your own time. These and other teaching-learning aids—computers, microfilm, video tapes, filmstrips—are yours to use as they fit your needs and objectives. But, although they can add immeasurably to your educational experience, they are no more than tools, useful only as instruments in the service of that most ingeniously engineered piece of learning equipment, the human brain.

A New Breed

Since human beings are the ultimate thinking machines, the expectations of students, whether first-time students or reentering ones, are quite understandably centered on the teaching staff. Regardless of the institution's prestige, the size of its grants, or the sophistication and extent of its technological equipment, the education provided is only as good as its faculty. It is in the interaction between instructor and student that the most meaningful learning transaction takes place. The tremendous expansion of colleges and universities, the increasing dependence of these institutions upon federal funds, the student protests of the sixties, and the entrance into higher education of large numbers of nontraditional students —all these forces have brought new pressures to bear upon faculty members, and in responding to these pressures they have moved further and further away from that traditional model of the professor as an ivory-towered "Mr. Chips," wholly dedicated to imparting the joy of learning to his students. As a returning student, you may be carrying an image like this in your mind, based on a favorite teacher from your school days, and certainly teachers who fit this description are still to be found on many campuses. However, they are becoming an endangered species, especially in the large universities. In coming back to school, you should be prepared for changing instructional styles and different teacher-student relationships. But if it's "Good-bye, Mr. Chips," who is taking the traditional professor's place in today's college scene? Here again, it depends very much on the kind of campus you've chosen for your reentry.

The community college is community-centered and therefore local; it is accessible, tuitionless or low-tuitioned, and easy to attend. It offers vocational training as well as courses in liberal arts. It attracts students of all ages, from varying backgrounds, and with abilities that range from somewhere near zero to somewhere near genius. To deal with such diversity of needs and capabilities, the community college teacher must be flexible, plugged into the concerns of the community, and, above all, able to *teach,* in the most basic, bread-and-butter sense of the term. Teaching in a community college does not require a Ph.D.; an M.A. is the usual requirement, and research, publishing, and consulting assignments are no feathers in the instructor's cap. (This is now beginning to change as unemployed Ph.D.'s seek out community college jobs and continue with their research and publishing in the hope of moving to the university.)

The university, by contrast, has a constituency that is national and even international. (The University of California has students from ninety-six countries.) Students at the university, having been filtered through the admissions process, are fairly similar in ability and in aspirations. In the university, the value placed on leadership in research far exceeds any value attached to undergraduate teaching. It is the graduate schools which are the jewels in the institution's crown, and the research and publications of its faculty are the stellar attractions which bring in funds from federal agencies and private foundations. A Ph.D. is required to teach at the university, but acquiring a Ph.D. does not involve training in pedagogy. Ph.D.s are trained in their academic disciplines, not in teaching methods, and once they have joined a faculty department, they continue to be committed to their field of study, realizing that their rewards and status will come from their research and publications rather than from their achievements in teaching undergraduates.

The neglect of undergraduate teaching in the university has fueled one of the hottest controversies in recent educational history. "Under respectable terms like consulting, research and scholarly publication, the neglect of students is concealed.... The routine problems of mass education... have fallen by default to graduate students who handle quiz sections, read examinations, listen to complaints and generally protect the professors from overexposure to the ignorant."[11] On the other side of the fence, faculty defenders of the "publish or perish" syndrome claim that it is research and publishing that keep the store of human knowledge alive and growing—that without this ceaseless effort to add to human wisdom, teaching would be an empty and sterile activity.

Some of the sharpest criticism of university faculty has been directed at their practice of absenting themselves from the classroom to act as high-paid advisers to government and business. Critics complain that since World War II, the contemplative, inner-directed professor has been overshadowed by the academic entrepreneur who spends more time in Washington than on the campus and who is more skilled at grantsmanship than at scholarship. The impact of the federal grant on the faculty is decried, even by some of those who are beneficiaries of government largesse. "It is a form of colonialism," says a social anthropologist, "because the grant agencies make us go where the money is, not where the problems are."

The race for grants, for status, and for choice consulting assignments not only has diverted attention and energy from the function of teaching but also has tended to pit faculty members against one another in the competition for academic rewards. Clark Kerr has described the faculty of our large universities as a group of competing entrepreneurs united by a common concern about parking. In a more serious vein, professors operating in today's college scene have been characterized as "knowledge technicians," as upwardly mobile as any corporate executive, "whose management of institute, bureau and center has its nearest counterpart in Washington or Detroit."[12]

How valid are these charges? Anyone who has spent some time at one of the megacampuses will attest that, yes, there is a breed of entrepreneurial faculty on board, more numerous in the sciences than in the humanities, very likely because it is the sciences which attract the choicest consulting assignments and the largest grants. (In an average year at a major university, the arts and humanities received $1 million in grants, while the sciences received $58.3 million.) And this new breed is not as interested in students as in promotion, tenure, and academic empire building.

But there are fresh winds blowing across the campuses, stirring up new attitudes and a new awareness regarding the university's obligation to its students. A growing number of institutions have instituted student evaluation of faculty members. Nontraditional students, many of whom must make substantial personal sacrifices for their education, are not content to be shunted off to graduate students who are acting as teaching assistants. And affirmative action policies, which are bringing women and ethnic minorities into the professorial ranks, are beginning to alter the teaching-learning environment in favor of a more student-centered instructional style.

Most important for you as a returning student is the changing attitude of the faculty toward the older student. In the sixties and earlier, the relatively few people over thirty-five who made the return trip to college felt like "second-class citizens" of the educational community. A former political science professor, John C. Ries, now a vice chancellor at UCLA, confirms that discriminatory patterns have existed which have placed older students at a disadvantage. Dr. Ries suggests that this has been especially prevalent at the graduate level and attributes it to the faculty's disbelief that anyone past the age of thirty can be serious about developing advanced academic credentials. There has also been a tendency on the part of faculty to regard older returnees as misfits who, having failed to make it elsewhere, have come back to school. But as mature students are increasing in numbers, they are gaining also in acceptance, and such prejudices are gradually disappearing.

Remember, too, that in the supersize institution that you will most likely be attending, your wide range of choices extends to the faculty. At the undergraduate level, you can usually count on there being more than one professor available to teach in a particular subject area. Consulting the student evaluations can help you in your selection of professors. Where there is no formal student evaluation procedure, you still have the option of attending the first class and then deciding whether the professor and you are likely to be compatible.

Though the faculty's role in your return to school is of first importance and though nothing can equal the intellectual excitement that a first-rate, dedicated teacher can generate, the fact remains that in college, unlike high school, the responsibility for your education rests with you, the student, rather than with the teaching staff. There may also be some truth in the familiar adage that "good students make good teachers." Since the consensus is that returning students are by and large of excellent quality, it can be expected that you and thousands of others like you who are undertaking this back-to-school adventure will make an important contribution to improving faculty performance in postsecondary education.

Campus in Transition: Closing the Reality Gap

Anthropologists tell us that in the world today there are people in every stage of evolution, from the Stone Age Tasaday in the Philippine jungles to the space-age peoples of technologically advanced nations like the United States and the Soviet Union. The same is true of the contemporary college scene, in which we can find all the stages through which higher education has passed, from the classical curriculum, which was the stuff of the early "gentry's education," to nontraditional and highly sophisticated scientific studies which are available to students of all ages, backgrounds, and income levels.

This multilayered campus, like the larger society, is in a state of transition, with familiar values, rules, and practices being challenged on every side. To accommodate yourself to the shift and flux of today's college life, you will need to develop a high degree of flexibility. Like the Greek god Proteus, who could assume a variety of shapes at will, you may find yourself making frequent adaptations to changing realities that bear little resemblance to your earlier expectations.

It will ease your adjustment considerably if, before registering as a student, you spend some time exploring the school you plan to attend. Most of the larger campuses have regularly scheduled visitors' tours which will acquaint you with the physical layout and with the resources and facilities that you will be using once you become a regular student. It is also possible to attend some of the large lecture classes as an auditor if there are seats available. This is a good time, before you come under the pressures of studying, to browse through the college libraries, stroll across the campus, stop for lunch at the campus coffee shop, pick up a book or two at the student store, and generally develop a sense of familiarity with the campus community in which you will be spending much of your time during the next few years. Then when the registration process is behind you and you're on your way to your first class, the feeling of strangeness will be less acute. One day, not too far off, you'll discover that the reality gap has been closed—that you are now a full fledged student and that although it isn't exactly the way you thought it would be, it's very much all right.

REFERENCES

1 William Marvel, "The University and the World," in Alvin C. Eunich (ed.), *Campus 1980,* Delacorte Press, New York, 1968.

2   Robert Ornstein, *The Psychology of Consciousness,* W. H. Freeman and Company, San Francisco, 1972.

3   Roger Kahn, *Why Students Rebel,* William Morrow & Company, Inc., New York, 1970.

4   Clark Kerr, *The Uses of the University,* Harper & Row, Publishers, Incorporated, New York, 1963.

5   Upton Sinclair, *The Goose-Step, Pasadena,* published by the author, 1922.

6   Patricia Cross, *Beyond the Open Door,* Jossey-Bass, Inc., San Francisco, 1972.

7   Study conducted by the University of Texas for the U.S. Office of Education, October 1975.

8   Fred S. Keller, "Goodbye, Teacher," *Journal of Applied Behavior Analysis,* Spring 1968.

9   *Learning to Use the Tools,* report of the Media Learning Resources Committee, UCLA, 1974.

10   J. R. Kidd, *How Adults Learn,* Association Press, New York, 1959.

11   Ronnie Dugger, "The Community College Comes of Age," *Change* magazine, February 1976.

12   Robert Nisbet, *On Learning and Change, Change* magazine, New Rochelle, N.Y., 1973.

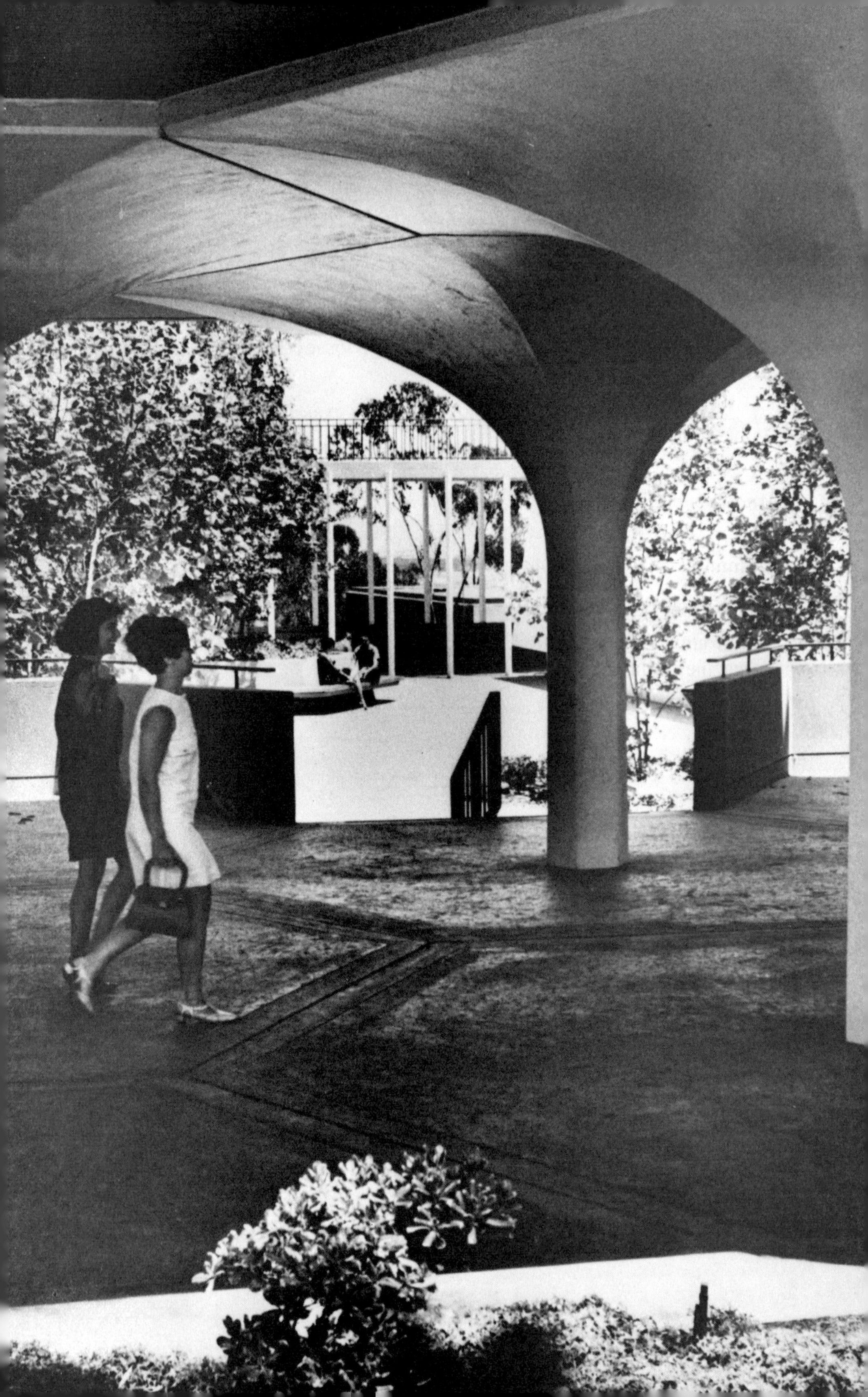

3 The School of Your Choice

I chose this university because, having put my husband through college, I felt it was my turn now, and I wanted the very best. Thirty-eight-year-old mother of two attending Stanford University.

Of all the decisions confronting the returning student, the most critical is: Which school? Yet in deciding to go back to school, many adults simply pick the college nearest their home, and that's the beginning and end of the decision-making process. Although location and convenience are important in choosing a school, many other factors should also be considered. In working with adults, we have found that the majority are unaware of these other considerations and, moreover, do not realize what a wide range of educational options and resources is open to them. A few decades ago the choices were far more limited, but today, by comparison, there is an embarrassment of riches awaiting those who wish to continue their education past secondary school. Choosing carefully and well from among the available options is particularly important for the returning adult, in terms of saving time, energy, and money and of avoiding the frustration of a poor first choice. This chapter will deal first with the large variety of educational resources available to the returning adult student. Then we shall take a careful look at the factors that you should consider in selecting the program best suited to your own educational needs.

WHAT ARE THE VARIOUS EDUCATIONAL AVENUES?

Resources in the educational world can generally be categorized into two broad areas—traditional and nontraditional. Traditional resources are usually the on-campus credit programs; they are formal, organized, and regularly scheduled, and they have some conformity over the years. Nontraditional resources include those programs, usually off campus, in which credit can be earned for study completed on the job, in fieldwork situations, or at home; in these programs study is scheduled and carried out by individual students at their own convenience.

TRADITIONAL EDUCATIONAL RESOURCES

The prospective adult student who looks to traditional educational programs will find extensive resources available. These include two-year colleges, four-year colleges and universities, and graduate and professional schools, as well as shorter programs, such as summer sessions and extension courses (offered at traditional colleges and universities), and specialized schools or colleges (for instance, colleges of music, computer technology, and business administration).

Two-Year Colleges

Two-year colleges—also called "community colleges" and, in some areas of the United States, "junior colleges"—have been a major focus for growth in higher education over the past twenty-five years. By 1975 there were two-year colleges available to American citizens in virtually every state of the Union. The returning adult student should consider both public and private two-year institutions as possible choices.

Public two-year colleges   People are usually aware of local two-year public colleges, mostly because these schools are very community-oriented (hence the name "community" colleges). These two-year colleges commonly have residence restrictions as a part of their entrance prerequisites (you must live in the district of a community college in order to enroll in its programs). Four types of educational programs are usually offered at these colleges:

1 Academic-transfer programs. A transfer community college program is a two-year academic curriculum that prepares a student to "transfer" to a four-year institution to complete a bachelor's degree. (In order to gain a sense of what the various academic fields are, you may refer to the list of academic curricula included at the end of this chapter.)

2 Technical or vocational training. Various types of technical or vocational training are usually offered by community colleges as terminal programs, that is, courses of study which are designed to lead to proficiency in vocational areas and which are terminated after a given period of time. (At the end of this chapter there is also a listing of vocational programs.)

3 Personal-development courses. The two-year colleges also provide courses or programs that enhance students' personal development by increasing their knowledge of subjects that they are interested in (for example, personal psychology and recreational skills).

4 Remedial education. Specially designed courses are provided to assist students in overcoming deficiencies in their previous education in such areas as reading comprehension, writing or composition, and mathematics.

In most cases, public two-year colleges have an open-admissions policy, which means essentially that people of all ages, regardless of their educational background, are eligible to enroll for as little as one course or as much as a full fifteen- to sixteen-unit program. It is for this reason that many adults returning to school find the two-year college a good avenue for reentry. Other positive characteristics of two-year colleges include:

1 A high emphasis on, and availability of, educational and occupational counseling

2 Short application deadlines

3 A relatively small-college environment (which makes for a more personalized educational experience than the bustling, densely populated environment of a large college or university)

4 Small class size

5 A well-educated, accessible faculty

6 Availability of part-time and evening classes

Perhaps the greatest advantage of the two-year colleges is that at these institutions, adult students are a respected and sought-after segment of the student population.

The two-year colleges generally have a degree system that grants an *associate of arts degree (A.A.)* for the two-year academic-transfer program (approximately sixty semester units); a *diploma,* or an *associate in science degree (A.S.),* for a two-year technical or vocational training program; and *certificates of completion* for a group of courses (lasting anywhere from two months to two years) that develop skills for specific occupations—for example, nurse's aide, teacher's aide, and various trade or industrial jobs.

One of the major advantages of attending a two-year college is the low cost involved (most two-year colleges have a tuition range from no cost to $500 a year, although the latter is an exception). Books and supplies may cost from $25 to $75, depending on the curriculum. Because these schools are community-based, the cost of transportation is generally reasonable.

Private two-year colleges The returning student often ignores the private two-year colleges as an alternative. Usually affiliated with a large university or a church, these schools offer a variety of programs both to people in the geographic area and to people from out of state. Because of their "private" status, the cost of attending such colleges is usually very high. However, in many cases these high costs, if one can afford them or manage to meet them with financial aid, may well be justified by the excellent quality and the flexibility of the programs such schools provide: special services, child care facilities, and adaptive-learning programs. The availability of a great variety of classes and the special interest generated by a close-knit, accessible faculty are other positive aspects of these types of schools. One should make sure that these schools are accredited, however, before actually enrolling.

Accreditation Accreditation is a key consideration when looking into private institutions. Basically, an accredited institution is one that has been evaluated and approved as meeting predetermined standards regarding its academic program, the extent and suitability of its curriculum, its faculty and administration, its library facilities, its financial viability, and its physical plant. Six regional accrediting agencies make these determinations. (See Appendix A for a listing of these accrediting associations.)

Accreditation is important mainly if an institution does not have it, since its lack means that the credit you get for courses there probably will not be accepted at other institutions either on a transfer basis or for graduate school application. As a means of evaluating your college record, employers often check to see whether the school you attended was accredited.

To find out more about specific public and private two-year colleges, you may refer to a variety of available publications that describe these schools in some detail. Bookstores (particularly those at colleges and universities) have them on sale. Most reference sections of even the smallest public libraries have copies of one or two. (You can also purchase copies of a publication directly from its publisher.) Some of the better-known references are listed in Box 1.

Box 1 Two-Year Colleges

American Association of Junior and Community Colleges: *Community, Junior, and Technical College Directory,* American Association of Junior and Community Colleges, Washington, 1975.

Cass, James, and Max Birnbaum: *Comparative Guide to Junior and Two-Year Community Colleges,* Harper & Row, Publishers, Incorporated, New York, 1972.

J. G. Ferguson Editorial Staff: *Ferguson Guide to Two-Year College Programs for Technicians and Specialists,* J. G. Ferguson Publishing, Chicago, 1971.

Gleazer, Edmund J., Jr. (ed.): *American Junior Colleges,* American Council on Education, Washington, 1971.

Graham, William R. (ed.): *Barron's Guide to Two-Year Colleges,* Barron's Educational Series, Woodbury, N.Y., 1975.

Richardson, Richard C.: *Student's Guide to the Two-Year College,* Prentice-Hall, Inc., Englewood Cliffs, N.J., 1968.

Four-Year Colleges and Universities

Is there a difference between a college and a university? Yes. Generally speaking, a university is an institution composed of several colleges and schools. In addition to a substantial offering of undergraduate studies in the liberal arts and sciences, the university offers graduate and professional training and doctorates in at least one field of study. Colleges, on the other hand, are usually four-year institutions, and some offer graduate work leading to a master's degree. In the first two years of both university and college programs, the student usually takes an exploratory sampling of courses; in the last two years the student is encouraged to concentrate on a "major" course of study. Academic fields of study vary a great deal from one college or university to another. In general, however, programs are similar to the ones outlined at the end of this chapter. The bachelor of arts (B.A.) and bachelor of science (B.S.) degrees are the major four-year degrees offered at these institutions.

Public four-year institutions Virtually every state in the Union has a public college or university system supported by tax revenues from the state. In many cases, states have both a state college system and a state university system. For example, in California, the State University system (which, before 1974, was called the State College system) is made up of nineteen campuses. Its major function is high-quality undergraduate education, as well as excellent programming at the master's level. Few Ph.D.'s are offered through this system. The University of California system is composed of nine campuses. Although undergraduate education is a part of its mandate, graduate education at the Ph.D. level and research are heavily emphasized. Usually state college systems are lower in cost and less rigorous in their admissions requirements than the university systems.

Public colleges and universities almost always have formal admissions requirements that include an evaluation of your high school record (regardless of when you graduated), in terms of grade-point average and prerequisite courses, and *any* college work done after high school graduation. In addition, certain entrance exams are required if you are applying to college for the first time. Transfer students from two-year colleges are required to have C averages if they are residents of that state; higher grade-point averages are required for nonresidents. Specific admissions information about individual colleges or universities can be obtained from their admissions offices, from state college and university relations-with-schools offices, and also from two-year college counseling offices.

Although the costs of attending a public college or university are certainly less than the costs of attending a similar private institution, they are not insignificant: The range of tuition fees is rising every year, the average yearly tuition now being between $600 and $800.

State colleges and universities tend to be considerably larger than two-year institutions. As a consequence, they often are "blessed" with more bureaucratic procedures with which you must deal than the two-year colleges are. On the other hand, in the four-year institutions you will also find a wider variety of course offerings and student services. Faculty members tend to be more heavily and highly, degreed than their colleagues in the two-year colleges. In some cases, classes are larger; often a teaching assistant (usually a graduate student), rather than a professor, acts as the instructor.

Although part-time attendance is becoming more acceptable, there is still some prejudice against the individual who is not a full-time student. The size of the university often dictates whether evening classes, which the returning student usually needs, are offered. Public four-year colleges and universities, have not adapted as well as the two-year colleges to adults as a part of their student population, although, of course, this situation varies from school to school. Generally, most adult students still have to forge their own way in public four-year institutions.

Private four-year institutions Private four-year colleges and universities provide perhaps the widest assortment of resources. These schools range from very small liberal arts colleges, sometimes affiliated with religious organizations, to large institutions like Stanford University in California or Columbia University in New York. Probably the most obvious factor about private institutions is the tuitions they charge, which range from $1,000 a year for a full-time program (at some of the smaller, lesser-known schools) to $5,000 or more a year at the bigger, more prestigious institutions. However, one should not automatically rule out these schools because of cost. Very often, particularly for low-income applicants, a variety of financial-aid opportunities are available. Even middle-income students can take advantage of loans, assistantships, and a variety of other ways of dealing with the financial aspects of going back to school (refer to Appendix A). Sometimes it is more cost-effective to attend a private school because of its greater flexibility in crediting units to your past educational or work experiences. In addition, the necessary element of a "supportive atmosphere" is present in many of the smaller private institutions.

Many publications describing four-year institutions are available. Some of these are included in Box 2 on page 60.

Graduate Schools and Professional Study

One might ask: after spending four or more years pursuing a bachelor's degree, why go on for a graduate degree? We have dealt in Chapter 1 with the general motivations for returning to school, but reasons for going on to graduate study are somewhat more specific. A 1971 study of adults at the University of California at San Diego indicated that they were interested in graduate study because they saw the end result as providing (1) a better job, (2) higher pay, (3) greater prestige, (4) higher status, and (5) greater flexibility.

Both public and private institutions offer graduate and professional study. Once again, we urge you to make sure that the school of your choice is accredited and, even more important, to check the accreditation of a particular school's program through its national professional organization (see Appendix C for a listing of these organizations). Many pro-

Box 2 Four-Year Colleges and Universities

> Barron's Editorial Staff: *Barron's Profiles of American Colleges*, Barron's Educational Series, Woodbury, N.Y., 1974.
>
> Berman, Susan: *Underground Guide to the College of Your Choice*, The New American Library, Inc., New York, 1971.
>
> Cass, James, and Max Birnbaum: *Comparative Guide to American Colleges*, Harper & Row, Publishers, Incorporated, New York, 1975.
>
> Dillenback, Douglas D., and Sue Wetzel (eds.): *The College Handbook*, College Entrance Examination Board, Princeton, N.J., 1972.
>
> Feingold, S. Norman, et al.: *College Guide for Jewish Youth*, B'nai Brith Vocational Service and Hillel Foundation, Washington, 1975.
>
> Furmiss, W. Todd (ed.): *American Universities and Colleges*, American Council on Higher Education, Washington, 1973.
>
> Hawes, Gene R., and Peter N. Novalis: *The New American Guide to Colleges*, Columbia University Press, New York, 1972.
>
> Lovejoy, Clarence E.: *Lovejoy's College Guide*, Simon and Schuster, New York, 1974.
>
> Thomson, Frances C. (ed.): *The New York Times Guide to Continuing Education in America*, Quadrangle Books, Inc., Chicago, 1973.

fessions have established their own accrediting agencies, which determine whether a school's program provides acceptable training for that profession. This accreditation is extremely important because very often it determines whether you will be able to be licensed in your profession (and therefore actually practice it). The American Medical Association accredits medical school programs, the American Bar Association accredits law school programs, the American Assembly of College Schools of Business accredits schools of business, and so on. Reference rooms of local libraries often have guidebooks describing graduate programs; these books indicate the accreditation status of specific programs. College career-planning or career-counseling centers also have this information on file. Finally, if neither of these resources is available to you, ask the professional organization in which you are interested to send you a list of its accredited schools.

Graduate study Graduate degrees are usually categorized at two levels: master's and doctorate. Some examples of the master's degree are master of arts (M.A.), master of science (M.S.), and master of social work (M.S.W.). The master's degree is granted for one or two years of full-time study beyond the bachelor's degree. The doctorate or doctor's degree is offered in a variety of forms also, including doctor of philosophy (Ph.D.), doctor, of law (J.D.), doctor of education (Ed.D.), and doctor of medicine (M.D.). A doctorate involves, minimally, three years of study beyond the bachelor's degree, and sometimes it requires as long as seven years.

Although individual programs of graduate study vary greatly from school to school, and even from department to department in the same college, two general areas can be described: academic programs and professional programs. Those individuals pursuing a master's degree in an academic area (history, sociology, engineering) usually spend one or two years taking courses. Sometimes written dissertations are required, and sometimes not. In pursuing a doctoral program, however, the usual sequence of events is as follows: being admitted after having taken the Graduate Record Examination (or perhaps another especially designated exam); taking a prescribed set of courses; taking either a written qualifying examination or an oral examination, or sometimes both, in the subject area after two years of study; and, finally, preparing a formal written dissertation or a research project (sometimes proficiency exams are required in one or two foreign languages as well).

Professional programs There is also a wide variety of programs available to individuals preparing for the professions, at either the Master's or the doctoral level. Sometimes professional training is a part of the bachelor's degree, or some specified courses beyond the B.A. may be required, as, for example, in the case of architecture, accounting, and certain types of engineering and teaching.

The process of preparing for graduate training in the professions usually involves taking courses during the undergraduate program that are prerequisites for entry into a professional program; taking an entrance examination (sometimes the examination is specific to a particular profession, like the MCAT for admission into medical school); gaining admission to a program; taking courses in the chosen field; serving an internship after the degree is obtained; and taking a licensing examination before working independently in the field.

Box 3 on page 62 contains some useful directions to graduate and professional studies.

Other Traditional Resources

Before moving on to discuss the nontraditional resources available to returning adult students, it is important to mention a few other traditional resources that are often ignored: (1) summer school or summer session programs offered through regular colleges and universities, (2) courses you take through the extension or continuing education divisions of traditional colleges and universities, and (3) specialized schools and colleges.

Box 3 Useful Directories to Graduate and Professional Study

> Berelson, B.: *Graduate Education in the United States*, McGraw-Hill Book Company, New York, 1960.
>
> Calvert, Jack G., et al.: *Graduate School in the Sciences: Entrance, Survival, and Careers*, Wiley-Interscience, New York, 1972.
>
> Chronicle Guidance Research Department (eds.): *Graduate and Professional Majors*, Chronicle Guidance Publications, Moravia, N.Y., 1973.
>
> Hegener, Karen C.: *Annual Guides to Graduate Study and Undergraduate Study*, Peterson's Guides, Inc., Princeton, N.J., 1974.
>
> Quick, Robert (ed.): *A Guide to Graduate Study Programs Leading to the Ph.D. Degree*, American Council on Education, Washington, 1969.
>
> Roose, Kennith D., and Charles J. Andersen: *A Rating of Graduate Programs*, American Council on Education, Washington, 1970.

Summer school Most colleges and universities provide a regular program of study during the summer that they call, not surprisingly, "summer school" or "summer session." Offering regular, transferable degree credit at both the undergraduate and graduate levels, summer sessions are usually shorter in length, and therefore more condensed, than regular school-year sessions. Although it is rather unusual, sometimes it is possible to earn a degree by attending a college during the summer. The most important feature of summer sessions to the returning adult student, however, is that there are no admission requirements; one has only to register for classes. Consequently, summer sessions provide returning adults with a unique opportunity to become familiar with campus life in a relaxed atmosphere. Students can meet and work with the faculty and test out their potential for returning to school on a regular basis. Summer study is also a useful way for students to explore a new field.

Extension: continuing education divisions College and university extension programs are usually self-supporting arms of the regular university program. Credit and noncredit courses are available, varying in length from one-day conferences and short lecture series to full-term courses and multiple-term certificate programs. Courses are offered not only on college campuses but also in many local, more convenient community centers. Although very few extension divisions are authorized to grant degrees, many offer courses that can be transferred to regular degree programs. (It is important to point out that most educational institutions accept only a *minimum* number of extension course credits; therefore, students should check with the college or university they plan to attend to see how many extension credits will be accepted, and under what conditions.) A most important feature of an extension pr⟨ ⟩ that one need not go through a formal admission process to regi⟨ ⟩ classes. In many cases, an adult student need only be present at th⟨ ⟩ meeting of a particular class. Courses with titles such as Math and Wr⟨ ⟩ Review for Going Back to School and Career Planning for Adults often provide the returning student with the confidence and skills that will make the actual return easier.

For more information about extension and continuing education programs, write to National University Extension Association, National Center for Higher Education, 1 Dupont Circle, N.W., Suite 360, Washington, D.C. 20036.

Specialized private schools and colleges Many educational institutions offer programs to students who are interested in certain kinds of advanced specialized training. For example, the Julliard School of Music in New York City offers a degree-granting program to individuals talented in music. There are similar schools for people who are interested in fashion, interior design, art, drama, theology, and optometry (to name a few). These institutions generally offer very practical kinds of instruction and pay little attention to the "liberal education" aspects of a student's development. Credit for study completed in these schools is sometimes transferable to a regular college or university, and sometimes it is not.

NONTRADITIONAL EDUCATIONAL RESOURCES

Experimental programs, adult programs, external degree programs, independent study, alternative degrees—these are just a sample of the variety of programs we shall discuss in this section. The major reason for this proliferation of program types is probably that nontraditional programs are relatively new to the educational scene, having been developed for the most part over the last five to ten years. Thus, although the nontraditional programs are here to stay, the forms and extent of this educational resource are still evolving.

What sparked the recent emergence of so many nontraditional programs? These programs developed (and are still developing) because of a number of phenomena: (1) During the examination of higher education that took place in the late 1960s, both young students and returning adult students began to seek educational avenues that were alternatives to the structured, usually inflexible ones available in the traditional institutions. (2) Also, partly as a result of the rapid obsolescence of knowledge (which makes periodic retraining a necessity), education is being looked at more and more as a lifelong or continuing process. In fact, in late 1975, the *Saturday Review* called lifelong learning an educational "boom."[1] A great variety of programs are consequently being developed to meet this need for continuing education, a need felt by people of all ages in our society. (3) Initially spurred by the women's movement of the late 1960s and early 1970s, whose proponents urged women to "develop themselves," and encouraged by the encounter and sensitivity movement, which supported "growth" and the development of one's human potential, more and more adults are making life-style and career changes that necessitate some form of reeducation. (4) Finally, and probably the most important reason for change in the educational institutions themselves, traditional university enrollments began to drop in the early 1970s. Colleges and universities consequently have had to look for alternative student markets in order to fill their growing economic void.

Many "traditional" kinds of students are now enrolling in nontraditional programs, especially those who want alternatives to their regular college programs. Basically, however, the alternative programs were designed for people who were denied access to, or who chose not to enroll in, traditional college or university programs (including the homebound; the physically, psychologically, or sociologically handicapped; the aged; those with scheduling barriers; the very mobile, such as the families of members of the armed forces, the geographically isolated).

Obviously, we cannot begin to describe every kind of program available because new programs are developing each day. We shall, however, identify at least six major types of nontraditional resources.

Experimental Programs within Existing Colleges and Universities

Mostly in response to the student "New Left" demand for more flexible educational opportunities, many traditional educational institutions are now developing programs that enable students to design their own educational programs with the help of faculty advisers. Actually, in order to meet the increasing demand for flexibility, schools are calling "experimental" many programs of study, ranging from a directed reading course or an independent study project to a complete four-year course of study structured by the student. Experimental programs in these institutions may thus include such various elements as attending regular college classes or special seminar classes, work-study experiences, independent study projects, courses at other colleges, study abroad, continued self-assessment of learning, or anything else a student proposes and can validate as an educational experience.

In many cases, experimental programs may serve as the university's or the college's testing ground, in that these programs provide opportunities to test out new ideas. The institution may then simply drop an idea if it does not work out or, if an idea proves successful, may integrate it into the regular university curriculum. The major advantage of enrolling in an experimental program within a traditional university or college setting is that the course credits you amass will probably be more readily accepted by other traditional undergraduate or graduate schools.

College Credit for Nonclassroom Activities

Did you ever stop to think how much you have learned from your own experiences, occupational and otherwise, even though you may not have sat through a year or two of classes to learn it? Returning adult students have available to them many shortcuts—that is, more direct routes—to gaining credit for their past activities outside the classroom. One of these routes is testing.

Credit for knowledge by exam For many years now adults who want to acquire a high school diploma—without actually having to go back to school—have been taking the tests of General Educational Development (GED). The success of these tests and of tests associated with the Advanced Placement Program of the College Entrance Examination Board (which offers college-level courses in high schools and prepares exams for which students, depending on their test performances, may be given credit or advanced standing in courses when entering college) has provided educators with the background necessary for developing a number of examinations that are of particular interest to the returning adult student. For a more elaborate discussion of entrance examinations and other credit opportunities, refer to Chapter 4.

External-Degree Programs
(Also Called "Extended Universities," "Special Adult Degree Programs," "Open Universities," and "Universities without Walls")

Within the nontraditional resources area, external degrees are probably the newest kind of degree and the least well known to the general public. Although most external-degree programs combine one or more of the nontraditional resources described in this section, there is no one resource so far discussed that can be said to have all the characteristics of this type of program. Cyril O. Houle, author of *The External Degree,* describes an external degree as "one awarded to an individual on the basis of some program of preparation (devised by himself or by an educational institution) which is not centered in traditional patterns of residential study."[2] Some elements characteristic of many of the external-degree programs now available are:

1 Degrees are granted for courses of study ranging from the two-year associate of arts to the doctorate.

2 In most cases the student is allowed to design and implement his or her own degree program on the basis of individual needs, talents, interests, abilities, and goals.

3 Many programs allow students to get credit for knowledge or training that they already have or for creative projects and products which they have completed before entering a program.

4 It is assumed that most external-degree course work and study will be completed away from the traditional campus at times and places that are convenient to the student.

5 Most external-degree programs provide the student with an academic adviser or tutor to help in designing and implementing the program of study. Contact may be in person, by telephone, through cassettes, through written correspondence, or by means of a combination of any of these.

6 Some external-degree programs include a student-institution contract that outlines the responsibilities of each to the course of study and sets a date by which the degree must be completed.

7 In many programs a specific major project, thesis, report, or product is a prerequisite for a degree (from the A.A. through to the Ph.D.).

8 Most programs require a minimum number of contact hours with an adviser and a limited amount of time "in residence" for orientation, evaluation, or seminar study.

Today, most students pursuing external degrees study certain specified subject areas, mainly the arts, education, the humanities, and the social sciences. Few individuals apply for external degrees in programs that require a heavy emphasis on very technical or scientific courses of study.

As is true of the programs themselves, costs directly attributable to enrolling in an external-degree program vary enormously. Some are fairly inexpensive (less than $1,000 for the entire degree), particularly when they are a part of a more traditional educational institution. Others can be as much as $8,000 to $10,000. There are no standard costs for external

degrees, and one really needs to shop around for the best "educati
buy."

To find out more about external-degree programs and where they are located, consult the resources listed in Box 4.

Box 4   External-Degree Programs

> Blaze, Wayne, et al.: *Guide to Alternative Colleges and Universities: A Comprehensive Listing of Over 250 Innovative Programs*, Beacon Press, Boston, 1974.
>
> Coyne, John, and Tom Hebert: *This Way Out: A Guide to Alternatives to Traditional College Education in the United States, Europe, and the Third World*, E. P. Dutton & Co., Inc., New York, 1972.
>
> Splaver, Sarah: *Nontradtional College Routes to Careers*, Simon & Schuster, Inc., New York, 1975.

Correspondence Study

Correspondence study has been available for many years and is particularly useful for the student who has unique requirements concerning when and where to study. Before you jump into a full program of correspondence study, you should be aware that most universities limit the number of units they will accept as credit toward a degree and that very few, if any, will allow a student to earn a degree solely by taking correspondence courses. Correspondence courses are appropriate for the student who wants to take a number of prerequisite courses before entering a regular curriculum or to prepare for certain proficiency examinations (for example, in language or writing). In some cases, correspondence study is aimed directly at helping students to pass the CLEP examinations.

The usual procedure for taking a correspondence course is the following:

  1   The potential student selects a school from which to take a course (one can get a listing of the accredited correspondence schools from the National University Extension Association).[3]

  2   The student submits an application form for a particular class and sends a check or money order for the course fee (most correspondence schools limit the number of classes a student may take at one time to two). The application form and required text order form are usually contained in the catalog. One can usually begin a correspondence course at any time.

3 The student receives a course-outline study guide, a list of assignments, and so on, and is given the name of the instructor to whom he or she will send completed assignments.

4 In most cases, when the student has completed the last course assignment, the correspondence school requires that he or she take a written final exam at some university-approved center.

Most correspondence study centers require that a course be completed within a one- or two-year period. Of late, some correspondence schools have arranged hours during which students may call their correspondence instructors and talk with them. Video tapes, cassette recordings, films, and records are also becoming more a part of correspondence study.

Instruction through Educational Technology

The electronics revolution of the 1960s made available what seems like unlimited educational opportunities to the would-be student. Although at present educational technology may still be in the infancy stage, numerous resources are becoming available almost daily. The following systems are now currently in use:

1 Course offerings through private, cable, and public television stations. A student can receive credit for watching "Introduction to Psychology," "Contemporary California Issues," or even the well-known "Ascent of Man" series, for example. Students can usually find out about these courses simply by consulting their own local newspaper or calling the local colleges for information about the availability and times of current offerings. As is the case with many other types of nontraditional resources, it is unlikely that a student could actually earn a degree by means of television courses alone, but these courses are now being offered for university credit. In order to receive this credit, students often must attend a few "contact sessions," located at centers throughout a viewing area. Although television stations are the medium through which courses are seen, it is up to the colleges and universities to offer specific credit for these courses. Sometimes a community college, private college, and public university all in the same area will offer credit for the same course.

2 Course offerings through radio. Radio courses resemble television courses, and are obviously limited to providing the student with information that does not require a "picture" to complete it. University music departments sometimes offer courses through the medium of radio. Once again, consulting the local newspaper listings is a good way of determining what, if anything, is available. As with television courses, the course credits are offered not by the radio stations themselves but by colleges in the area.

3 Video cassettes as a means of instructing. Community "learning centers," libraries (public and university),[4] adult schools, public school in-service education centers, colleges and universities, businesses, and university extension offices are just some of the places where one might be able to view video cassettes and earn credit for another form of off-campus learning. At some future point it is projected that students will be able to "check out," in person or by mail, video recordings that will be replayed on their own home units.

4 Courses in newspapers and magazines. Conceived of, and developed by, Caleb A. Lewis, of the University of California, San Diego extension, and supported initially by the National Endowment for the Humanities, a whole new method of transmitting knowledge has been made available to the public through the courses-by-newspaper project. One can earn credit for a newspaper course simply by reading a newspaper essay once a week, enrolling with the appropriately affiliated college or university, and completing the required assignments. Over 400 newspaper organizations and 230 affiliated universities have been offering courses with such titles as The Future of Man, American Issues Forum, and Oceans: Our Continuing Frontier. Popular magazines are beginning to see the potential promise of such projects for their subscribers, and it is not too farfetched to suggest that newspaper and magazine courses may be widely available at some future time.

There are many other forms of nontraditional learning resources that have not been mentioned in this chapter. Existing resources of this type are too numerous to account for in this book, and new ones are being formulated and experimented with constantly. We advise students to keep their eyes open for all new opportunities that do become available. Certainly your local library is one of the best sources of information on new developments. The resources listed in Box 5 should also prove helpful.

CHOOSING A SCHOOL

At this point you should know something more about the alternatives open to you as a returning adult student. As we have said before, knowing what is available is only one part of the process of deciding to go back to school. The next step is actually the most important one—selecting the best program for you. In order to choose wisely, you must consider a

Box 5 Nontraditional Learning Resources

Brooks, Jean S., and David L. Reich: *The Public Library in Nontraditional Study,* ETC. Publications, Homewood, Ill., 1974.

Dye, Carl M., and Gerald B. Flora: *Directory of College Transfer Information,* Monarch Press, New York, n.d.

Jensen, Beverly J.: *College by Mail,* Arco Publishing Company, Inc., New York, 1972.

Lewchuk, Ross C., and Richard A. Ungeia (eds.): *National Register of Internships and Experiential Learning: A Guide to Off-Campus Study Programs and Opportunities,* Acropolis Books, Washington, 1973.

National Media Programs, University of California Extension, San Diego and La Jolla, Calif., 1976.

Wax, Rosalie H.: *Doing Fieldwork: Warning and Advice,* The University of Chicago Press, Chicago, 1971.

Wurman, Richard S. (ed.): *Yellow Pages of Learning Resources,* The M.I.T. Press, Cambridge, Mass., 1975.

whole series of factors. Although it may be all right for the younger student to explore by actually enrolling in one institution after another (in order to finally find the "right one"), needless to say, most adults don't have time for this luxury. (Actually, neither does the younger student, but "finding oneself" through trial and error is considered more appropriate for adolescents than for adults, who usually have many more responsibilities and time strictures than their younger counterparts.)

Almost everyone faces the selection process feeling overwhelmed by the number of resources and by a lack of knowledge of how to choose. Too often, returning students make a quick decision based on expediency and emotional factors, rather than moving through a planned process that results in a wise choice. The returning student should set up certain requirements, establish priorities, and demand that certain criteria be met. When making up your own set of criteria and priorities for wisely selecting a college to reenter, you might consider some of the following:

1 Physical characteristics of the college
   a Location. Is it near your home? Is it in your state? Is it located in the city or in the country? Is it located on 160 acres, on one city block, or in various parts of a city?

   b Type of institution. Is it a university? A four-year college? A two-year college? Is it a private or a public institution? Does the college have a religious affiliation?

c Size of the student body. Is it very small to small—under 500 to 2,000? Is it medium-sized to large—2,000 to 10,000? Is it very large—over 10,000?

d Kinds of students. What is the enrollment by sex? What is the religious and racial makeup of the student body? What is the average socioeconomic standing of the students? What is their intellectual caliber? How many adult students are on campus? What is the geographic representation of the student body?

e Enrollment figures for specific programs. What is the size of the undergraduate, graduate, or departmental program you are interested in?

f Yearly costs. What are the costs for tuition, student fees, books, child care, food, and housing? How many of these costs must you assume?

g Educational philosophy. Is the college traditional or experimental? Are the students encouraged to participate in decision-making processes?

h Reputation. What are the college's admissions standards? How is its faculty rated? Where do its graduates get jobs or go for further schooling? What do its students think of the college?

i Accreditation. Are the total institution and its specific professional programs properly accredited?

j Campus atmosphere and environment. Is it a pleasant place? Are the buildings and grounds kept neat? Is the campus safe for both day and evening classes? Does the campus suit your temperament—are you comfortable there?

k Calendar plan. Is the campus on a semester, trimester, or four-quarter system? Does the system make any difference to you? Are summer sessions available?

l Transportation and housing. Is the college easily accessible by car or transit system? How much time would a commute require? What are the parking facilities? Is on-campus housing available for adults? What types of housing are available off campus?

2 Academic program

a Admission characteristics. What are the application deadlines? Is early admission possible? What, if any, admission tests are required? What are the specific entrance requirements? How flexible is the institution in dealing with the admission issues specific to adults? How competitive is admission to the college? Is credit for work experience and exams given?

b Residency. What are the residency requirements? Is part-time study permitted?

c Degrees, programs, and courses. Does the college offer what you are interested in? What is the scope of basic courses available in your field? Are upper-division or graduate-level courses offered in your areas of interest? Are the classes large or small? Is a sufficient variety of courses available at times that are convenient for you, such as days, evenings, or weekends?

d Graduation requirements. What are the specific requirements for graduation? How long will it take you to graduate?

e Nontraditional resources. Are resources such as independent study, seminars, work-study programs, television courses, programmed learning courses, and study abroad available?

f Grading system. What is the system? Is it a traditional A-to-F system? Are some pass/fail options available?

g Special programs. Are there programs in such areas as women's studies, ethnic studies, and environmental concerns?

h Faculty. What is the ratio of faculty to students? How much individual attention can the faculty give to students? Is it important to you to have access to faculty members on a one-to-one basis?

3 Facilities and services

a Facilities and services offered specifically for adult students. Is there a reentry program? Is there an adult-student association? Is there a special gathering place for adults on campus?

b Housing. Is university housing available for single adults? Is university housing available for married students?

c Learning resources. Has the university developed, specifically for adults, either credit or noncredit review courses in math, reading, or writing? Are tutors available? Are study-skills classes offered?

d Athletic programs. What types of programs are available? Is the physical education department oriented to adults as well as to younger students? Is general physical fitness of concern? Are intramurals an integral part of campus life?

e Child care. Is child care available on campus, and what is the cost? Are fathers as well as mothers eligible to use such services? At what times of day and night are the services available? What is the quality of the child care facilities?

f Financial aid. Is financial aid available? Are there knowledgeable financial-aid counselors available, trained specifically to deal with adult concerns? Are part-time work opportunities available on campus?

g Veterans' affairs. Is there an active VA office on campus? Is it able to help both young and older veterans?

h Health, mental health, and career-planning services. Are these services available, and to what degree are they oriented to the adult student?

i Libraries. What are the facilities? Are there comfortable places to study? Is the library open at times convenient to you?

j Special student needs. Are there services and facilities especially developed for handicapped students?

k Food services. Are dining halls for use only by dormitory students? Are food-service centers also student gathering places? Are there coffee shops? Are the services open in the evenings?

l Student centers. Are there places where students and faculty members can meet informally? What is the nature of student activities? Is the cultural life rich?

4 Special considerations in choosing a nontraditional program
  a Accreditation. Is this special type of program accredited or in the process of being accredited?

  b Supportive services. Have special services been developed to meet the specific needs of nontraditional students, including counseling and tutoring, for example? Are there places where students can meet informally?

  c Degrees. What is the meaning of the nontraditional degree offered? Does it have value in the job market? Will other educational institutions accept this degree as preparation for advanced programs? Are there time limits for completing the degree?

Once you know what your options are in terms of returning to school, you can make a really informed choice. Take a look at the various factors outlined above and list the ten or fifteen that are most important to you, perhaps even assigning priorities. Then visit the school, walk around the campus, talk with the instructors, and eat in one of the dining rooms. Perhaps the most important thing for you to do is to talk with adult students on the campus who are taking courses in the areas that interest you. Your "gut" reactions are very important, and you should have some sense of belonging on a particular campus.

In choosing a specific school to attend, remember that educational institutions will be "choosing" too; this is especially true of the more competitive, prestigious institutions. It might be wise to apply to a number of colleges. Be sure to include one at which your acceptance is virtually guaranteed and also one or two (perhaps your first choices) at which your acceptance is in question. Never eliminate any possibilities until you have at least had an opportunity to explore with the institution *personally* what your chances are for admission. Very often, a few admission spots will open up; many admissions officers have a high degree of flexibility in setting aside some admissions places under "unusual" circumstances. We have found that, particularly for adults with a high degree of motivation and a sense of purpose, rules can be bent, changed, relaxed, avoided, or ignored. Exercise persistence and thoroughness in obtaining information; remember that interviews are especially important in getting results.

POSSIBLE VOCATIONAL OR TECHNICAL FIELDS OF STUDY IN TWO-YEAR COLLEGES

Agriculture. Includes nursery and landscape technology, forestry and wildlife, agricultural technology.

Business.

Education. Includes nursery school aide, instructional assistant, library technician.

Health services. Includes emergency medical care, dental assisting, medical assisting, nursing.

Office technologies. Includes bookkeeping, data processing, medical-clerical work, secretarial work.

Technical services. Includes air-traffic control, computer technology, instructional media, micrographics, pilot training, surveying, technical writing.

Trade and industry. Includes air conditioning, architectural drafting, automotive repair, commercial art, machine shop, power sawing, television service and repair.

Trade and industry apprenticeship. Includes automotive, barbering, bricklaying, carpentry, ironworking, machinist, painting.

Public services. Includes library assistant, law enforcement, fire control, mortuary science, social work.

This listing is only a sample of how vocational and technical fields of study are organized. Consult your local two-year college for specific course offerings.

POSSIBLE ACADEMIC FIELDS OF STUDY IN TWO-YEAR COLLEGES AND FOUR-YEAR COLLEGES AND UNIVERSITIES

Academic disciplines are specific branches of learning. Generally they are grouped as the *natural sciences* (the physical and biological sciences); the *social sciences* (psychology, sociology, anthropology, economics, political science, and sometimes history); and the *humanities* (which usually include fine arts, history, languages, literature, and philosophy).

Agriculture and environmental sciences. Includes agronomy, animal husbandry, forestry, horticulture, wildlife management.

Biological sciences. Includes anatomy, biology, botany, ecology, genetics, marine biology, microbiology, nutrition.

Business. Includes accounting, banking, finance, hotel management, industrial relations, management, marketing, real estate, secretarial science, transportation.

Communications. Includes journalism, radio, television.

Education. Includes counseling and psychological studies, educational administration, curriculum and instruction, special education.

Engineering. Includes aerospace engineering, chemical engineering, civil engineering, electrical engineering mechanical engineering.

Fine arts. Includes architecture, art, art history, cinematography, drama, environmental design, music, photography.

Health sciences. Includes administration, medical technology, nursing, occupational therapy, physical therapy, public health.

Home economics.

Humanities. Includes English, foreign languages, literature, philosophy, history, theology.

Information and computer processing.

Mathematics.

Physical sciences. Includes astronomy, chemistry, geology, oceanography.

Social sciences. Includes anthropology, economics, history, political science, psychology, sociology, urban and rural studies.

This is only one way in which academic programs of studies are organized by colleges and universities. Each school has its own unique method of presenting its course work. There are, in addition, new courses of study such as interdisciplinary programs, women's studies, and East African studies that are beyond this usual order of courses. There are also professional fields such as medicine, social work, business, and law. The best way to determine what a particular school is offering is to consult its catalog.

REFERENCES

1 *Saturday Review,* Sept. 20, 1975, pp. 14–29.

2 Cyril O. Houle, *The External Degree,* Jossey-Bass, Inc., San Francisco, 1973.

3 *Guide to Independent Study through Correspondence Instruction,* National University Extension Association, Washington.

4 Libraries are becoming a major resource to the independent learner. Under the auspices of the Office of Library Independent Study and Guidance Projects of the College Entrance Examination Board (888 Seventh Avenue, New York, N.Y. 10019), libraries are providing new services and resources in supporting adults in their efforts to be "self-directed learners." Libraries in the following areas have these programs: Atlanta, Ga.; Denver, Colo.; Baltimore, Md.; Woodbridge, N.J.; Miami-Dade, Fla.; Portland, Maine; St. Louis, Mo.; Salt Lake City, Utah; Tulsa, Okla.; and Cleveland, Ohio.

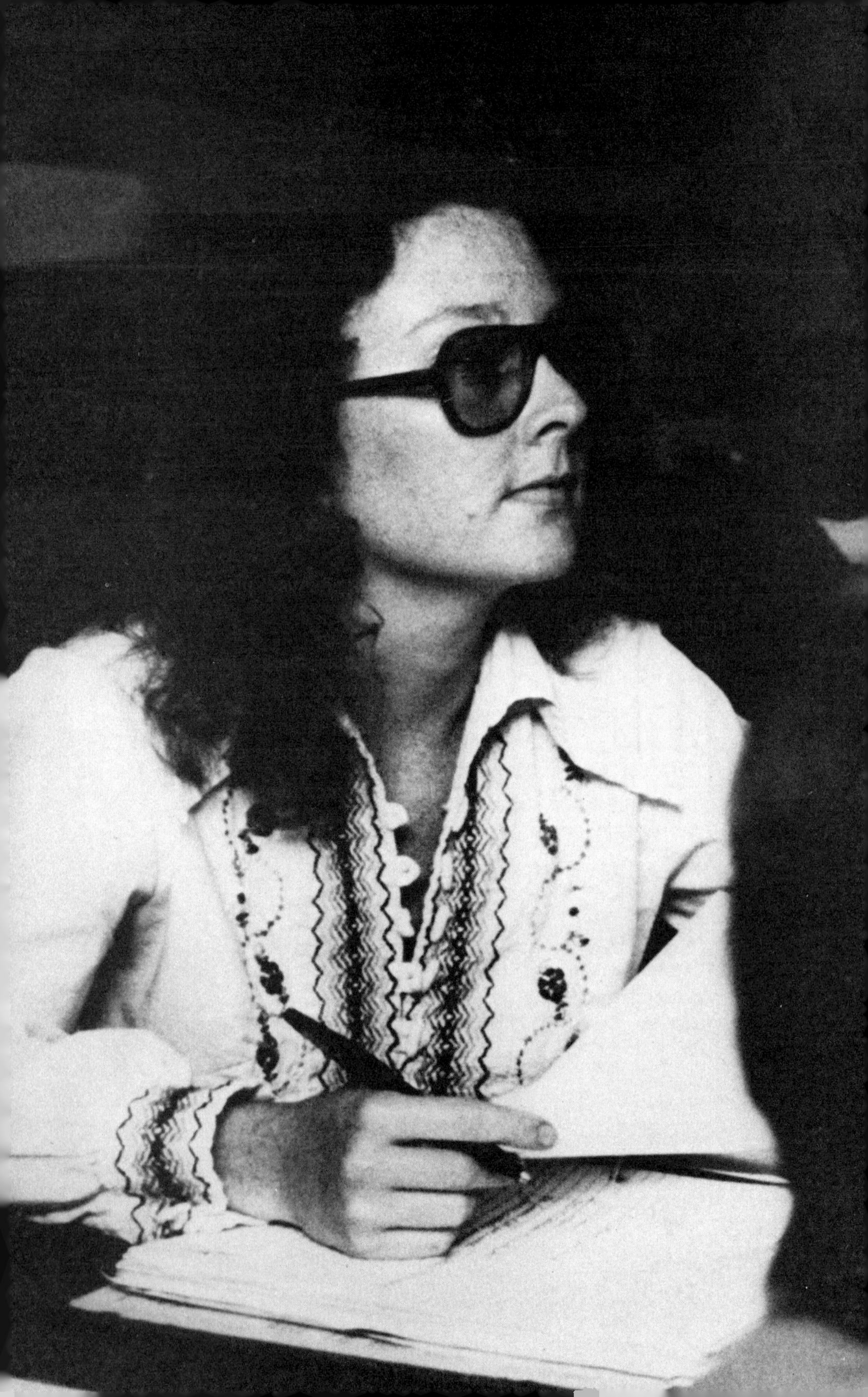

4 Getting Past the Gatekeepers

The problem is that students, regardless of age, are treated like children. Undergraduate counselor, UCLA.

Since higher education was designed primarily for the young, the admissions process in four-year colleges and universities has been geared to traditional students, whose school experience is either directly or not very far behind them. However, as a result of pressure from mature and other nontraditional applicants, admissions policies and procedures are changing shape and taking on new and unexpected dimensions. Of all the changes occurring in higher education, the innovations which affect the point of entry will probably have the most far-reaching significance for adults seeking to continue their education.

To understand how admissions policies work and how they may

affect your application for admission to an institution of higher education, it is helpful to have some knowledge of how these policies have evolved. Colleges and universities have historically operated on an exclusionary principle which, simply stated, says that criteria should be established for letting certain people in and keeping other people out. This principle is still at work, although the criteria have gone through various changes and a new and complex set of answers is being generated to the question: Who should have access to higher education?

FROM ARISTOCRACY TO EQUAL OPPORTUNITY

In its early history, higher education was regarded as an exclusive preserve for the training of young men from upper-class families. Before the land-grant movement, those who attended the private tuition colleges—Harvard, Princeton, Yale—came from high-status, moneyed backgrounds. They were as close to an aristocracy as America had ever produced, and being born into this elite was virtually a guarantee of admission to college. Young people going to college at this time were expected to fulfill only two requirements: (1) They had to be able to afford a college education, and (2) their station in life had to require it. "For generation after generation," Henry Adams tells us, "Adamses and Brookses and Boylstons and Gorhams had gone to Harvard College, and although none of them, as far as known, had ever done any good there or thought himself the better for it, customs, social ties, convenience and above all, economy, kept each generation in the track . . . all went there because their friends went there, and the College was their ideal of social self-respect."[1]

The land-grant universities signaled the end of this aristocratic era in higher education and the beginning of a new order which opened the gates to those who could earn the right to a college education instead of acquiring it by birth. Advocates of the land-grant idea questioned such gatekeeping practices as tuition which excluded the children of working people, and they challenged the curriculum, which they felt was unrelated to the needs of the new clientele. Education, in their view, should prepare young people for well-paying jobs and professional careers.

This called for a new emphasis—on academic merit rather than social class. In place of aristocracy, we now had meritocracy, which produced a new set of gatekeeping practices in the form of grades and test scores. The principle of meritocracy is summed up in a statement from a 1954 study by the Commission on Human Resources and Advanced Training: "The nation needs to make effective use of its intellectual resources. To do so means to use well its brightest people, whether they come from farm or city, from the slum section or the country club area, regardless of color or religious differences but not regardless of ability."[2]

The rise of the meritocracy has been generally considered a progressive step, bringing higher education closer to the American democratic ideal. But, ironically, the meritocrats were setting up some obstacles of their own and replacing one set of gatekeepers by another. True, the gates had been opened wider, but it was still assumed that only a fairly small percentage of the population had the ability to benefit from a college education. In the 1940s and 1950s, when the principle of meritocracy was at its peak, studies of the potential college clientele placed the figure at no more than 25 to 35 percent of the population.

Today, though meritocracy is still the ruling principle, it is being challenged by the rise of an egalitarian view which claims that the prevailing definition of academic merit is narrow and rigid and that it reflects the abilities and aspirations of a middle-class, technologically oriented sector of the society. According to this argument, "merit" is not culturally neutral, and college entrance tests based on "aptitude" produce different results when taken by the son of a successful surgeon, a black youngster from the ghetto, a housewife in her forties, and a Mexican American whose parents are Spanish-speaking farm workers.

The fairness of merit criteria comes into question when one considers the continuing relation between college attendance and income levels: The most recent Census Bureau figures indicate that families with incomes over $15,000 are four times as likely to send their children to college as families with incomes under $3,000. Further, since the merit principle holds that the rewards go to the deserving, those who are unable to pass through the gates tend to blame themselves rather than the "system" for their failure.

Citing the high individual and social costs of these practices, proponents of the egalitarian principle favor an "open-admissions" policy which would make higher education available to all those with a high school education who want to go to college, regardless of their ability to meet the established criteria of academic merit. Whether this principle will ultimately replace meritocracy or not, its influence is being felt in college entrance attitudes and policies. In returning to school at this time, your experience with the admissions process in higher education will be shaped mainly by meritocracy, but elements of the newer egalitarian approach will also be at work as you make your way past the gatekeepers.

RUNNING THE OBSTACLE COURSE

The roadblocks on the mature applicant's path through the admissions office vary considerably with the type of institution. The community college is favored by a majority of older students primarily because of its open-admissions policies. As we saw in Chapter 2, the public two-year college, in fulfilling its mission to serve the community in the widest possible sense, extends its embrace to all those residing within its district who are eighteen years of age or older. Most community colleges do not even require a high school diploma.

But these two-year institutions have their limitations—of space, for one thing. Classes fill up quickly, and it may be difficult to find a place in the courses you need for your program. Also, because of their vocational orientation, community colleges offer a limited range of enrichment courses in the liberal arts, fine arts, and social sciences. And there are returning students who prefer the learning environment of a four-year college or university, with its many cultural amenities and facilities, and who want these advantages right from the beginning.

If you are among those who have decided to apply directly to a four-year college or university, you will find that the admissions process is not as simple and routine as in a two-year college. But this is to be expected, since, admissions procedures in the four-year colleges and universities have been developed for the traditional student, who moves in lockstep from the secondary to the postsecondary level. We have seen in Chapter 3 how the application blank addresses itself to these younger students. In addition, our inventory or obstacles on the mature student's path to admission includes requests for letters of reference from recent teachers, passing of examinations that assume recent exposure to facts, difficulties in transferring credits, reliance on dated records, ingrained attitudes of admissions directors and counselors, bureaucratic impersonality, and the narrow definition of "academic merit" in accordance with the meritocratic principle. Although these practices and attitudes are rarely the result of official policy, they tend to place older students at a disadvantage.

In a report on male undergraduates, it was found that middle-aged students were disturbed by the fact that admissions people and counselors tended to discount or even ignore their nonscholastic life experiences.[3] Their impression is borne out by admissions practices in many public colleges and universities that do not take account of applicants' nonacademic achievements. This leads to such absurdities as requiring a returning student who has spent ten years in a high-level management position to take beginning courses in management in order to earn credits toward the undergraduate degree. It can be unnerving to reentering students to discover that, in the milieu they are seeking to enter, none of their hard-won learning experiences are of any value unless they can be measured in academic units (as we'll see later on in this chapter, the problem of crediting life experiences is receiving increasing attention in higher education).

But the barriers that loom largest for nontraditional students are the entrance examinations which are used to "process" applicants for undergraduate admission. These standardized national tests, together with your high school records (or, if you're seeking graduate admission, college records), are the basis on which your application will be either accepted or rejected. Although standardized tests for college admission have been given since the turn of the century, it is only in the past two decades that the practice has become nationwide. There is some disagreement among administrators concerning how much reliance is placed on the tests; a University of California admission officer says that except for those in English composition, the tests are used mainly for "statistical purposes." But most college and university officials believe the tests serve an important purpose in providing a standard national measurement for students of widely varying ability.

Like all examinations, these tests generate some degree of anxiety, regardless of the age or experience of the persons taking them. For the mature applicant, the anxiety level tends to rise in proportion to the number of years he or she has been out of school. If, for example, you have spent the past fifteen years seeking out bargains at the supermarket, preparing nourishing casseroles, and chauffeuring children to music lessons and orthodontists, an entrance examination will seem more formidable to you than to a recent high school graduate, for whom taking tests is a familiar routine.

Learning all you can about the kinds of tests you are likely to encounter along the admissions route can be helpful in overcoming your fear of the unknown. The examinations discussed below are the ones most commonly used by the nation's colleges and universities for denying or granting admission to undergraduate standing.

GENERAL EDUCATION DEGREE TEST (GED)

If you left school before obtaining your high school diploma, your first step is to apply to your state department of education for information about taking the High School Equivalency Examination, more familiarly known as the GED, or General Education Degree. This program is administered nationally by the American Council on Education, but each state has its own policies and procedures, which vary mainly in terms of administrative methods. In most states, an adult who achieves a satisfactory score on the High School Equivalency Examination is eligible to receive a high school equivalency diploma or certificate, which is the legal equivalent of the diploma issued by a high school. Most colleges will admit a student whose High School Equivalency Examination scores are in line with their admissions requirements for high school graduates and will accept the scores in place of a high school transcript.

The GED has been designed to make it possible for adults, whatever their age, who did not graduate from high school to have their academic knowledge tested without having to go through an educational routine designed for youngsters. The examination, which is given at official GED test centers (your state department of education will tell you which is the one nearest to you), consists of a series of five tests. Since the total testing time is ten hours, with two hours allotted to each test, the examination is given over a two-day period. If you fail to make the minimum required score on one or more parts of the test, you may retake those parts later.

The testing areas cover the five fields that make up the major areas of a typical high school curriculum:

Correctness and effectiveness of expression

Interpretation of reading materials in the social studies

Interpretation of reading materials in the natural sciences

Interpretation of literary materials

General mathematical ability

If you are planning to take the GED test, you are advised to begin studying early, spreading your study over a period of several months rather than attempting to "cram" at the last minute. Books containing practice GED tests are available at bookstores and libraries, and as is the case with all standardized tests, it is the steady, day-to-day practice that will produce the best results. You may also wish to enroll in a GED preparation program, which is offered in many adult schools around the country.

The following is a sample question from the test on correctness and effectiveness of expression:

> Directions: Each of the following groups consists of four words, one of which may be misspelled. On the answer sheet, blacken the space under the number corresponding to the number of misspelled words. If no word is mispelled, blacken the fifth space.
>
> **1** (1) horrified (2) procede (3) subjunctive (4) dynasty
>
> **2** (1) ferocious (2) judicious (3) automation (4) honorific

Since "proceed" was misspelled, your answer would look like this:

```
1        2        3        4        6
| |      ■        | |      | |      | |
| |      | |      | |      | |      | |
```

84 SO YOU WANT TO GO BACK TO SCHOOL

Sample questions like this one in all five testing areas are available in the practice book, which also offers a helpful self-evaluation profile to be used with a diagnostic test which is a replica of an actual GED test.

SCHOLASTIC APTITUDE TEST (SAT)

Every year, on six Saturday mornings, approximately 1½ million students gather at thousands of test centers throughout the nation and abroad to take the three-hour Standard Aptitude Test; this test and the achievement tests in specific fields of knowledge make up the "college boards." These tests, which are designed by the Educational Testing Service in Princeton, are taken to meet the entrance requirements of some 1,500 colleges and universities. The SAT consists of a verbal section and a mathematical section, plus a thirty-minute test in standard written English, intended to reveal the student's ability to write expository essays. This third section was added recently in response to the concern of many colleges over the fact that entering students are unable to write clearly and accurately; it is used not for admissions purposes but for postentrance placement in freshman English courses.

Here is a typical question appearing in the verbal section of the SAT (questions of this sort test the extent and quality of your vocabulary):

> Directions: Each question below consists of a word in capital letters, followed by five lettered words or phrases. Choose the lettered word or phrase that is most clearly *opposite* in meaning to the word in capital letters. Since some of the questions require you to distinguish fine shades of meaning, consider all the choices before deciding which is best.
>
> 6 COMPOSURE: (A) analysis (B) alertness (C) contrast (D) agitation (E) destruction

The word "composure" means calmness or self-possession. Choices (A), (C), and (E) can be eliminated, as they are clearly not opposites of calmness. Although choice (B), "alertness," suggests mental activity and attentiveness, its opposite would be a word specifically suggesting lack of attention. The correct answer is therefore choice (D), "agitation," which means emotional disturbance or excitement. When this question was used, it was correctly answered by 67 percent of the students.

This question, like the others in the verbal section, does not appear especially difficult or complicated, and yet the preparation of such a test question involves 150 steps and may take as long as two years. The tests are designed to serve as measuring rods, capable not only of assessing academic aptitude but also of differentiating between different levels of ability; thus they vary considerably in degree of difficulty. The verbal section of the SAT tests your vocabulary and reading skills using four types of verbal questions: antonyms, analogies, sentence completions, and reading passages.

The mathematical questions test your problem-solving ability in three areas: arithmetic reasoning, elementary algebra, and informal geometry. These are designed to measure abilities closely related to college-level work. Two kinds of multiple-choice questions appear in the mathematical portion of the SAT:

1 Standard multiple-choice questions (approximately two-thirds of the test)

2 Quantitative comparison questions (approximately one-third of the test)

The following is a typical multiple-choice question from the mathematical section:

Directions: In this section solve each problem using any available space on the page for scratchwork. Then indicate the *one* correct answer in the appropriate space on the answer sheet.

The following information is for your reference in solving some of the problems.

Circle of radius r:
   Area = πr^2
   Circumference = $2\pi r$
   The number of degrees of arc in a circle is 360.
   The measure in degrees of a straight angle is 180.

Triangle:
   The sum of the measures in degrees of the angles of a triangle is 180.

   If $\angle$ CDA is a right angle, then

(1) area of $\triangle$ ABC = $\dfrac{AB \times CD}{2}$

(2) $AC^2 = AD^2 + DC^2$

Definitions of symbols:
   $<$ is less than $\leq$ is less than or equal to
   $>$ is greater than $\geq$ is greater than or equal to
   $\perp$ is perpendicular to $\parallel$ is parallel to

Note: Figures which accompany problems in this test are intended to provide information useful in solving the problems. They are drawn as accurately as possible EXCEPT when it is stated in a specific problem that its figure is not drawn to scale. All figures lie in a plane unless otherwise indicated. All numbers used are real numbers.

11 If 16 × 16 × 16 = 8 × 8 × P, then P =
(A) 4 (b) 8 (C) 32 (D) 48 (E) 64

The answer is (E). Seventy percent of the students answered correctly.[4]

How well do the tests perform their function? There is some controversy about this in higher education circles. Standardized tests are sharply criticized by many academic traditionalists and by those in the humanities who claim that there is no way to standardize aptitude as it relates to the learning experience at its deepest and most significant levels. Others, particularly those trained in psychometrics, maintain that the tests are excellent tools and that they do their job well.

The SAT tests are scored by a formula that has been designed to discourage guesswork. The raw score is arrived at by the number of correct answers minus the number of wrong answers. (One quarter of a correct answer is deducted from each incorrect answer as a correction for haphazard guessing.) Test takers are advised to avoid haphazard guessing but to attempt informed guesses if they think they have enough knowledge to eliminate one or more answer choices.

The completed tests are shipped back to the Educational Testing Service in Princeton, where computers transfer the answers to magnetic tape and score them. The ETS computer center has a remarkable record of accuracy: More than 99 percent of the tests are scored without error. In order to resolve any questions about the accuracy of the scores, answer sheets are kept on file for a year. Students frequently retake the tests in order to raise their scores. The mean in recent years has been 440, which represents a decline from the 1963–1964 national average of 475.

The decline in the SAT scores in both the math and verbal sections is considered by critics of American education to be evidence that high school academic performance is deteriorating. The following are among the explanations offered to account for the decline: faultiness of the tests themselves, which are not keyed to present-day educational realities; television watching, which undermines verbal skills; a changing pool of test takers, including more students from disadvantaged backgrounds and more housewives whose learning skills have declined; and changing cultural values among the young, as a result of which the tests are taken less seriously. In any case, in most colleges and universities around the country the consensus is that standardized tests are here to stay and will continue to influence admissions policies for the foreseeable future.

It costs $6.50 to take the SAT and $11 to take achievement tests, although the fees may be waived for low-income students. (For further information, write to Educational Testing Service, Princeton, New Jersey 08540.)

COLLEGE-LEVEL EXAMINATION PROGRAM (CLEP)

The movement to grant credit for off-campus learning is a direct result of the entrance of mature and other nontraditional students into the world of higher education. Credit for prior learning attempts to "recognize learning that has resulted through experience before the student sought to enroll for college programs or which occurred when he or she was enrolled though not under the supervision and auspices of the institution . . . it includes all types of out-of-classroom experiences that result in learning judged to be of college level. . . ."[5]

The mechanism most commonly employed to evaluate and assign credit for learning that has taken place before the applicant's college entrance is the examination. The theory behind such tests is that knowledge at the college level should count for college credit, regardless of how it was acquired. Of the prior-learning tests administered nationally, the most fully developed and best known are the College Level Examination Programs (CLEP) exams. Sponsored by the College Entrance Examination Board of Princeton, New Jersey, CLEP was begun in 1965 and was introduced to colleges and universities in 1966. CLEP was intended to facilitate transfer for students and also to promote career mobility by assisting adults who wished to continue their education in order to meet licensing and certification requirements or to qualify for higher-level positions. Since it is possible to receive as much as one year's college credit through the CLEP examinations, this method of gaining entry represents a considerable savings in time and money for returning students.

The CLEP examinations are given at test centers throughout the United States during the third week of each month. Anyone may register and, for nominal fees, take one or several of these examinations. Two groups of exams are offered: (1) five general exams (sixty minutes long) covering English composition, the humanities, mathematics, the natural sciences, and the social sciences and (2) more than forty subject exams (ninety minutes long) covering subjects offered in specific college courses such as those in American government, behavioral sciences for nurses, elementary computer programming, and Western civilization. The tests are multiple-choice and are designed to test materials usually covered during the first two years of college—what educators refer to as the "common elements of areas of subject matter." The College Entrance Examination Board does not grant college credit itself; rather, it provides the means by which institutions of higher education can assess off-campus credit toward the degrees they offer. According to the CEEB, more than 1,500 institutions in all fifty states now offer credit on the basis of CLEP scores. CLEP examination scores are expressed on a scale of 200 to 800, with a mean of 500.

The general exams are designed to measure growth in knowledge similar to that achieved by college sophomores. By contrast, the subject examinations are designed to measure learning in terms of its equivalency to learning that would be achieved in specific college courses. As the CEEB puts it, these subject exams "stress concepts, principles, relationships, and applications of course materials." The following is a typical CLEP exam question from the general examination group in the humanities:

> Which of the following characters is INCORRECTLY paired with the novel in which he appears:
>
> (A) Heathcliffe . . . Pride and Prejudice
> (B) Pip . . . Great Expectations
> (C) Jake Barnes . . . The Sun Also Rises
> (D) Rochester . . . Jane Eyre
> (E) Clym Yeobright . . . The Return of the Native

The correct answer is (A).

Here is a typical question from the subject exam category in educational psychology:

> According to Piaget, a child's speech during the earliest stages of language development is directed primarily toward
>
> (A) himself
> (B) his mother
> (C) inanimate objects
> (D) modifying his social environment
> (E) modifying his physical environment

The correct answer is (A).

As you might expect, the CLEP exams, which represent a departure from traditional academic entry procedures, have not escaped criticism. Institutions using CLEP have been charged with granting credit without regard to what the test averages represent, as a result of which "students are acquiring college credits for knowledge that is partly subcollegiate, partly unclassifiable, and in some cases, trivial in quantity."[6] But CLEP also has its staunch defenders, who maintain that, among the many advantages they offer the mature student, CLEP exams are a good means of transforming the life experiences and nontraditional education activities of the average American housewife into college credit. An experimental CLEP program at the St. Louis campus of the University of Missouri is offered as an example. The purpose of the program was to assess the ability of mature women to qualify for college credit through CLEP. Over a two-year period, almost 900 women took a CLEP exam, and 58 percent earned a credit-recommending score on at least one of the five subtests of the general examination.[7]

If you decide to take a CLEP exam, you should keep the following points in mind:[8]

It is not necessary to answer all the questions on a test correctly in order to get an acceptable or even a high score.

Institutions that use the CLEP exams differ greatly from one another in the scores they designate as passing and in the total amount of credit they allow. Be sure to check with the school of your choice to determine whether and to what extent it credits CLEP exams.

You may have your scores sent only to yourself if you wish, or you may have them sent directly to the institution you are planning to enter.

CLEP examinations may be repeated. Students wishing to retake a CLEP exam must send a request for permission to repeat the test along with a registration form to the College Board at least four weeks in advance of the new test date. The general examinations may be repeated after three months, and the subject examinations after six months.

COLLEGE PROFICIENCY EXAMINATION PROGRAM (CPEP) AND REGENTS EXTERNAL DEGREE EXAMINATIONS (REDE)

These tests provide another way of earning credit for nonacademic experiences. Established by the New York Board of Regents in the early 1960s, CPEP offers credit through examinations in more than twenty-five subject areas in the arts and sciences, education, health, nursing, business, and foreign languages. The REDES are given in the fields of nursing, business, and foreign languages. As with the CLEP exams, the New York State Education Department does not actually grant CPEP/REDE credit directly; more than 200 institutions in New York State, Connecticut, Illinois, Idaho, and Oregon grant credit on the basis of their determination of minimally acceptable scores. The examinations are also used in New York State to meet state teacher certification and licensure requirements.[9]

OVERCOMING THE OBSTACLES

Entrance examinations, though they may seem forbidding, can actually work to the advantage of the returning adult. Since they test your reasoning power and your ability to comprehend, rather than an accumulated store of information, you may in fact be better prepared for these tests than the recent high school graduate. Your additional years of living have given you added experience in developing your capacity to think, observe, and evaluate, and the fact that this has been taking place outside the classroom does not reduce its value as mental equipment. Like many mature students, you may be misjudging or underestimating your abilities. Taking stock of your assets is one way to shore up your confidence.

What about the charge that the tests are stacked against nontraditional applicants and those from minority cultures? This criticism is based on the relatively poorer scores of blacks and lower-income applicants. Studies have shown that the SAT predicts college performance as accurately for blacks as it does for whites both in traditionally black colleges and in integrated colleges. The score differentials do not result from bias in the test but from the test's reflection of unequal educational opportunities. Efforts to develop a culture-free, nonverbal test have been unsuccessful so far. One problem is that blacks score higher on the verbal questions of the SAT than on the mathematical and spatial questions. Most of the nonverbal tests show a surprisingly high correlation with the verbal tests they are designed to supplant. And the only true culturally neutral tests, such as a series of mazes, do not reveal anything that might be useful to college admissions officials.[10]

Whatever the inadequacies or biases of the tests, the most prudent course is to approach them on their own terms. Collections of sample tests are available at most bookstores and can also be obtained from the Educational Testing Service and the College Entrance Examination Board. As is true of the GED, practicing with these tests can help you gain facility and improve your speed in answering the questions.

You can also take advantage of a variety of opportunities for upgrading your verbal and math skills, which may have become rusty since you left school. Remedial programs are available at adult education centers, community colleges, extension divisions, and other centers. Your state department of education can supply you with a list of these programs. The time you put into practice and preparation will go a long way toward reducing your anxiety about taking the tests, and it is anxiety rather than lack of ability that is most likely to handicap you.

Remember, too, that if you are not satisfied with your performance, you can retake the examination. Also, the exams are only one aspect of the college entrance procedure. When an admissions officer considers your application for admission, several pieces of information will enter into the final determination: the application form itself, which provides a certain amount of personal data; your standardized test scores; and your grade score as revealed on your high school transcripts, together with transcripts of any previous college work you may have completed.

For mature students, the grade score, exhumed from long-buried and long-forgotten transcripts, can present more of a roadblock than the standardized entrance exams. To illustrate, let's take the admission requirements of a university north of Chicago:

1   Students with no college work (first-time freshmen)

   a   Students who graduate in the upper half of their high school graduating class from an accredited school are eligible to apply for admission. There is no specific sequence of course work required.

   b   Students who graduate in the lower half of their high school class (state residents only) may be considered if their ACT scores are sufficiently high to compensate for low class rank. (ACT—for American College Testing programs—is comparable to the SAT and is used primarily by institutions in Southern, Western, and North-central states.)

2   Students with college work (transfer)

   a   To be considered for admission, students who have attended other colleges must have earned a cumulative C average from all colleges attended and must be in good standing at the last college attended full time.

   b   Transfer students who have earned fewer than thirty semester hours of credit will be classified as freshmen and must also meet freshman admission requirements.

Now let's apply these requirements to a woman in her early forties who graduated from high school twenty-five years ago and went on to earn twelve units of college credit before dropping out to marry and raise a family. Having decided to return to college for a degree, she sends for her high school and college transcripts and discovers, to her dismay, that her high school grades were lower than she remembered. It all seems a bit hazy now, but she does recall problems at home and other distractions which interfered with her studies at the time. Her twelve college units showed a grade improvement—she remembers that she found the college atmosphere liberating and that she pitched into her studies with enthusiasm—but those credits are not sufficient to lift her out of freshmen status. At this point, her SAT scores become a critical factor. Suppose, however, that they are not high enough to compensate for her low high school average and that, as a result, her application is rejected.

What recourse is open to her? The most obvious route is the two-year college, with its open-admissions policies. But if she has set her sights on the university, she can appeal her case by requesting a personal interview with an admissions officer. Despite the rigidity and impersonality of university bureaucracies, admissions officers can be human and sympathetic and, especially in the case of nontraditional students, have been known to bend the rules when there seemed to be sufficient justification for doing so.

THE HIGHER YOU GO . . .

If your educational program includes graduate school, you will soon discover that, at this level, the exclusionary principle is in full force. The reasons for this are not hard to pinpoint. Graduate education is expensive for the institution as well as the candidate. One estimate puts the cost to society of educating a Ph.D. at $50,000, and the cost to the candidate can run anywhere from $10,000 up, with the "up" figure rising sharply if one includes earnings lost during the period of study.

Graduate school is also highly demanding, and the professor/student ratio is relatively small, with students requiring and usually receiving a large amount of individual attention from the faculty. As a result, the number of students who can be accommodated is limited; places are at a premium, and the gatekeepers must be particularly diligent in identifying students who, according to the prevailing educational philosophy, are most qualified and therefore most deserving of admission.

In the winnowing-out process, which often requires difficult and complex decision making, admissions officers are seeking to ensure that the highest standards of achievement are maintained so that society can be served by doctors, lawyers, engineers, and other professionals whose competence is beyond doubt. The undergraduate degree may reflect a wide spectrum of knowledge and intellectual attainment, but the advanced credential, conferred upon those who will hold the most influential and responsible positions, has always been reserved for the most meritorious.

All this has meant that graduate school, the channel to professional occupations, has been virtually closed off to nontraditional students who do not have the background or training to meet the rigorous entrance requirements. The mature student has had a particularly difficult time since most graduate admissions officers do not believe that anyone past the age of thirty can have the dedication or capability necessary for law, medicine, or other advanced studies. Additionally, the investment in a lawyer, doctor, or other professional is seen as paying dividends over a longer span of time in the case of younger graduates.

But despite these factors, the strongholds of graduate education are beginning to yield to changing social pressures. In fact, here, where the stakes are highest and the admissions policies tightest, we can see signs of a contest developing between the meritocratic principle and the egalitarian view. As graduate enrollments decline in some areas and as Ph.D.'s find their job opportunities dwindling, graduate admissions directors are being encouraged to take a new look at the role and policies of their schools.

A study of graduate education reveals several emerging trends, including:

> A reduced rate of research and development expenditures and hence a reduced demand for new Ph.D.'s in such activities

> A continuing decline in the total amount of financial support available to full-time graduate students

> Increased enrollment demand by nontraditional graduate students, such as older students, part-time students, nonresidential students, nondegree students, minority students, and women returning after child rearing

In view of these new developments, the National Board on Graduate Education has called for graduate schools to pay greater attention to "new clienteles" and to experiment with less traditional forms of graduate education:

> What will be needed are expanded opportunities for nontraditional forms of graduate education serving nontraditional graduate students. During the next decade, graduate education must make the transition from a system that has tended to follow a single model of advanced education to the increasing diversity required by changing demographic and economic circumstances. The greatest responsibility for adapting to changing circumstances necessarily lies with the institutions themselves.[11]

What this adds up to is that the prospects for the nontraditional student who wants to go on to advanced study are brighter than they have been in the past. If you have that extra measure of stamina and dedication and are prepared to invest the necessary time, hard work, and money, you should be able to gain admission to graduate school regardless of your age. And if you are from a minority background, affirmative action policies will be working in your favor. In its compendium of graduate and professional school opportunities for minority students, the Educational

Testing Service points out that "as a black, Chicano, Puerto Rican, or native American college graduate, you are distinctive. Many graduate and professional schools will want to look at your credentials and will want to get to know you better."

The Graduate Admissions Process

At the graduate level, admissions requirements are usually based on grade average, graduate qualifying examination score, letters of recommendation, and a statement of purpose.

Grades Generally, graduate admissions offices prefer letter grades to the various forms of ungraded work such as "pass," "credit," and "satisfactory," which is something to keep in mind during your undergraduate years. Credit for cooperative or experiential education or for life experience also complicates the task of screening applicants. But none of these pose insuperable obstacles. According to the admissions office of Northeastern Illinois University, "If you are bright and prepared for graduate work, you should be able to establish these facts in some way or other. Students in Northeastern University's, University Without Walls program (UWW), for instance, receive neither credits nor grades for their work, but have had a high degree of success in obtaining entry to graduate schools."

Qualifying exams Depending on your goal, you will be taking one of the following qualifying examinations for entrance to graduate and professional schools:

1   GRE. The General Record Examinations are generally given in October, December, January, February, April, and June. The GRE program offers both an aptitude test and advanced tests in nineteen subjects. Registration closes approximately three weeks before the test date. Most graduate departments that require the GRE prefer that their applicants be tested in October. A fee of $10 is charged for the aptitude test. Each advanced test also costs $10. Write to the Educational Testing Service, Box 955, Princeton, New Jersey 08549, or Box 1502, Berkeley, California 94701, for registration forms.

2   MAT. The Millers Analogies Test requires the solution of a series of intellectual problems stated in the form of analogies, most of them verbal. Write to the Psychological Testing Corporation, 304 East 45th Street, New York, New York 10017, for information about the examination and the test center nearest you. Fees vary from center to center.

3   LSAT. The Law School Admission Test for students interested in

attending law school is given in October, December, February, April, and July. The fee is $14. The Law School Data Assembly Service (LSDAS), which summarizes and reports transcript information, costs $8. Registration forms may be obtained from LSAT, ETS, etc.

4 ATGSB. Students planning to attend business schools that require the Admission Test for Graduate Study in Business should write to ATGSB, Educational Testing Service, for registration forms. The test is given in November, January, March, and July. The fee is $12.

5 MCAT. The Medical College Admission Test is given to applicants for admission to medical schools. The test is given in October and May. The registration fee is $20, and arrangements for taking the test must be made directly with MCAT, Box 451, American College Testing Program, Iowa City, Iowa 52240.

6 DAT. Students planning to attend dental school should take the Dental Admissions Test, which is given in October, January, and April. The test fee is $15. For further information, write to the Division of Educational Measurements, American Dental Association, 211 East Chicago Avenue, Chicago, Illinois 60611.

7 TOEFL. Many graduate and professional schools require that foreign students take the Test of English as a Foreign Language. The test fee is $12, and information is available from TOEFL, Box 899, Princeton, New Jersey 08540.

Practice tests are available for the above, and the test-preparation strategies recommended for the GED and the undergraduate entrance tests can be used with these graduate qualifying examinations.

Statement of purpose This provides a good opportunity for you to personalize your application and, as an older student, to make a virtue of your maturity. Although the statement of purpose does not ordinarily count as heavily as the grade average and test scores, it can, in marginal instances, make the difference between acceptance and rejection. A statement of purpose does not have to run more than a couple of pages, though some have been known to reach ten pages or more, and it should be a clear, accurate expression of your reasons for wishing to undertake advanced study in a particular field.

The following is offered as an example of a brief, simply expressed statement of purpose. It was submitted by a forty-seven-year-old woman, with a bachelor's degree and some experience teaching at an adult school, who applied to a graduate school of education. Although neither her college grade score nor her GRE test scores were competitive with those of other applicants, she was accepted in the graduate program.

Statement of Purpose

I am convinced that continuing education is one of our best hopes for the future, both as a source of personal enrichment and as a means of helping people to comprehend and deal with the complex and critical problems of our time. The past few years have clearly demonstrated how important it is for adults to be able to participate intelligently in their community affairs. And as we move from a society of abundance to one of scarcity, we will need more trained and committed educators to help adults rethink their values, learn new skills, and develop personal resources for their later years.

But granting the above, why, it may well be asked, should someone of my age wish to pursue graduate study in adult education? Here I must offer a bit of autobiography. Like so many women of my generation, I did not plan for a professional career. I married soon after graduating from college, and though I held a number of jobs, I never considered these to be other than stopgaps, something to fill the time until I began raising a family. During the time my children were growing up, I occasionally took extension courses at the nearby university. These courses made me aware of how much I missed the intellectual stimulus of studying; they gave me a new vision of what I could do with my life, of how I could grow in new directions.

I realized that I wanted more than anything to be involved in some way with education. It was a realization that came late in life. But I also discovered that, in maturity, I could be a far better student than I had been in my college days. My undergraduate years were fraught with personal and financial pressures that made it difficult—at times, impossible—to achieve a superior academic record. And like many girls of that era, I had been led to believe that it was not important for me to do well in school or prepare for a career since my destiny was to be marriage and a family.

Now with my children grown and leading lives of their own, I believe I can bring a more receptive mind to my studies as well as a framework of experience in which to place the ideas and concepts provided through lectures and books. Having gained so much from continuing education personally, I have become somewhat of an advocate or missionary for the "cause." In pursuing a graduate program in adult education at this time, I hope to continue my own learning in a disciplined manner and, in time, to make some worthwhile contribution to the field.

Letters of recommendation These should be solicited from professors who have had an opportunity to become familiar with your undergraduate work. Even in the impersonal atmosphere of the multiversity, you will find that the majority of the faculty members are approachable and genuinely interested in helping students continue their education. It is a good idea to inform the professors in your major field as early as possible that you intend to go on to graduate school; this will encourage them to take a special interest in your progress and to do what they can to help you.

In some instances, letters of recommendation may come from nonfaculty sources. For example, if you have been employed at an occupation that is related in some way to your chosen field of graduate study, a letter from your employer or a colleague may be acceptable; you should check this out with the institution, however.

Frequently, a personal interview is part of the graduate admissions procedure, and this gives you an opportunity to fortify your application by presenting your case for admission in a person-to-person rather than a bureaucratic setting.

Institutional Response

Around the country, admissions offices are taking a fresh look at their entrance requirements in view of the new kinds of applicants who are turning up at their doors. The decline in the SAT/ACT testing scores is also helping to focus attention on the fairness and effectiveness of standardized examinations. One of the institutions that have responded to these developments is Bowdoin College in Brunswick, Maine, which has eliminated the SAT test as a requirement for admission. College officials report that "the option not to submit scores is taken each year by about 50% of incoming freshmen, many of them proving to be among Bowdoin's best students. This program was undertaken to eliminate a certain artificiality which such tests impose and to permit a more realistic assessment of each prospective student's total potential."[12]

Grade scores, too, are coming in for sharper scrutiny as it becomes more apparent that grades are not always a dependable measure of ability. Several studies have shown that there is, in fact, no correlation between grades and achievement in adult life. Recent innovations in grading, such as pass/fail in place of letter grades, are forcing a reconsideration of grades in the total admissions picture. While very little official action has yet been taken in this area, there has been a noticeable softening in admissions-office attitudes toward the grade average, and graduate schools are increasingly taking note of other aspects of a student's background, especially when dealing with older students with diverse experience. In the same vein, a few institutions are no longer requiring transcripts which are more than ten years old.

Affirmative Action

The purpose of affirmative action programs at both the undergraduate and the graduate levels is to break the cycle of inadequate educational opportunity among minorities and women and to increase their representation in higher-level jobs and professions.

It has long been a practice of colleges and universities to set aside a percentage of their total enrollment for "special actions," or to applicants who do not fit the standard admissions procedures. This percentage, which varies with the institution (at the University of California, it is 2 percent), has been known as the "athlete's exception," but in accordance with affirmative action policies, it has been expanded to include women, minority applicants, and those from low-income backgrounds. Another encouraging feature, since nontraditional students frequently need help in sharpening their learning skills, is remedial education programs, which are proliferating on college and university campuses.

In some graduate schools, special programs have been designed to develop an admissions system which supplements the rigid objective requirements with subjective factors in order to make it possible to admit students whose chances would otherwise be very slight. In effect, such programs set up two admissions systems: the regular system, which is based almost exclusively upon grades and test scores, and the special admissions program, which also considers grades and tests but which places emphasis upon letters of recommendation, interviews, and personal histories as well. In considering grade scores, which combine the undergraduate grade-point average with the qualifying examination score, the permissible minimums are lower for special students than for regular admissions.

This dual admissions system has been challenged in court in what has become known as *De Funis* v. *Odegaard and the University of Washington*. The case arose in 1970, when, Marco De Funis applied to the University of Washington Law School; he was rejected, although his test scores and college grades were such that he would have been admitted if, instead of being Jewish, he had been a black, a Filipino, a Chicano, or an American Indian. De Funis asked the Supreme Court to declare that the Washington admissions practice violated his rights under the equal protection clause of the Fourteenth Admendment. The case was dismissed by the Court as moot when the law school admitted De Funis and said he would be permitted to graduate regardless of how the case came out. But though the question has not been legally resolved and the case dealt with the issue of ethnic background rather than age, it has implications for mature applicants, who frequently require special consideration in order to be able to compete fairly. This is one aspect of the admissions process which the courts may have to deal with definitively in the future.

SPECIAL PROGRAMS FOR ADULT LEARNERS

The programs described in this section are a small sampling of the new kinds of degree programs that have been developed especially for adult learners. Programs like these are expected to multiply rapidly as educational institutions attempt to accommodate their new clienteles.

The Board of Governors Bachelor of Arts Degree

This program was designed expressly for the working adult, and the requirements and nature of the degree were developed to make it possible for qualified adults to earn a college degree while pursuing careers or carrying family responsibilities. The degree is awarded directly by the Board of Governors of State Colleges and Universities of Illinois upon recommendation of any of the five universities under the direction of the board. This particular degree can be earned at any one or combination of the following universities:

Chicago State University

Eastern Illinois University

Governors State University

Northeastern Illinois University

Western Illinois University

The two key features of this program are its flexibility and the fact that adults can receive credit toward the bachelor of arts degree by means of evaluation of their adult learning experiences that are college equivalents. The primary intent of the program is to make higher education available to adults in a way that is compatible with their life style and responsibilities and to recognize that college-equivalent learning and skills can be achieved in a variety of ways.

No major subject area is required for this program, but a student may pursue a major or concentration if he or she wishes to do so. The program staff advises the student in terms of meeting overall program requirements, but academic direction in specific subjects or discipline areas is provided by the academic departments. Students in the program, like all other students registered at the university, have access to its full counseling, academic, and other resources. Those with educational or career goals that presuppose specific academic preparation (such as state teacher certification or admission to graduate studies) are counseled to select course work in areas that would meet these objectives.

The BOG/BA degree has full legal value and standing, and the experience of the five universities administering the program indicates that the degree has proved in practice to be as acceptable as degrees received in the more traditional programs.

New Directions

A program intended for women who either had not taken a degree or had not attended college at all, this was launched at the Westchester campus of Pace University in 1965. Specific features of the program include special scheduling, supportive counseling, and a distinct administrative structure. A later evolution in programs designed for adults is the Bachelor of Professional Studies program; this is directed toward students of proved competence in various fields and provides equivalent academic credit up to a possible three-year total for experience, creative attainment, and professional achievement. Enrolled in the program are bankers, engineers, actors, writers, television personalities, and many others. Evaluation of experience is directed by the dean of continuing education, supported by faculty committees competent in specialized areas.

Bachelor of General Studies

This degree program was developed by the University of South Carolina for mature and other nontraditional students who do not fit into the university system and who find that the traditional curriculum is irrelevant to their needs. The program is designed to accommodate new or changing areas of study and to offer the new learners a more personalized instructional plan. After admission to the General Studies program, each student plans an individual curriculum in consultation with a faculty advisory committee; the faculty advisers represent areas of study in which the student is most interested.

Degree Based on Demonstrated Competence

Developed by the Worcester Polytechnic Institute in Worcester, Massachusetts, this degree represents three innovations in undergraduate education at the Institute:

1   A change from granting degrees on the basis of course credits to granting them on the basis of demonstrated competence

2   The development of independent study and project work, requiring about one-quarter of a student's college effort

3   The introduction of video tape as a critical component of self-instruction

University without Walls

Empire State College of the State University of New York designed this program, which permits students to pursue their education with only occasional on-site contact with the college. The college consists of learning centers, located around the state, where a cluster of faculty has gathered. Students come and, guided by the faculty, design a degree program that meets the college's learning objectives and their own objectives. Students may receive credit for prior learning, either school or nonschool. This credit takes the form of advanced standing toward the degree. There are two basic steps in the program: (1) The student prepares a portfolio of prior learning that is related to the degree plan, and (2) the college evaluates the portfolio.

The first task faced by the student is the identification of learning which might be recognized and which relates to his or her goals. This is not a simple process, since few people think systematically about their experiences or how they might relate to their educational goals. For this reason, the experience of preparing the portfolio is regarded as educational in itself.

After this process is completed, the student must acquire the necessary documentation. Finally, the completed portfolio is presented to an administrator, who submits it to a learning-center evaluation committee. A date is set, and the portfolio is evaluated by a committee that may include outside evaluators.

The Goddard College Adult Degree program offers another approach to academic credit for off-campus learning. Advanced standing can be granted for "critical life experience." This procedure employs a petition through which the student describes extraacademic experiences thought to be of "significant educational worth." The petition is filed after consultation with an adviser, who guides the student through the intricacies of the petition process. (For example, every item of documentation must be listed, and the petitioner must provide a detailed narrative of the experience, explaining how the learning gained from the experience fits in with current plans.) A committee on evaluation then reads the petition and, subject to appeal, decides whether acceleration is justified. Like the Empire State program, Goddard focuses on the educational process and therefore emphasizes the value of preparing the petition as an educational experience in itself.

CREDIT FOR LIFE EXPERIENCE

The institutional response to the needs of adult learners that looks most promising is the crediting of "life experience" as practiced by Goddard, Empire, and other institutions. In itself, the idea is not new—Antioch College has granted credit for work experience for many years—but the range of creditable experiences has been widening to reflect the increasingly diverse experiences of the new learners. Life experiences that merit college credit may now range from military and Peace Corps ser job experience and even voluntary and domestic activities.

A study conducted by the Center for Research and Develop Higher Education at Berkeley in 1972 revealed that, of the 1,185 institutions queried, the following percentages would grant credit for the activities listed:[13]

	Percent
Cooperative work experience	35
Volunteer work in a community agency	28
A completed work (book, piece of sculpture, or patent, for example)	17
Study abroad sponsored by groups other than educational institutions	16
Participation in a local community theater, orchestra, or civic activity	14
Completion of formal courses of instruction conducted by business, industry, or government agencies	14
Election to the position of student-body officer or active participation in institutional governance	10
Sensitivity-training or encounter-group experience	7
Attendance at classes at a local free university or a local experimental college	6
Unsupervised foreign travel	6
Other	8
No information or no such credit granted	28

Two kinds of learning are usually assessed: (1) that which is comparable to learning achieved in college-level courses and (2) that which is not necessarily comparable to traditional academic learning. As a rule, students seeking such credit are expected to take the responsibility for identifying the specific skills and knowledge they have acquired in their life experience and to convince the appropriate educational officials that this experience is related to their educational objectives.

CREDIT FOR MILITARY EXPERIENCE

The Commission on Accreditation of Service Experience (CASE), established by the American Council on Education, evaluates military educational programs and recommends to civilian colleges and universities the number of credits to be awarded for each military course. (Credit evaluations can be obtained *only* by university officials.) Examinations are usually not required. It is important to point out, however, that civilian colleges and universities usually accept a CASE/OEC recommendation only if a comparable course is offered through that university (in other words, if a university does not offer a course in automotive repair, it is very unlikely that it would accept credit for military training in that area).

The Office on Educational Credit of the American Council on Education also evaluates noncollegiate educational programs, including those sponsored by such groups as business, industry, government, and labor unions. Because many of the educational experiences offered by noncollegiate organizations are comparable to the content of college-level courses, the OEC has established a credit advisory service to help educational institutions assess individual experiences and recommend that credit be given for certain of these experiences. Again, it is up to the individual educational institution to determine whether credit will be given, how much, and for what purposes.

CREDIT FOR VOLUNTEER AND HOMEMAKING COMPETENCIES

The life experiences of women who have been engaged in homemaking and community activities are gaining recognition through such programs as the Conference on Accrediting the Competencies Women Acquire from Domestic and Volunteer Work. Sponsored jointly by the Educational Testing Service and the Council of National Organizations for Adult Education, the conference is developing three workbooks to assist adult learners in receiving academic credit for skills acquired in volunteer work and homemaking activities. One workbook will be designed to help colleges in crediting these skills and competencies; another will guide the student in articulating volunteer and homemaking experiences; and the third will be directed to the volunteer agency that requires help in specifying goals, assessing its volunteer needs, and evaluating the performance of its volunteers.

If you are interested in receiving credit for your volunteer or homemaking skills and experience, your initial step should be to contact local colleges to determine whether they have previously credited or are at least open to the idea of crediting nontraditional learning. You will need to find out from the colleges what kind of information and documentation they would need in order to consider granting credit. The office or individual to contact varies from one institution to another, but some possibilities would include the vice president for academic affairs, academic deans, ombudsmen, department chairpeople (in the area in which the credit may be granted), the continuing or adult education office, and the women's program office.

Also, if you are presently engaged in volunteer activities or if you are involved with training volunteers, here are some things you can do to make your experience more creditable:

> Keep a record of the purpose of the training or the activity and the learning which took place. A syllabus is a helpful tool.

> Keep work samples whenever possible.

> When leaving or when completing work with a particular project or volunteer agency, be sure to get a recommendation from your supervisor or from a professional with whom you have worked.

> Try to understand and be able to articulate fully not only what was involved in an activity but also why it was carried out.

The accreditation of skills acquired through domestic activities has so far been meeting with greater resistance than volunteer accreditation; this type of activity was not even included in the Berkeley survey mentioned earlier. If you plan to seek this type of credit, you will have to be prepared to specify very clearly which of the skills among those you have acquired are most relevant to the college experience. Some potential areas of credit are budgeting, horticulture, child development, and learning disabilities. Again, keeping work samples and documentation to support your acquisition and effective use of these skills will be helpful in obtaining credit toward your degree.

As we would expect and as is borne out by the Berkeley study, it is the nontraditional institutions that are more likely to grant this type of credit; however, traditional institutions are becoming increasingly aware of the need to give more serious consideration to crediting life experience, particularly when the experience conforms to academic learning. A good example is the case of a former New York City policeman in his late thirties who was eager to get into counseling. He had studied for several years in a Franciscan seminary, had analyzed the Japanese social system while stationed in Tokyo during his military service, and had learned a good deal about law and human behavior while employed as a law officer in the public morals division. An evaluation committee at the traditional college he wished to attend determined that his life experiences were worth 30 of the 128 credits necessary for a bachelor's degree.

Proponents of life-experience accreditation maintain that since adult learners bring a rich inventory of experience with them, it makes little sense to start them off at the same place as an eighteen-year-old freshman.

For mature students who wish to accelerate their college education, credit for life experience is like time and money in the bank, and as this trend gains further acceptance in the foreseeable future, the new learners will find the admissions process working for instead of against them.

PLANNING FOR ADMISSION

Once you are familiar with the various steps involved in the admissions process, you are ready to develop a plan of action that will get you past the gatekeepers in an orderly and efficient manner. Your plan should take the form of a timetable working back from the deadline for filing applications; this will give you a clear idea of when you should be doing what.

Your first step is to check out the admission deadlines of the school you have chosen to attend. (You can, of course, apply to as many institutions as you like; there is a filing fee of about $20 for each application.) For institutions on the trimester system, which may require that applications be filed anywhere from four to ten months prior to the beginning of the quarter, your schedule for filing might go like this, depending upon which quarter you wished to enter:

Quarter	Classes Begin	Applications Due
Fall	Last week in September	June 5
Winter	First week in January	July 1
Spring	First week in April	October 1

With these dates as your starting point, you can proceed to schedule the various steps that are involved in the admissions process. Let's assume that you are planning to enter a four-year state college which is on the semester system and that you wish to enter in the fall. (Bear in mind that in many institutions you can be admitted only in the fall and that failure to apply on time means losing a year.) You have been informed by the admissions office that classes start in mid-September and that applications must be in by August 15 (the time span is usually shorter in institutions which are on the semester rather than the trimester plan). Here, then, is a sample timetable that would help you in your planning:

Classes begin: September 18

Application due: August 15

Pick up application blank: August 1

Send for high school and/or college transcripts: July 1

Take SAT/ACT or GED tests: April (or earlier, to allow time for retaking the test if you are dissatisfied with your score).

Begin preparing for SAT/ACT tests: December (or as soon as possible following your decision to apply). Allow four to six months for remedial training in your math and English skills if these have grown rusty.

If you are seeking credit for life experience, make sure, first of all, that the institution you're applying to grants this type of credit; then allow at least six months for identifying and documenting the experiences you wish to have credited. (Time requirements for this will vary considerably from institution to institution, according to the criteria being followed by the evaluation committees.)

For admission to graduate school, build into your schedule sufficient time for soliciting letters of recommendation, for drafting a statement of purpose, and for having a personal interview, where this is part of the institution's admissions procedure.

As you move along in your admissions plan, there may be moments when you experience varying degrees of frustration and anxiety, but when you open a letter that begins with the words "We are pleased to notify you that your application to undergraduate [or graduate] standing has been approved," suddenly it will all seem eminently worthwhile and, in its own way, an important part of your new learning experience.

REFERENCES

1 *The Education of Henry Adams: An Autobiography,* Houghton Mifflin Company, Boston, Sentry Press edition, 1961.

2 Quoted in Patricia K. Cross, *Beyond the Open Door,* Jossey-Bass, Inc., San Francisco, 1972.

3 Edith Waters, "The Other Generation Gap: Admission Procedures for Adult Students," Journal of College Student Personnel, November 1971.

4 1975–1976 Admissions Testing program of the College Entrance Examination Board.

5 "Current Practices in the Assessment of Experiential Learning," *Cooperative Assessment of Experiential Learning,* Working Paper no. 1, Princeton, N.J., September 1974.

6 Edward Caldwell, "Analysis of an Innovation (CLEP)," *Journal of Higher Education,* December 1973.

7 M. C. Fagin, *CLEP Credit Encourages Adults to Seek Degrees,* College Board Review no. 81, Fall 1971.

8 For more specific information, write to CLEP, College Entrance Examination Board, 888 Seventh Avenue, New York, N.W. 10019.

9 For further information, write to CPEP/REDE, Room 1919, 99 Washington Avenue, Albany, N.Y. 12230.

10 Diane Ravitch, "The College Boards," *The New York Times Magazine,* May 4, 1975.

11 *Outlook and Opportunities for Graduate Education,* National Board on Graduate Education, Washington, 1976.

12 *Current Ventures in Undergraduate Education,* The Ford Foundation, New York, 1974.

13 Commission on Non-Traditional Study, *Diversity by Design,* Jossey-Bass, Inc., San Francisco, 1973, p. 128.

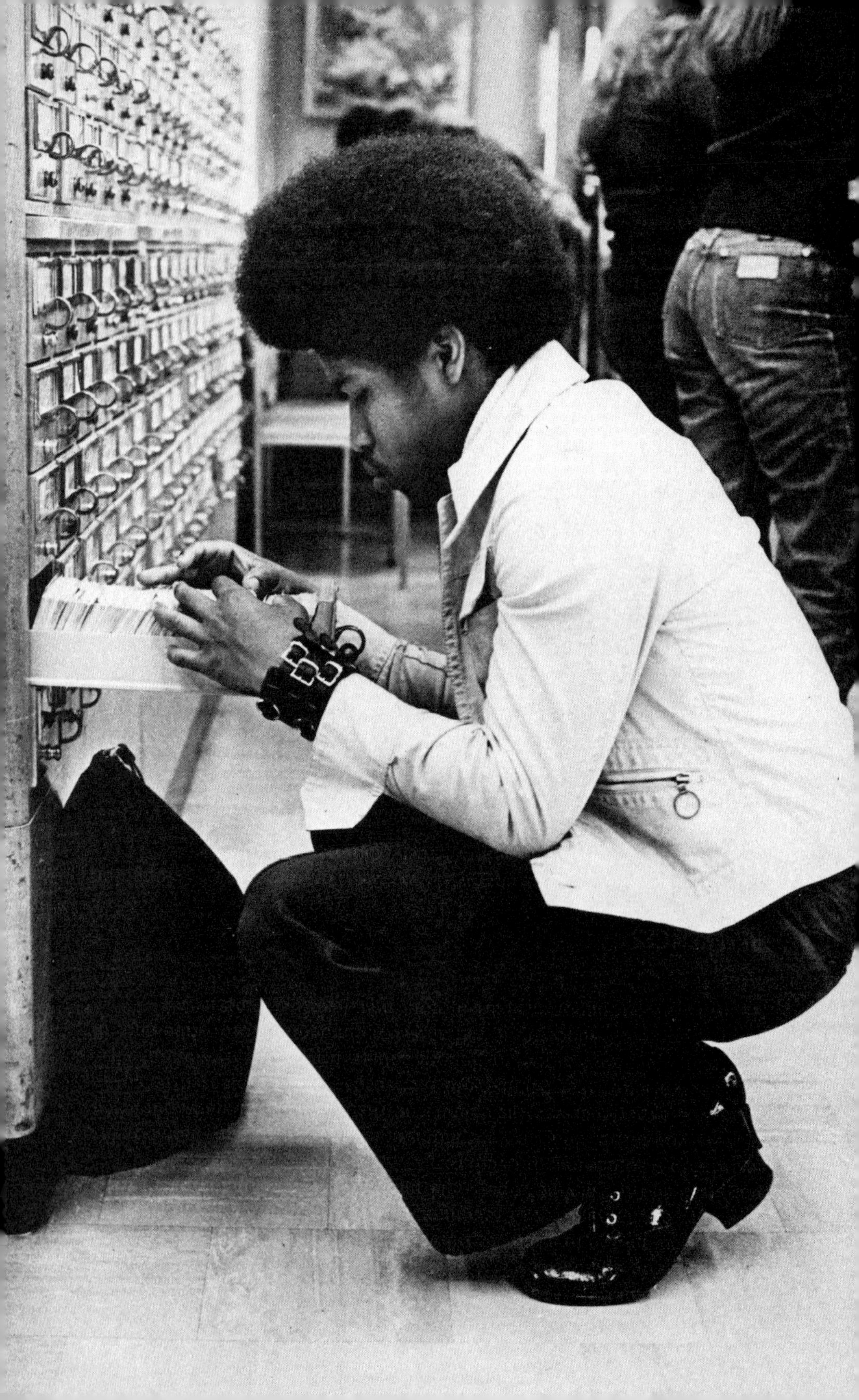

5 Resources to Help You along The Way

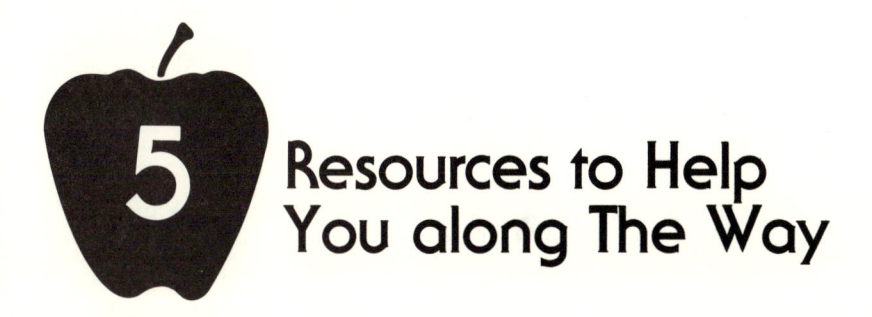

This time I am learning to use the institution and shape it to my needs rather than being used and shaped by the institution. Forty-six-year-old woman who has returned to college for the second time, with an eight-year lapse in between.

Adult students returning to campus who have adjusted their expectations, in line with the information given in Chapter 2, will discover that there is much about college life that is familiar. Despite the new technologies, professors continue to teach by delivering lectures. Examinations are given with unfailing regularity and still strike fear in many a student heart. Students complain about faculty lack of interest, while faculty bemoan the lack of student involvement.

    The adult student who has been away from school for some time might therefore be jolted by the youthful appearance of both students and faculty but would also find that the general pace and tone of the college experience are largely familiar. One area that has changed a great deal, however, is student services. There now exists on almost every college and university campus an incredible array of programs designed specifically to help students maximize their learning experience. Financial services, psychological services (or counseling services), recreational athletics, childcare facilities and programs, veterans' offices, and programs for the physically limited are just a sampling of what is currently available. It is absolutely critical that adult students become fully aware of what help is available. It is even more important that they fully utilize all those services which will aid them in their reentry into school.

A WORD TO THE WISE RETURNING STUDENT

Before launching into a comprehensive description of what to look for in student services, we would like to deal very directly with what we have found to be a major problem for the adult student: Because of both ignorance and fear, most adults tend to underutilize services. First of all, many adults are so grateful at having been "allowed" to enter the hallowed halls of a higher educational institution that they try very hard to be no trouble to anybody. As a result, they tend not to ask questions or to be presumptuous in any fashion; they fear that if they somehow rock the boat, they will be banished from the campus forever. Second, adult students often feel ashamed about asking for help. After all, isn't it degrading for a forty-year-old man to have to talk to a psychologist at a counseling center about how frightened he is in the classroom? And why should a grown woman have to learn how to read more effectively? Student loans must be for somebody else (those who are indigent or fiscally incompetent)—how could a person who has managed his or her own family finances for the past fifteen years apply for financial help?

Remember that, as an adult student, you will deserve all the help you can get and that you are paying for the vast array of services that are available. Only in the last decade or so have these services been developed, as university administrations began to appreciate that students must be dealt with as whole persons with a variety of needs rather than as one-dimensional educable components. Interestingly enough, it is often the so-called best institutions (those which are most selective and most rigorous in their academic demands) that provide the richest, most diverse set of service programs. Harvard University, for example, was one of the first colleges to offer a reading-improvement program because it found that many of its highly qualified students had only moderate reading skills. Similarly, Stanford University has recently reported that more than two-thirds of its undergraduate student body receives financial aid of some kind through its Financial Services Office. These examples are cited to let you know that you need not be indigent, mentally deranged, or simply youthful to utilize university services.

One further piece of information: You need not wait until you are actually enrolled in a college to begin making use of at least some of its services. Indeed, in some areas, such as financial aid, it is absolutely critical that you begin anticipating your needs before the academic experience begins. Likewise, the best time to evaluate your study skills and perhaps begin some remedial work is before you begin school, rather than when you are in the midst of a study crisis. Summer sessions, which are open to nonmatriculating students, are a good place to begin working on these problems. Some study-skills centers may also be available to students before they actually enroll in classes. Certain service areas, however, will be available to you only *after* you have been admitted as a student. Thus as you begin to investigate colleges initially, find out what facilities and services are open to you as a nonstudent and make use of them.

It is important to note at this point that not all services exist at all colleges. You may be surprised, however, to find that considerably more are available than you thought. As we have indicated in other chapters, it is important that you be direct in your requests, active in your search for services, and willing to make use of whatever is available.

FINANCIAL AID

What kinds of expenses are you likely to incur in going back to school? Of course, your expenses will vary a great deal depending on such factors as whether you are going to move to a new location, whether the school is private or public, and whether you are married or have children. In general, your expenses may include the following:

Tuition, registration, and other required student fees

Books and supplies

Child care

Transportation

Clothing purchases and maintenance

Increased expenses for convenience foods, and for eating out

Housing costs

Recreation and entertainment

Medical and dental expenses

How can you meet these expenses? One possible way is through obtaining financial aid.

Some years ago the financial-aid office of a college or university might have consisted of an administrator, his or her assistant, and a couple of clerical people. Their major job then was to award a limited number of scholarships and to help students with emergency loans. Most public colleges and universities had low or no tuition, which meant that the cost of attending such institutions was relatively low. At private colleges or universities, most students (or their families) were expected to take full responsibility for financing all educational costs.

Over the past twenty years, however, two major changes have occurred within the financial-aid world. The first change was the large investment of federal dollars distributed to veterans through the GI Bill during the years following World War II, the Korean war, and the Vietnam war. The second change occurred during the 1960s, when equal educational opportunity became a significant issue at institutions of higher learning all over the United States. At this time it was acknowledged that many people were being denied the opportunity for further education solely because of their limited financial resources. Simultaneously, many educational institutions recognized the homogeneous nature of their student populations and began to take a greater interest in attracting students from a wider variety of backgrounds (including those who were part of a minority because of their educational or socio-economic background and sometimes even because of their gender—for example, women were admitted for the first time to colleges and universities that had been traditionally open only to men).

Types of Financial Aid

Because most institutions at this time have taken the stance that no person is to be denied the opportunity to go to school because of inadequate financing, there are a large number of financial resources available to help meet educational expenses. Financing resources are not limited to those who are at low-income levels; there are also resources for individuals in the medium-income levels. The kinds of financial aid available generally fall into several categories, which we shall now describe. (For more information about financing a college education and financial aid, refer to Appendix A.)

> 1 Scholarships and grants. Scholarships and grants are direct payments to students of money that does not have to be repaid. Scholarships are usually awarded on a competitive basis for specific levels of academic achievement and financial need; grants are usually given for financial need.

2 Loans. There is a wide array of loans available to students who are in financial need. Most loan programs allow students to borrow money at very low interest rates (3 percent and up) and repay the loan after they have completed their undergraduate or graduate studies. In some cases the college itself has loan money available for distribution; in other cases, the financial-aid office administers a loan program for a second party (like the state or federal government or a private foundation).

3 Work-study. Work-study is a federal government program which provides jobs for students who have demonstrated financial need. The federal government pays a percentage of a student's hourly wage, and the employer, off or on campus, pays the remaining amount.

4 Emergency loans. Open to *all* registered students, emergency loans are short-term, no-interest payments of money to students who are in the emergency situation of experiencing immediate fiancial stress. Students are required to pay back the money within a specified period of time.

How to Apply for Aid

If you think you need financial aid, your chances of getting it are vastly improved if you apply carefully; that is, you should take specific steps at specific times. It is very important that you observe deadlines set by financial-aid offices because aid is given out only during certain times of the school year. If you miss the deadlines, little money is left over. The following steps are the usual ones for requesting aid:

1 As you look at colleges initially, contact their financial-aid offices for information about their resources. At the same time, ask for a financial-aid application and a financial-aid form (the latter used to be called a "parent's confidential statement"). Many colleges and universities require *all* students, young and old alike, to submit a needs-analysis document to an independent financial analysis corporation for a financial evaluation. The best known are the American College Testing Program and the College Scholarship Service. The corporation, in effect, examines the student's assets, income, and expenses and determines what amount the student should be expected to pay and what amount of financial aid he or she should receive from outside sources. In the case of self-supporting individuals, many financial-aid offices require supporting documents to indicate their own particular independent financial status. Most require (*a*) income tax returns dating back one or more years, (*b*) proof that the indiidual has not been claimed as a dependent by his or her parents for one or more years, (*c*) a document establishing that the individual has not lived with his or her parents for one or more years, and (*d*) proof that the individual has not received more than $600 from his or her parents for one or more years. A college or university may also request a copy of a financial-aid transcript from adults who are transferring from another postsecondary institution, whether or not they received aid from that school or not. You should know that all the information you give to the financial-aid office will be kept in strict confidence and that information may not be forwarded to other offices on or off campus without your consent.

2 *Fill in the information asked for on all forms and mail the forms to each postsecondary institution you are applying to.* One important piece of advice: Be sure to keep duplicate copies of all applications, forms, and correspondence you turn into a financial-aid office. This will save you a lot of time and frustration if the office should misplace your materials.

3 After receiving your forms and the analysis of your financial situation, the financial-aid office will put together a "financial package" for you which will indicate how much you will be expected to pay on your own and what other financial possibilities are open to you through the school and other sources. *At this point, you should make appointments with the financial-aid offices of the schools you are considering seriously to find out what packages have been put together for you.*

Most schools require that you be an enrolled student before they actually give you money. Once you are enrolled, the financial-aid office can tell you how payments will be made by the various aid sources assigned to you.

Many adults ignore financial assistance as an alternative because they feel it is inappropriate, for various reasons, to apply for it. These people should realize that the vast majority of funds being awarded are public dollars coming from federal, state, and local taxes; they should recall that they probably have been contributing to these moneys for any number of years and are now eligible to receive some of it back. Because finances often wind up being one of the most significant barriers a student faces in returning to school, we suggest that you explore the options in this area thoroughly. There are many other pressures associated with going back to school—why have a problem where one need not exist?

ACADEMIC SERVICES

Let us assume that you have just received a letter of admission to a college and that you are planning to be a half-time student during the next fall term. The admission notice comes in May, classes begin in September, and you are still somewhat confused about a number of issues, including these: What will be your major? Which courses should you take? If you took Psychology I when you were last in college, do you now take Psychology II? Because all this sounds very confusing, your initial response is probably to wait until September to get it all straightened out, right? *Wrong*! We suggest that you arrange immediately to see one of the people with whom you may be spending a good deal of time over the next few years—the academic adviser.

Academic Advising

What is an academic adviser? Generally speaking, an academic adviser is a person who helps students translate university requirements into individual courses of action that lead to the earning of degrees. In a large university an academic adviser may be attached to a college such as the college of arts and letters or the college of engineering. In a smaller college or university, the academic adviser is more likely to be attached to a counseling office or an admissions or registrar's office. Academic advisers are knowledgeable about such things as degree requirements and course sequences, and they are adept at interpreting all those college regulations that are generally outlined in the college catalog.

Questions that you might want to ask an academic adviser include the following: What courses do I need to take in order to graduate with a B.A. in sociology? What kind of schedule can I arrange as a part-time student? What courses outside my major must I take in order to meet the college's general graduation requirements? What are lower- and upper-division courses, and how many of each must I take? What kinds of nontraditional courses are available on campus (such as independent study and work-study programs)? How can I map out a course program for the next two years?

A good time to ask for an academic adviser is during the summer before you return to school (if you are returning in the fall). This is a time when advisers are bound to be less pressured by numerous student problems and probably more available to provide you with thorough counseling. By the way, the best academic advisers are those who know how to make the rules work for you as a student (by bending, interpreting, or petitioning). The worst ones are those officious people who are awed by the regulations, who exaggerate their own importance as interpreters of the rules, and who indicate that the letter of the law must prevail—those who exude an attitude of: "No, you can't." "No, it is not possible." "No, it's against the rules." If you happen into the latter type, change advisers as quickly as you can—yes, it is possible to do this—because your academic adviser may have a great influence on whether your college experience is smooth-running or not. We shall now discuss some other academic services that will make your experience at college easier and more worthwhile.

Faculty Adviser

Another resource whom you should contact as early as possible is a faculty adviser (assuming, of course, that you have an academic major in mind). A faculty adviser is a professor assigned by an academic department (such as psychology, literature, or urban and rural studies) to help students with issues related to majoring in that particular field. When you are ready, call a departmental office and ask for their list of faculty advisers. Perhaps a more effective approach would be to go to the office yourself and talk to the administrative assistant or other adult students about your specific needs. Every department has a few special people— those who seem to enjoy working with students and who do it comfortably and without rancor. Make sure that you get to see one of them.

Ask a faculty adviser questions such as the following: What is the emphasis of the psychology department on this campus? Clinical? Research? Psychoanalytic? Behavioral? What are the opportunities for doing fieldwork in this major? I am interested in children—is there any way that I could integrate my volunteer work at the local nursery school with a course in developmental psychology? What about graduate study—is this a department that can offer me a graduate program once I have earned my B.A.? I am planning to take social psychology and abnormal psychology in the fall—how do I get the reading lists so that I can begin my preparation this summer?

There is a definite difference between an academic adviser and a faculty adviser. For instance, do not ask the faculty adviser about anything in the catalog. The faculty adviser may have skimmed the catalog when he or she arrived on the campus but probably has not looked at it since. Most faculty advisers are just not prepared to answer technical questions about university requirements. These should be directed to the academic adviser, the expert on rules and regulations. On the other hand, if you ask the academic adviser questions about the technical aspects of any major, you are likely to receive misinformation or no information at all. Academic advisers tend to be generalists who know everything about everything; faculty advisers tend to be specialists who know mainly about their own specific field or department.

Study-Skills Programs

In all probability, as a returning student, you are concerned about your capacity to function successfully in the academic world. If so, you are not an unusual case. Most students are worried about their abilities but make the common mistake of confusing their abilities with their actual skills. When we speak of ability, we are referring to a *basic capacity to learn*. Most adults who have functioned in any educational setting before are capable of returning to academia again. What they usually lack, however, is *skills*—reading, study, mathematical, and writing skills. Before the adult-student "boom" began, colleges and universities discovered that many of their young, bright students lacked these same skills. As a means of helping their students compensate for their educational "gaps," institutions began to develop programs called "adaptive-learning programs," "study-skills programs," or "learning-assistance programs." Although the comprehensiveness of such programs varies from institution to institution, a number of resources are routinely offered.

Reading Programs

As mentioned earlier, many college students read with only moderate speed and comprehension. Additionally, it has been found that after a few years of higher education, students may tend to give the morning newspaper the same ponderous attention they do a physics textbook. Since professors in most classes assign a great deal of reading and expect this reading to be accomplished in a brief period of time, if there is one single factor that can thoroughly handicap a student's academic progress, it is poor reading skills. Reading programs, in the form of either classes or groups, first measure reading speed and comprehension and then systematically help students individually to build up their skills in these areas.

Study-Skills Programs

Significant progress has been made in the area of study skills recently. Only a few years ago the issues stressed were such seemingly obvious ones as the necessity for a quiet, well-lighted place to study and the importance of spacing your study rather than trying to cram. Currently, awareness of *learning processes* has greatly expanded the repertoire of skills that are taught. In the most sophisticated study-skills programs, you learn about the process of cognitive organization, maximum methods of recall, the use of mnemonic aids (ingenious memorizing techniques), and so on. These programs may also provide opportunities to learn test-taking techniques; for example, you may be taught different approaches to use in taking objective and essay examinations. Finally, such programs can help you develop methods for both recognizing and dealing with test anxiety, which is important because taking an examination in a relaxed mood can significantly improve your overall ability to perform well. Learning all these techniques gives you a decided advantage. Students who have taken study-skills classes have been shown to perform consistently better than their not-so-well-trained peers. Interestingly enough, it has been found that study-skills classes are often attended mainly by the strongest students, who are trying to change their B's into A's, and are avoided by the weaker ones, who feel that appearing at such classes would somehow be a sign of weakness. The message should be quite obvious.

Writing-Skills Programs

For as long as we can remember there has been a significant discrepancy between the writing skills that most students gain in their high school classes and what is generally expected of them at the college or university level. Although special transition programs—unfortunately known as "dumbell English" classes—have been offered for some years, writing-skills programs have now been beefed up to accommodate the rising number of poorly prepared young as well as older students. Such programs are most often staffed by upper-division or graduate students who help writing-skills students prepare papers that are perhaps due in their other classes. This type of learning helps students to gain skills while they are completing assignments for other classes—a double bonus.

Mathematical-Skills Programs

More and more, mathematics is being used as a basis for approaching all fields of knowledge. Although a few years ago one took math courses in preparation only for "hard" science programs, today even the "soft" social sciences are utilizing mathematical concepts to deal with their complex subjects. In addition, recent research has shown that the lack of mathematical skills consistently has eliminated both women and minorities from gaining access to the so-called powerful fields and to positions of authority in general. In response to these findings, many campuses are beginning to develop nonthreatening, understandable courses that help students develop their mathematical skills. Often placing an emphasis on eliminating the fear of math, a typical math-skills program initially tests students to determine what skills they have and then develops individualized learning programs for students on the basis of their test performance. If need be, in such programs one may even begin working on addition without fear of being ridiculed. The best programs allow for a high degree of interaction between instructor and student and urge the student to progress at his or her own individual pace.

COUNSELING SERVICES

In addition to the types of financial and academic services we have described, returning students will find services that will probably be incredibly helpful during their college experience—the counseling services. These services cover two broad areas: psychological counseling and counseling on career planning and placement issues.

Psychological Counseling Services

Less than fifteen years ago, most colleges and universities were just beginning to recognize that an educational experience could be highly stressful and that this stress could have a negative effect upon a student's ability to function effectively. In addition, researchers found that often the students who needed help the most were those who were achieving and productive, not just the so-called goof-offs. Consequently, many institutions began to hire mental health specialists to help students identify and deal with the stresses they were undergoing.

Originally, psychological services were created to aid those students who were experiencing exceptionally troublesome problems. The counseling office was often hidden in a remote part of the campus. Students who made use of the service were secretive and ashamed. The counseling office itself often contributed to this air of mystery by maintaining an extraordinarily low profile on campus. This situation, of course, was the outgrowth of most institutions' original conception—that such services were designed to provide counsel to a small number of temporarily distressed students.

After World War II, a large number of adult students—returning veterans—suddenly flooded campuses and brought with them a whole new set of unique concerns. These socially mature, highly motivated students were faced with such questions as where to concentrate their energies, what to choose as majors, and how to integrate their personal interests and academic strengths with their long-term vocational goals. In response to these needs, many campuses created vocational counseling centers, where students could begin exploring "who they were" and where they could make reasonable vocational choices on the basis of such exploration. Once again, the original conception of these centers was that they were to service a small number of specific students—certainly not to meet any kind of general campus need.

Interestingly enough, over the years large numbers of students (many more than had originally been predicted) began to use both types of services—to seek help with matters of personal distress as well as with problems concerning choice of majors and vocational planning. In fact, students' concerns that seemed to originate in one area—say, feelings of personal inadequacy and confusion—would often wind up focusing on another area (for example, uncertainty about the reason for being in school or about the value of education). And students who sought counseling in order to deal with issues of vocational decision making often ended up exploring issues of personal development. What began as a small service area soon became just the tip of the iceberg. Today a majority of students come to the counseling services looking for help in resolving problems they have regarding themselves, their relationships, their goals, and their futures. Most colleges and universities have responded to the growing use of these services by increasing the size of their psychological staffs and making the counseling services maximally available to all students.

Psychological counseling services in the 1970s have therefore become quite extensive: Almost every college and university has one if not two or three offices specifically designated to provide psychological services for students. The names of the agencies vary, but common ones include "counseling center," "psychological services center," and "mental health unit of the health service." It is not unusual for more than half of the students at a college or university to have contacted one of these offices during their time on the campus. In addition, the centers have changed in terms of what they do. Rather than merely waiting for students to appear for help, they are also attempting to prevent problems before they arise. For example, it is now common for a counseling center to offer workshops on such issues as goal setting, test anxiety, sexuality, interpersonal communication, and even the special problems of the returning student. Irrespective of the university or name of the office, the goal of the counseling services is to provide students with an opportunity to deal with a problem while it is still in the infancy stage rather than allowing it to develop to a point where it significantly interferes with academic performance.

Most important, there has been a significant change in the institutional attitude toward the existence of such agencies. Rather than seeing them merely as places where students in trouble receive help, now universities recognize that such services significantly aid the *natural* development of students—that, indeed, these services act as adjuncts to the educational aims of the campus.

How to use psychological counseling services As a returning student, you might find the following suggestions regarding the use of the psychological counseling services helpful: If in the beginning stages of your return you are confused or even uncertain about what your major in college should be, it might be a good idea for you to go through some vocational counseling (sometimes also called "life-style counseling," "interest counseling," and so on). Such programs usually take from two to four weeks (meeting once or twice a week) and involve talking with a counselor and taking a number of interest, aptitude, and personality tests. The focus of this process is to help you to sort out your interests, skills, and abilities so that you can arrive at a vocational goal and make choices appropriate to that goal.

We also suggest that you inquire as to whether any transition programs are being offered specifically for the adult student. Existing programs of this sort may address problems having to do with being a single parent, developing new roles, maintaining self-esteem, resolving difficulties with one's spouse, or dealing with one's children and parents.

You should realize that at various times during your academic career problems will probably arise. You, like any of your fellow students, may experience periods of anxiety, confusion, depression, or lack of ability to concentrate. Rather than suffering stoically or using your friends or family as your primary source of help, we strongly suggest that you make use of the counseling services that are on campus. (By the way, many university counseling centers make their services available to students' spouses and children.) Further, we suggest that you do this when you *begin* to experience some sense of distress, rather than waiting until you feel overwhelmed. Remember, you will be a part of the majority in seeking help, not somebody who is strange or unique. Also, when you go to the counseling office, be sure to ask whether there is a specialist on the staff who is experienced in helping adult students. If so, at least initially ask to see that person.

In most instances, counseling services will respond directly and appropriately. The earlier you make contact, the greater the likelihood that your problem can be resolved quickly. You may be seen individually, or you may be asked to join a group of people who are dealing with similar concerns—it really depends on the nature of what is bothering you. In this as in other areas, we urge you not to hesitate, not to hold back: If you have a problem, seek help!

Career-Planning and Placement Services

Colleges and universities are aware that most students entering or re-entering school expect their campus experience to help them significantly in finding meaningful and financially rewarding work after graduation. Given the recent economic downturn and consequent unemployment, students are demanding even greater institutional concern about the practicality of their education. In some cases, institutions of higher learning are responding to these needs through their career-planning offices.

Traditionally, these offices have helped students articulate the relationship between their area of academic concentration and their area of future work. They have tried to answer such questions as: What can people with a B.A. in sociology do when they graduate? What jobs are there in industry for a chemistry major? If I am too old to get into medical school, what other kinds of health science alternatives are there? What is the best way of presenting myself in a job interview? In addition to helping students make the transition from student to worker more smoothly, career-planning offices also bring potential employers to the campus and give upper-division students an opportunity to talk with them about potential jobs.

The career-planning agency sometimes is able to provide students with work-study experiences. These are opportunities for students to spend part of their time in an actual working situation either for money or for academic credit. This experience enables the student to begin some early, precareer testing of the likelihood of being satisfied in a particular kind of work environment. Often associated with the career-planning agency is the student employment service, which offers part-time employment to students, sometimes on campus and sometimes in the community.

Like the counseling offices, career-planning agencies offer specalized workshops for students; these deal with such issues as résumé preparation, effective interviewing techniques, and getting the job you want. Career-planning offices may also have information available about special work fellowships, summer appointments, and federal, state, and local clerkship programs. It is amazing how many students really do not make use of these university services and at the same time complain bitterly about their inability to find meaningful work.

Our advice to the adult student who wants to use the career-planning offices is this: Early on, form a liaison with someone on the office staff who is a specialist in your area of academic concentration. If you are planning to work while you are a student, enlist the help of your specialist in acquiring a job so that your on-campus experience is enhanced by your practical experience. The adults student who does this may very well be in a better position than younger students because many employers prefer to hire individuals who are more experienced and more mature as trainees or interns. Job hunting is one of many situations in which your age may be an advantage in competing with your fellow students.

HEALTH SERVICES

There is an incredible range of health services available to students. At one extreme, a college may view students' physical health as their own individual responsibility and, aside from providing a referral list of community physicians, do little else. On other university campuses (particularly where there is an attached medical school), health services may be offered that surpass those available in the finest private health centers in terms of both variety and quality.

If there is a health service on campus, it is probable that its use is restricted to full-time students. If you are a part-time student, contact the health service and find out whether you can make use of the student health program if you pay supplementary fees. Once again, don't take the first "no" as a certain answer; there seems to be a growing opportunity for part-time students to pay student fees voluntarily and thus become eligible for many of the services that were previously denied them.

Once you have learned whether you can participate in the health service plan, the second thing is to find out about supplementary health insurance. Because most student health services are available only during the academic year, if you wish to have continuing coverage through the summer, it will be necessary to buy a supplementary insurance policy. Ordinarily, the payment is a very modest one, considering the amount of services for which you will be contracting.

In addition, many colleges and universities are now offering students the opportunity to purchase health insurance that will cover the spouse as well as children. In most instances, such coverage costs considerably less than comparable coverage from a private insurance company and represents a combination of an excellent buy and quality service. We suggest that adult students carefully compare their current health insurance program with the one offered by the college or university, and then decide which is best.

When you do seek medical care from the student health services on your campus, keep the following suggestions in mind: First, find one physician whom you like and see whether you can have continuing appointments with that person. Because they don't realize that they have this option, most students end up seeing a new doctor each time they visit the health service. Although this is not necessarily bad, most people are better served and more comfortable if they have a continuing relationship with just one doctor. Second, most health services are geared to serve the majority student—those who are late adolescents or young adults. Consequently, these services are not as prepared to deal with the unique medical problems that older students might have. Interestingly enough, according to Dr. Robert Allen, director of health services at the University of California at San Diego, the so-called unique problems of adults hardly ever show up in campus health centers; most adult students are treated for the same problems that younger students present—colds, sore throats, and upset stomachs. Perhaps the most useful advice we can give you is to provide your university physician with a complete medical history, which should include any idiosyncratic or chronic problems that may have developed over the years. Having this information will make it possible for the health center to respond to your illnesses with much greater care. Third, inquire as to whether there are specialized health service programs available. For a small supplementary fee, many health centers offer such services as birth control clinics, emergency dental care, and optometric care. Once again, it is advisable to make specific inquiries at the student health center about these programs, which many students might not know about at all. Finally, since the added stress of your new role as a student may overtax you to the point where physical illness could result, make sure that you take good care of your health.

OTHER SERVICES AND PROGRAMS

Up to this point we have described financial aid, academic services such as advisory and study-skills programs, counseling of various sorts, and health services—the services most likely to be available to, and used by, students in general. What follows is a listing of other services and programs that may be offered on your campus.

Child Care

The increasing number of students on campus who have children has led many colleges and universities to begin developing their own child care centers. Sometimes these centers are part of an academic program, such as an education department's early childhood laboratory center. These centers emphasize child development and usually provide a rich and varied experience for the children who attend. Other universities offer child care under the sponsorship of the parents themselves. Under these circumstances the agency is run jointly by an administrator hired by the university and the students themselves. The students are expected to help with the supervision and teaching in the center. The cost is usually about 50 cents an hour; in addition, a student parent is asked to commit a certain amount of time (two to ten hours a week) to working at the center. If the college you are attending does not offer any child care, you may want to begin the process of setting up such a facility. Services of this kind are most often developed as a result of student need and demand (and hard work).

When campuses have no actual child care facilities, they are often able to refer parents to reliable off-campus individuals or agencies through the student activities center. Of course, the quality of the child care that is available varies significantly. For women who are mothers, child care may be the most crucial issue to resolve in going back to school. Unless they feel good about the care their children are receiving, it is virtually impossible for them to go to classes, let alone concentrate on their studies.

Legal Services

Over the last ten years many campuses have begun to develop legal counseling services for students. These programs often provide counseling at no fee or on a low-fee basis and help students with a wide array of problems. The most common legal issues dealt with by these agencies are divorce proceedings, landlord-tenant problems, lawsuits resulting from automobile accidents, and minor criminal actions. Sometimes legal services are restricted only to giving counsel and do not cover court appearances. However, in these cases the on-campus agency helps students to find competent, low-cost counsel in the community. Legal counseling is perhaps the newest kind of service to be offered on campuses.

Housing Services

Although ten or fifteen years ago the primary housing available to students consisted of shared dormitory rooms, this situation, too, has changed in recent years. Now many colleges and universities provide a variety of living arrangements for students, ranging from the traditional dormitory room to apartments, housing cooperatives, and special areas set aside for students with families. The housing office on campus often can be helpful in locating nearby housing in the university community through its listings of good rentals, houses that become temporarily available as faculty or staff members leave for sabbaticals, and so on.

A new but growing phenomenon is the single adult student who chooses to live in university housing with younger students. Obviously, these adult students give up some degree of autonomy, but they find that the convenience and sense of community are well worth the lack of privacy.

Veterans' Affairs and Services

If you have spent more than ninety days on active duty in one of the branches of the armed forces, you may be eligible for VA benefits. These benefits vary according to when you were in the service, the length of your service, and the kinds of benefits you have previously used or asked for. It is well worth your while to find out whether any support or services are due you. The best place to inquire about such matters is at the veterans' affairs office on campus. On some campuses the veterans' program will be housed in an office with the student financial-aid services; on other campuses it will be an individual program with its own office.

Services for Returning Students

As the numbers of adult students have increased on campuses, some colleges and universities have developed services and centers designed specifically to meet their unique needs. Examples of these services are the Center for Continuing Education at the University of Michigan and Services for Returning Students at the University of Texas. Such programs usually offer special educational counseling for people who have interrupted their formal education and brush-up courses in math, writing, and reading. The most important function of these programs and services is that of providing a home base where adults can meet with one another to share problems and insights and where they can receive help from professionals as it is needed. In some cases, these services are a microcombination of all the services provided on a campus, organized in one place for adult students.

Services for Handicapped Students and Special-Interest Groups

Facilities and services for handicapped students are another resource provided by some campuses. There are also a variety of student-interest organizations ranging from chess teams to hang-gliding clubs. Often there are women's centers and men's centers and special programs for ethnic students. Whoever you are and whatever your interests are, it is highly likely that the college or university you are attending offers a program or service that you need or would enjoy. Therefore, if at the end of your first term you still feel alien, disconnected, or unwelcome, it may be that the fault lies with *you* rather than with the institution.

Finally, many colleges and universities have orientation programs for new students, the most extensive of which take place just before the fall term. Often, less elaborate replications of these orientation programs take place every academic quarter or semester. Unfortunately, these programs are geared mainly to the traditional—that is, younger—undergraduate or graduate student, and it is still a rare college that provides special reentry programs for the adult student. We suggest, however, that it is to your advantage to attend the orientation program. It may be your only opportunity to hear a comprehensive description of the services and programs available to students on your campus. It provides a chance for you to ask questions of relevant people—those who work in the various service offices, as well as university faculty and administrators. It also gives you an opportunity to begin meeting your fellow students and to gain an appreciation that they, too, are experiencing uncertainty and confusion as new students.

In conclusion, we again urge you, as an adult student, to feel free to make use of every resource that a campus has to offer. If you have a special need, be sure to ask for help, and do not accept the first "no" you hear as the final answer. If you have a need that cannot be met, perhaps you can be instrumental in having a new program or service created—for example, a special program for returning adult students, a seminar series for dual-career families, (families in which both wife and husband have careers of their own), or a group that meets to discuss the problems and rewards of being a part-time parent and part-time student. By starting something new, you will be helping not only yourself but your fellow returning adult students as well.

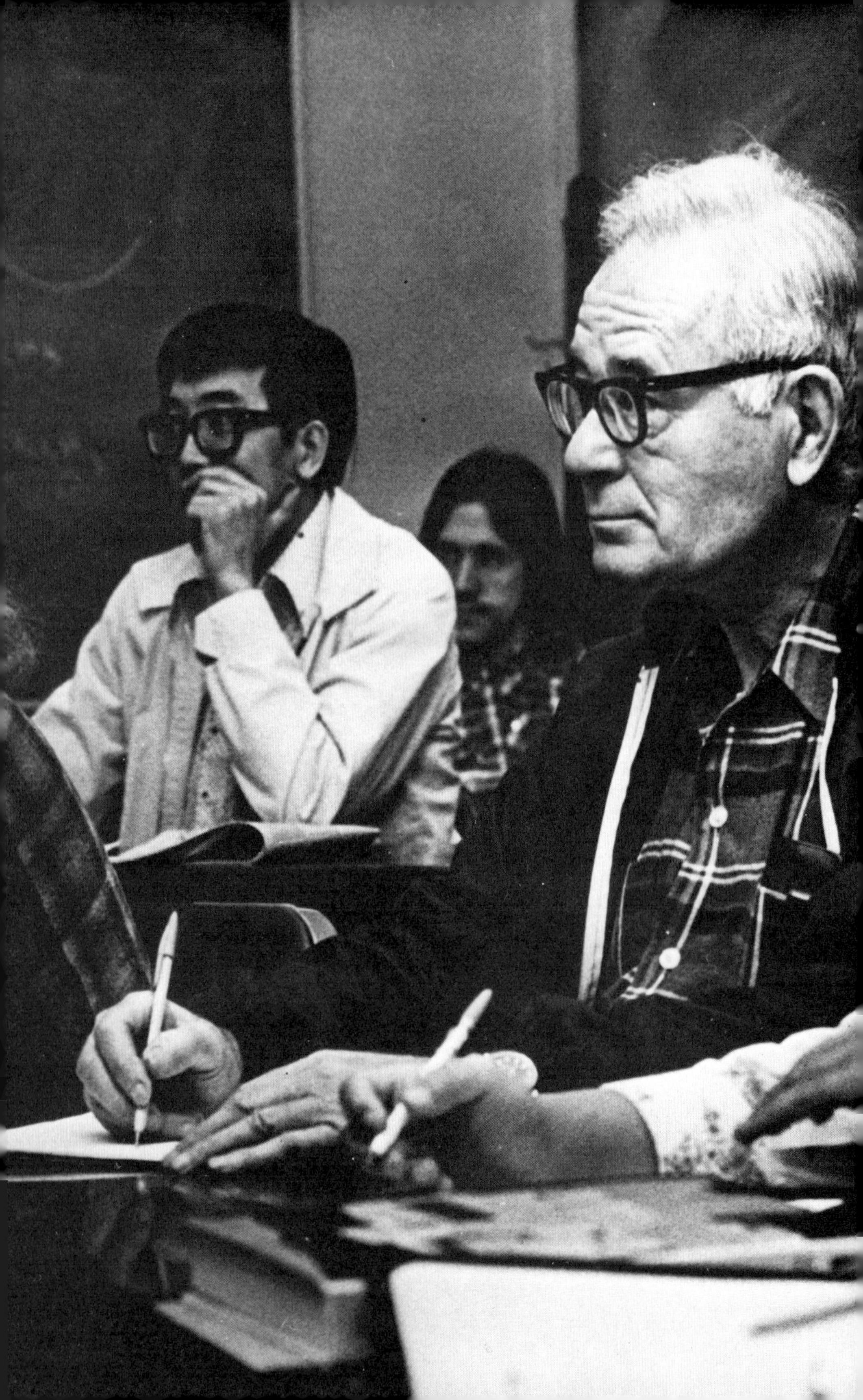

6 Myths about Maturity

I had thought that intelligence and memory decline in advanced adulthood except for a few outstanding people, but now I believe this is a myth. I am beginning to feel that I might even be capable of competing with our wonderful youth. I finished my second semester with an A in all five subjects. Sixty-year-old grandmother attending Westchester Community College.

In our acutely age-conscious society, most of our interest and attention have been devoted to the early years. The years of adulthood and maturity have been a neglected area, the "dark ages" of human development. The middle years have somehow failed to capture the imagination of poets, painters, and scientists. In medicine, pediatrics has been an established field since the middle of the nineteenth century, and adolescent medicine and gerontology have made rapid gains in our own time. Search through medical dictionaries for a definition of "adulthood," however, and you will find either that the term "adult" does not appear at all or, if it does, that it is defined as "fully grown and mature; a fully grown individual."[1]

But what does it mean to be "fully grown and mature"? Here the dictionaries fail us too, with little more to offer as a definition of "mature" than "to become ripe."

According to the standard view of middle age, it is a quiescent period, when, with the cares and turbulence of youth safely behind one, life settles into a comfortable pattern. It is a time when risk and adventure are replaced by routine and stability, when personal identity has become fixed, and when choices have narrowed or disappeared. In Shakespeare's "seven ages," middle age takes the form of "the justice, in fair round belly, with good capon lined, with eyes severe, full of wise saws and modern instances, and with little to look forward to beyond the final stage: second childishness and mere oblivion, sans teeth, sans eyes, sans taste, sans everything."[2]

In a variation on this theme, the middle years are frequently depicted as a time of desperate yearning after lost youth. The woman suffering from the "empty nest" syndrome has been served up again and again as a rather ridiculous and pathetic figure—menopausal, overbearingly matriarchal, struggling vainly to retain some vestiges of her fading charms. Her male counterpart comes off somewhat better, since men are assumed to be less concerned about aging than women, but he, too, is seen as preoccupied with his declining virility, which he seeks to restore through affairs with younger women.

The scenario of middle age is a familiar one, and its recurring motifs are those of loss and failure. Sexual appetites and powers diminish. Marriages go sour. New liaisons are attempted, but rarely succeed. Careers no longer bring satisfaction. Children grow up and go off, leaving their parents feeling vaguely guilty and inadequate.

How well does this picture reflect the realities of the maturing process? For adult learners to be able to distinguish the realities from the myths is a top priority since it is these myths that have been largely responsible for discouraging the mature student's educational ambitions. Happily, our exploration into the subject comes at a time when there is an upsurge of interest in the middle years. Hardly a week goes by without the appearance of an article, a book, or a new study dealing with this time of life. The midlife identity crisis, discussed in the first chapter, is beginning to be seen as a manifestation of growth that ranks in importance alongside puberty. New questions and new ways of looking at maturity are springing up as it becomes apparent that people in their midyears are simply not behaving in accordance with the conventional wisdom.

Much of this developing interest in adulthood has been spurred by the larger proportion of older people in the population, a phenomenon occurring not only in the United States but in many parts of the world as well. The expectation of life at birth has continually increased throughout the centuries. It was eighteen years in ancient Rome and twenty-five in the seventeenth century. In the United States, the proportion of people over sixty-five was 2.5 percent in 1850 and 4.1 percent in 1900; today it is close to 10 percent. In France, the life expectancy is sixty-eight for men and seventy-five for women; in the United States, it is seventy-one for men and seventy-seven for women. The figures are comparable in other industrially advanced nations.

What this means is that, for the first time in history, there is a greater proportion of older versus younger people in the population. It is this demographic change, with all that it portends for the future, that is responsible, more than any other factor, for the shift away from an exclusive preoccupation with youth toward a growing concern with adulthood.

ARE THERE LIMITS TO GROWTH?

During the early history of our educational system, it was commonly accepted that learning capacity falls off sharply after the early twenties and that memory is diminished and concentration reduced as the individual arrives at a mental plateau where he or she remains until the inevitable decline into old age. These assumptions were given credence by a series of tests that were administered to adults in the years after World War I. One such study that received considerable attention was conducted by Harold E. Jones and Herbert S. Conrad and was entitled "The Growth and Decline of Intelligence."[3] The tests were administered to 1,191 selected subjects who ranged in age from ten to sixty. When the scores were plotted against chronological age, the results seemed to show rapid intellectual growth to about sixteen years, some growth to about eighteen to twenty years, and a gradual but steady decline thereafter.

On the basis of these examinations, Jones and Conrad stated that tests of vocabulary and information were the least valid indicators of intelligence and that speed was a major factor in the measure of intelligence. A premise underlying the study was that adults could be considered equivalent in all respects, this despite the fact that at the time of testing, the twenty-year-olds had had considerably more formal schooling than the sixty-year-olds.

Another influential study that provided a more optimistic view of adult learning capacity was conducted over a period of years by E. L. Thorndike at Columbia University. These experiments were based on the performance of people from the ages of fourteen to fifty in tasks of many kinds such as learning to translate a message into code, to acquire an artificial language, and to memorize poetry. Thorndike came to the following conclusions about adult learning as a result of the tests:

> The most advantageous period for learning is between twenty and twenty-five years of age.

There is a decline in the capacity for learning, of approximately 1 percent per year, from this period to about age forty-two.

The influence of intellect upon the curve of ability to learn in relation to age is slight.

Although the Thorndike experiments advanced the cause of adult learning, the results continued to favor the young as learners, which is understandable in view of the concepts on which the tests were based:

The results were determined by the rate of speed at which the tasks were performed.

As in the Jones-Conrad studies, the subjects, though of different ages, were assumed to be alike in all respects except for age.

The tasks selected were laboratory or schoolroom exercises, with little relation to real-life experience.

The tests assumed that learning is primarily a matter of practice, regardless of the quality of the teaching.

These assumptions, which placed the adult learner at a disadvantage, grew out of a widespread misperception about how adults learn and about the learning process in general. There has always been, and no doubt will always be, a large amount of confusion and controversy about how learning takes place. Part of the problem is that learning is so dynamic, and at the same time so amorphous, that it is difficult to pin it down. Augustine once said: "I know what time is, but don't ask me." Much of what we know cannot be accounted for, and how we acquire our knowledge often defies scientific analysis.

Learning can be thought of in many ways—for example, as acquisition and mastery of what is already known about a subject, as the extension and clarification of one's individual experience, and as a means of testing ideas and solving problems. In a larger sense, learning is growth, change, and development; it is a process that begins at the moment of birth and continues until death or as for as long as the individual is capable of functioning as a sentient being. Learning is as natural to human beings as breathing and just as necessary to survival.

By the time a child enters school at the age of five or six, he or she has already learned a great deal—in fact, there are educators who claim that these early years of learning are the most important of all in shaping the individual's perception of the universe and his or her place in it. The significant change that takes place when children enter school is that learning becomes institutionalized; it is now directed toward social objectives, toward equipping them with the skills and knowledge that will help them find a suitable role in the social structure.

During the early years of this century, when industrialization was occurring at a rapid pace and the children of immigrants were being Americanized primarily through the schools, learning became equated with schooling. It was the schools that were expected to keep the "melting pot" simmering so that children from a wide variety of ethnic backgrounds could be transformed into functioning citizens of the new nation. The melting-pot concept, hand in hand with the idea of education as the principal route to upward mobility, disregarded other kinds of learning.

This attitude toward education can be found in the early tests of adult learning capacities, such as those conducted by Thorndike. The emphasis on speed, rote learning, and school-related tasks and the standardization of the test takers typify an approach which excludes noninstitutionalized capacities and abilities. Understandably, when adults whose schooling was behind them were forced to compete with youngsters who were daily being trained in institutional routines and exercises, the adults came off second best.

This below-standard performance of adults offered aid and comfort to the "hole-in-the-head" theory of learning, which continues to hold sway in some educational quarters, particularly those of the traditional variety. This theory represents a view of learning:

> . . . as if it were some process by which an entrance is somehow forced into the brain and facts are poured in or stamped in. The process is seen as a simple one. Organize your facts carefully; use repetition and other devices to make sure that they are properly injected into the mind. One concomitant of this notion is that the heads and minds of children are regarded as easier to penetrate, as less cluttered than those of adults."[4]

The hole-in-the-head approach also places teachers and students in an unbalanced relationship in which the teacher is the active agent and the student is the passive receptor.

THE LEARNING REVOLUTION

In recent years, as many educational assumptions have come under attack and as nontraditional education has been on the rise, a slow but steady reappraisal of the earlier theories and practices has taken place. The current revolution in education, which is one of the products of the sixties, places learning in an entirely new context. In this view, learning encompasses far more than what is taught in school; an accumulation of facts does not add up to an education, and though adults may have special educational needs, this does not place them in a second-class category. It is becoming clearer all the time that there are no limits to growth, except those which are self-imposed, socially imposed, or both.

These conclusions, which have not yet permeated the popular consciousness, have been arrived at through the work of psychologists, psychotherapists, sociologists, and other practitioners who are providing fascinating new insights into the mystery of learning and growth. One of the leaders in this field is Dr. Lissy Jarvik, professor of psychiatry at UCLA and chief of psychogenetics at the Brentwood Veterans Hospital, who has been studying the intellectual functioning of an aging population for several years. She has found that generally there is no decline in knowledge or reasoning ability—not only into the thirties and forties but into the sixties and seventies as well. Her study concerns 136 pairs of identical twins, first examined when they were more than sixty years old. As she followed the twins along into their seventies and eighties, they generally did not show the expected intellectual decline.

The decline in psychomotor speed which showed up in earlier studies is validated by the Jarvik experiments. The speed of mental operations increases up to the age of fifteen, remains stable from fifteen to thirty-five, and then begins to diminish. People over sixty perform poorly on intelligence tests when they have only a limited time to complete them (as is the case with all standardized admissions tests). But if they have all the time they want, they may do as well as people in their twenties or thirties. As the Jarvik tests show, where speed is not a factor, there is a great deal of intellectual stability. (And there are actually few learning areas outside of physical education where the speed factor is important.)

The most common learning complaint of older people is that their memory is not as good as it once was. But Dr. Jarvik's studies have shown not only that the young and the old have an equal ability to learn but also that their memory too is often equal. Much of what is called "loss of memory" may be due to inadequate learning in the first place, possibly caused by some factor such as hearing trouble, impaired vision, inattention, or trying to learn at too fast a speed. This interpretation is supported by another series of tests carried out on 3,000 persons in Holland which showed that memory decreased only with great age, but less among intellectual than among manual workers, less among former specialized craftsmen than among unskilled laborers, and less among those who were still working than among the retired.

Dr. Jarvik found that mental deterioration among older people is often a symptom of depression. What is misdiagnosed as mental deterioration can frequently be corrected by counseling, psychotherapy, or antidepressant medication. Dr. Jarvik notes that because of a cultural stereotype about older people and loss of memory, when an older person can't remember something, it is attributed to age, but when this happens to a younger person, a reason unrelated to age is offered.

Another learning problem that is common to people in their middle years and later is a decline in adaptability. It becomes more difficult to adapt to new situations and to deal with unfamiliar circumstances and concepts. Learning a foreign language or attempting to deal with a new symbol system—molecular physics, for example—presents greater problems for older students. Mature persons tend to develop a "mindset," and according to Simone de Beauvoir, "Once they have adopted the set, they are most reluctant to let it go. Even when they are faced with problems to which the set no longer has the least reference, they still cling to it. This means that their possibilities of learning are very much reduced. All powers such as observation, abstraction and synthesis, integration and structuration in which adaptation is a necessary part, diminish after thirty-five. . . ."[5] A discouraging note, but then she adds, "particularly if they are not exercised."

Here is a key to learning in maturity that appears again and again in current research on the subject. In vocabulary tests, for example, people with limited education show a decline in their later years, whereas among those who have had more education and have continued to be intellectually active, vocabulary retains its level and may even grow richer. All the tests and statistics point to an unmistakable conclusion: The higher an individual's intellectual level, the less likelihood there is that his or her powers will decline. Mental capability, like muscle tissue, atrophies with disuse; for the mature learner, the golden rule is: If you keep on using your memory and intelligence, you can preserve them unharmed.

De Beauvoir makes the point that "there is a great deal of intellectual work performed without any relation to age. Professional skill, technical ability, sound judgment, and organization can compensate for the weakening of memory and of resistance to fatigue, and for the difficulties of adaptation."[6]

There is also the compensating factor of motivation, which has long been recognized as a critical component of the learning process. In a 1955 paper on age-related changes in learning, the psychologist James E. Birren, who is director of the Gerontology Center at the University of Southern California, says: "The person who has a successful and ego-satisfying career is one whose accomplishments are noteworthy, relative to his expectations and accomplishments; there is a close congruence between the 'actual self' and the 'ideal self.'"[7]

In the area of motivation, mature students appear to have an edge over the young. College administrators, faculty members, and counselors are almost unanimous in proclaiming the higher motivation levels of adult students. Younger students, particularly if they have had no learning experience outside school, often lack a sense of direction in their college years, but men and women who return to school in midlife usually have, as we've seen in the first chapter, clearly identifiable reasons for continuing their education. These men and women, we can assume, have been able to translate their motivation into action because of the closeness between their actual and ideal selves that Birren has noted.

But there are mature persons for whom a serious gap exists between expectations and accomplishments. These people refuse to look at themselves honestly and analytically; they develop a defensiveness which, as Birren puts it, "is reflected in a lack of desire to explore the new and unfamiliar." This defensiveness is often found in maturing individuals whose self-concept has been shaped by age stereotypes. Agism as a form of prejudice is as insidious as racism or sexism and is equally threatening to the healthy development of the individual identity. The fear of growing old is universal, but it is especially acute in technologically advanced societies like ours, in which economic usefulness is age-related.

One of the ironies of aging is that although it is something that happens to all of us and although it is continuous from the cradle to the grave, it is usually perceived as an unfortunate event that occurs quite suddenly and unexpectedly. "You are young, and then you are middle-aged, but it is hard to tell the moment of passage from one state to the next. . . . Changes have taken place . . . but you are hardly aware of them, because the ice has ground so slowly down the valley."[8]

This way of thinking about maturity is linked to the belief that an adult is fully formed by the time adolescence is over—that once a person has passed puberty, his or her identity is fixed. But new discoveries about maturity and aging are yielding a very different view of how adults grow up.

BIOLOGICAL AND CULTURAL CLOCKS

When does middle age begin? When does it end? Is there a precise moment at which an individual can be described as old? Psychologists and therapists who specialize in aging are in agreement mainly about the difficulty of locating specific age boundaries. According to the experts, aging is an individual matter which is determined by a complex set of factors, cultural as well as biological. Because the criteria for "youth" and "maturity" vary from one society to another as well as from one individual to another, any attempt to measure age by the usual chronology of clocks and calendars can be misleading.

Not even in physiological development do we find across-the-board consistency. Signs of puberty vary considerably, with menstruation occurring in girls anywhere from ten to seventeen years (in the United States today most girls begin to menstruate at around age twelve or thirteen) and with enlargement of the testicles occurring in boys between the ages of nine-and-one-half and seventeen-and-one-half. These changes, which mark the onset of adolescence, signal the beginning of the reproductive period. At the end of the reproductive cycle, we have the menopause, which may occur from age forty-five to age fifty or more. Aging, as the gerontologist Howell has said, "is not a simple slope which everyone slides down at the same speed. It is a flight of irregular stairs down which some journey more quickly than others."

Thanks to medical science, the journey is becoming a safer and pleasanter one. Today, the body is protected against many diseases and infirmities and can retain its vigor and resilience into advanced age. In terms of physical strength and dexterity, variations among people in the same age group may be as great as, or greater than, variations among those of different ages. There is no striking difference between the powers of a fifty-year-old and those of a sixty-year-old. Maximum muscular strength is reached at the age of twenty-seven. In sixty-year-olds it has diminished no more than 7 percent in comparison with forty-eight- to fifty-year-olds. Even manual skills—which, as we've seen, show the greatest decline with age—change little between the ages of fifteen and fifty. Between sixty and sixty-nine, the time needed to perform a task involving manual skills increases by merely 15 percent.

In general, it can be said that the physical follows the mental. As long as the intellectual powers retain their strength and resilience, the body has a good chance of remaining healthy. A severe intellectual or spiritual shock often leads to a deterioration of the body's physical capability. But here again, this depends on the individual and on how he or she can cope with, and rise above, such psychic disturbances.

MILESTONES OF MATURITY

From a biological perspective, we may speak of puberty, menopause, and the climacteric as being the milestones of adult life. (Menopause is the cessation of menstruation, and the climacteric is a corresponding phenomenon in the male, characterized by a decline in sexual activity and ability. However, in current usage the two terms have become synonymous.) But as a psychiatrist who specialized in adulthood has remarked, "The landmarks of such a subdivision are also too far apart to provide us with sufficient rungs on the ladder to match the many other important events that characterize adult life."[9]

What are these important milestones in adult life? Of the many investigators who have attempted to locate and define the stages of adulthood, three whose work has special relevance for adult learners are Carl

C. Jung, Erik Erikson, and Roger Gould. In the period following Freud, whose theories of development focused on children, Carl Jung addressed himself to the life stages after puberty. He defined "youth" as the period between postadolescence and adulthood, a time when childhood aspirations are put aside and the individual is concerned with developing sexuality and self-esteem. This part of the life span represents a general broadening of the life perspective.

The next stage is located by Jung between the ages of thirty-five and forty, at which time some personality changes begin slowly to make their appearance. Childhood traits repressed during youth may reemerge at this time, and there is a general reappraisal and reshuffling of goals and interests. These changes gradually become stabilized, and by the age of fifty, there is a marked decline in adaptability; rigidity and intolerance are seen as characteristics of the years from fifty onward.

Erik Erikson has made a major effort to discover the dimensions of adult identity by looking at the entire life cycle. Whereas Shakespeare posited "seven ages of man," Erikson sets forth eight phases, each governed by the tension between counterforces. (See Figure 3 on page 141.) It is this tension and the individual's adaptation to it that define adult identity for each stage. Each stage has its specific "task" to accomplish, but there are no neat divisions between the stages; rather, the adult is contained in the child, and the child in the adult, and the entire life cycle is held together by external and internal bonds and linkages.

For Erikson, life begins when childhood and youth come to an end. At this time, the individual is directed toward work or study for a career, sociability with members of the other sex, and, in time, marriage and a family. There are three stages of adulthood in this scheme. First is the period following adolescence, which is motivated by the development of intimacy and the tension between intimacy and self-absorption. This stage involves relationships with members of the other sex and of the same sex and with oneself as well. But, as Erikson emphasizes, "It is only after a reasonable sense of identity has been established that real intimacy with the other sex, or for that matter, with any other person or even with oneself is possible."[10]

The young, who are unsure of themselves, shy away from interpersonal intimacy; as they develop inner confidence, they seek intimacy in the form of friendship, leadership, love, and inspiration. These attachments represent an attempt to define one's own identity by discussing with others one's plans, wishes, and expectations. Failure to establish satisfying relationships at this stage may lead to isolation or to repeated attempts and repeated failures. The problems that arise in so many young marriages can be traced to the obligation placed upon the partners to act as mates and parents before they have completed the work on themselves;

THE INTERPLAY OF SUCCESSIVE LIFE STAGES

	1	2	3	4	5	6	7	8
H. Old age								Integrity vs. despair, disgust: *Wisdom*
G. Maturity							Generativity vs. self-absorption: *Care*	
F. Young adulthood						Intimacy vs. isolation: *Love*		
E. Adolescence					Identity vs. identity confusion: *Fidelity*			
D. School age				Industry vs. inferiority *Competence*				
C. Play age			Initiative vs. guilt: *Purpose*					
B. Early childhood		Autonomy vs. shame, doubt: *Will*						
A. Infancy	Trust vs. mistrust: *Hope*							

Figure 3 The interplay of successive life stages

MYTHS ABOUT MATURITY

they are not ready for "twoness" until they have each achieved true "oneness."

The counterpart to intimacy is isolation, the readiness to withdraw from and repudiate those relationships which seem threatening to one's own development. This occurs as the individual moves away from self-absorption into cooperative and competitive relationships, gradually forming a circle of partners in friendship and sex. The task for this stage is to find oneself in another.

The second stage poses generativity against stagnation, and it represents that time of life which is devoted to the establishment of the next generation. Parenthood is the usual means of accomplishing this task, but Erikson suggests that the same purpose can be pursued in other ways, through productive activities that absorb the individual's creative energies. What is really important at this stage in the growth of a healthy personality is to find a satisfying way of investing oneself in the future. Adults who fail at this may regress to a sense of stagnation and begin to indulge themselves as if they were their own only children.

In his work with adults at this stage, Erikson observes, particularly in young parents, an inability to arrive at their full development. He finds the reasons in early childhood impressions, in faulty identifications with parents, in excessive self-love, and in a lack of faith, a lack of a "belief in the species," which is an important motivation for parenthood and all creativity. "To make be" and "to take care of" are essential to the formation of identity at this phase.

In the third and final phase of human development, which is the fruit of the preceding two stages, integrity vies with despair for control of the adult personality. By "integrity," Erikson means taking care of things and people and adapting onself to the "triumphs and disappointments of being." It is a stage characterized by acceptance—of one's life as being one's own responsibility and as being what it had to be. It is a time of coming to terms, of participating as a follower as well as accepting the responsibility of leadership. There is a sense of comradeship with men and women who have lived at other times, a feeling of kinship with humanity. At the same time, the drive toward integrity makes one ready to defend the dignity of one's own life style against all others. As in the earlier stages, failure to accomplish the task associated with this phase carries its price, which is despair and an often unconscious fear of death. Despair is expressed in the sense that life is short and that one's choices are few; it may also take the form of cynicism and self-contempt.

The sequence of Erikson's life stages depends on the proper development of each at the proper time; the rate of development is determined by the makeup of the individual and the nature of the society in which the personality unfolds.

Thus, we have considerable individual variation within an ongoing process of adult growth. As psychiatrist Roger Gould sees it, it is a process that directs the individual toward greater self-tolerance and an appreciation of life's complexity. Whereas Erikson speaks of "tasks" for the various phases, Gould sees a series of roles for different times of one's life. The success with which these roles are carried out is related to the specific theme or needs of the life stage at which they are assumed. Gould's observations, based on his study of people in seven age groups ranging from sixteen to fifty and beyond, have convinced him that "the precise ages at which changes occur are a product of an individual's total personality, lifestyle and subculture."[11] He takes issue with prevailing notions of adulthood which deny the fact that adults grow and change—"children change; adults only age"—and according to which adults are expected to remain essentially the same for a half century or so.

Gould believes that growth in adults involves arriving at new beliefs about oneself and the world. It requires "thoughtful confrontation" with oneself and others so that conflicts between past and present beliefs can be reconciled; in this way, new values are developed that reflect the adult experience at a particular stage of life.

The theories of human growth which we have surveyed are important to adult learners because they are helping to overcome the myth of a static adult personality, a myth which has kept many people in their midyears from pursuing higher education. The individual's attitude toward being middle-aged is another psychological factor that may serve as either an impetus or a deterrent to learning.

SELF-AWARENESS IN MATURITY

If, as we are discovering, there are no discernible boundaries between one age or stage and another, how can we map out that terrain known as "adulthood"? What does it mean to be "middle-aged"? According to Lissy Jarvik, a better term than "ages" or "stages" would be "transitions," and while stressing the individual nature of cyclical change, she offers two cues for identifying the middle years: the sense of having reached the peak of achievement in whatever is important to you and the feeling that you can still change your world instead of having to adapt to it. The transition from middle age to old age is signaled by the tendency to measure time from death rather than birth.

The awareness of middle age is very much a part of our contemporary consciousness, of a society that is struggling to break free from youth worship and confront the demographic realities of its time. Research on the middle years is still in its preliminary stages, but as the inner life of the mature person becomes better known to us, some useful insights emerge for those who are considering a midlife change but who may have some doubts and questions about its timeliness.

From an extensive series of in-depth interviews with men and women who have had educational and social advantages, it appears that, for such a group, middle age is a time of heightened self-assessment.[12] Chronological time is not important; the life cycle is viewed in relation to various contexts: one's body, one's career, family. A business executive regards himself as having reached the pinnacle in his career, and yet because his children are still young, he feels he has a long way to go before achieving his family goals.

Midlife people see themselves as bridge builders within their families and also in their work and their communities. A corporation executive says: "One of my main problems now is to encourage young people to develop so that they'll be able to carry on after us." But the task of bridge building, particularly in regard to the younger generation, can set off shock waves of age recognition. Here is a forty-eight-year-old who graduated during the Great Depression: "Today's young people are different. They've grown up in an age of affluence. When I was my son's age, I was much more worldly, what with the problems I had to face. I was supporting my father's family at his age. But my son can never understand all this—he's of a different generation altoghether."

Or the shock may come from the other direction, from the sudden awareness of a parent's aging, as in this woman's account: "I was shopping with my mother. She had left something behind on the counter, and the clerk called out to tell me that the 'old lady' had forgotten her package. I was amazed. Of course, the clerk was a young man, and she must have seemed old to him. But the interesting thing is that I myself don't think of her as old—she doesn't seem old to me."

Male-Female Differences

In certain respects, men and women experience middle age differently. Women tend to mark the passing of time and their own aging by events having to do with the family: the birth of children, graduations, anniversaries. Even unmarried women tend to think of middle age in terms of the husband and children they might have had. "The things that bothered me in my thirties about marriage and children don't bother me now," a single woman remarked, "because I'm at the age where many women have already lost their husbands."

Men, on the other hand, find their age cues outside the family—most frequently in their work and in their bodies. The competitive work setting to which men have historically been conditioned provides them with their keenest sense of age status (as more women enter business and the professions, there are indications that the work setting is replacing the family as a reference point for feminine life stages). A man may first become aware of growing old when younger associates begin treating him in a deferential manner or presenting challenges to his competence and authority.

Men are more profoundly affected by biological changes than women are. Despite the menopause, women show less concern about their own health than their husbands'; concern with widowhood (or, as it has been called, "rehearsal for widowhood") is fairly common among women with husbands in their forties and fifties, a concern that is substantiated by statistics which show widows outnumbering widowers four to one. For men, bodily changes occurring in midlife are the mose dramatic age indicators. "Mentally, I still feel young, but suddenly one day my son beat me at tennis," is the way one man expressed it. Another said, "It was the sudden heart attack of a friend that made the difference. I realized that I could no longer count on my body as I used to do."

By contrast, women often experience a sense of physical release and an upsurge of energy at this stage. Typically, a woman, now that she is free from domestic responsibilities, will speak of new interests and enthusiasms, while at the same time her husband is expressing boredom, a sense that life is becoming stale, flat, and unprofitable. A history professor said: "I'm afraid I'm a bit envious of my wife. She went to work a few years ago, when our children no longer needed her attention, and a whole new world has opened to her. But myself? I just look forward to writing another volume, and then another volume. . . ."

Other differences between mature men and mature women show up in what they worry about. In the following order, women worry about their children, their husbands, their parents, and themselves. A man's worry list places the family as a single unit at the top, followed by himself and his image and then his parents.[13]

Role confusion, in regard to marriage and parenthood, is prevalent in midlife, and it is accentuated when the children grow up and leave home. Raising the children has absorbed most of the time and energies of many married couples; personal plans and interests have been shoved aside "for the sake of the children." In effect, they have been child-raising teams, and now that their "generativity" task has been completed, they are faced with "stagnation." But as Erikson's theory suggests, the completion of a cyclical task at one stage leads to equally important and challenging tasks in succeeding age cycles. It is only when adulthood is thought of as a no-growth period, defined entirely by parenthood, that the "empty nest" appears as a void across which husband and wife can no longer communicate.

The way middle age is experienced differs also in relation to income and social strata. Higher-income people in their midyears see themselves as being "in command," whereas those in low-income groups have a sense of being manipulated by forces beyond their control. Those in the middle- and high-income groups are more upwardly mobile and more likely to identify with a structured life style based on achievement and status. Working-class people tend to think of middle age as beginning earlier than middle-class people do. For instance, a top business executive places life divisions at thirty, forty, and sixty-five; he considers a forty-year-old "mature," with middle age arriving not before fifty, and old age at around seventy. An unskilled worker sets age boundaries at twenty-five, thirty-five, and fifty and regards forty as middle-aged and sixty as old.

As this survey of adulthood indicates, the concept of middle age is fluid and open-ended. What was once regarded as old age, the years from forty to sixty, is now considered the "prime of life." The middle years, like childhood and adolescence, are now seen as a time of change and growth, of intense self-questioning, of a search for purpose and identity. Far from being a tranquil time, it is fraught with problems and crises which may lead to severe personal and family disruptions. It is also a time of great challenge and opportunity, a time to explore the inner self and capitalize on one's newly discovered resources.

MAKING THE MOST OF MATURITY

To the midlife person seeking higher education, Shaw's remark that "youth is wasted on the young" must at times seem painfully apt. Here you are, struggling to mesh your studies with all your other obligations and responsibilities, and there they are, the young ones, going through college the traditional way—the easy way, as it must appear through many an adult viewfinder. They seem to have everything going for them, especially those who are living at home: no time-consuming domestic cares, no money worries, plenty of freedom, and all that bounce and verve and energy.

Aside from the fact that this is far from an accurate picture of today's hardworking, often hard-pressed young college student, it also overlooks a whole range of benefits and advantages that accrue to the older, re-entering student. From our expanding knowledge of the middle years, we are beginning to realize that this is a most favorable time of life for undertaking new learning experiences. A prerequisite for adapting to the demands of a new life style is an understanding of maturity, of its possibilities as well as its limitations.

The most valuable asset that mature students bring with them is their life experience. The notion of the seventeenth-century philosopher John Locke that a child's mind at birth is like "white paper, void of all characters," has been debated through the centuries, but only those who subscribe to the hole-in-the-head theory of learning would consider a *tabula rasa*, or clean slate, more conducive to learning than a mind with some "characters" written on it. For it is becoming clearer all the time that intelligence does not function in a vacuum, that learning needs some soil to take root in, and the richer the soil, the better the learning.

As you map out your educational program, your life experiences can serve as your surveying tools. If you have been employed at a job or a succession of jobs, what strengths and weaknesses did you discover in yourself in the course of your work? If your time has been spent mostly in homemaking, what did your family relationships as well as your hobbies and community activities reveal about your tastes and aptitudes? Have you discovered that you are more people-oriented or more thing-oriented? Are you happier making something with your hands or spinning something out of your head? Do you respond better to visual or auditory stimuli? Since your maturity means that you have had more time and more opportunity to test yourself in a variety of situations, you have a better chance of arriving at some accurate answers.

The tendency toward self-examination, which, as we've seen, comes through strongly in the midyears, can also work to your advantage. For the young, the past is foreshortened, and much of it has been spent in a state of dependence. Maturity not only gives you more of a past to guide you toward the future but also offers you a view of yourself as an autonomous being as well as an individual involved in a network of relationships—as if you were seeing yourself simultaneously in close-up and at a distance. Self-knowledge, arrived at in this way, is an excellent foundation for any educational program, whether it is intended for self-renewal, career advancement, or both.

Making the most of your maturity may also involve a change in values, and this can present a formidable stumbling block to people in midlife. Attitudes that have become deeply embedded in the consciousness are not easy to dislodge, and a set of attitudes that have become crystallized can lead to the "mindset" referred to by de Beauvoir. Since this tends to close one off to new stimuli and impressions, it can be a deterrent to learning. This does not mean that values built up over a lifetime must be suddenly and drastically revised. What it suggests is that an open, accepting approach to new ideas is important for continuing one's education. It also affirms the Erikson-Gould thesis that the "task" or "role" suitable for one stage of life may not be appropriate for another.

MANIFESTO FOR MATURE LEARNERS

Entering successfully into the life of a student means recognizing the practical requirements of learning at this time of your life. It means not only compensating for such limitations as a decline in speed and strength but also, beyond that, structuring the situation so that learning becomes easier. This might include such obvious ploys as carrying a light, low-pressure course load, even if this means that it will take you longer to reach your goal; making sure that you have optimum physical conditions for studying, such as good light, privacy, and easy access to the books and materials you need; and freeing yourself from all unnecessary burdens and tensions that erode your time and energies. For example, you may have to give up, for the time being, some of the social, civic, and recreational activities that you used to enjoy—in other words, you may have to budget your time and energy. More basically, you must realize that, as an adult, you have educational needs that deserve special consideration from professionals in higher education as well as from other adult students.

While most professionals in adult education will readily admit that mature students studying in a variety of nontraditional situations have learning requirements and capabilities that are different from those of young students in traditional settings, the question of what precisely these differences are is less likely to produce a consensus. These professionals, like others, bring to their field of diversity of opinions and conclusions, and in a field as dynamic as continuing education, hard-and-fast formulas are particularly difficult to come by.

However, from research and experience, both here and in other countries, eight principles emerge to provide a manifesto for learning in maturity:

1   Adults respond positively to learning in which the information has some personal meaning for them (this is also true of younger students, as the cry for "relevance" indicates, but it is intensified in adults). Because of this, adults are especially receptive to "affective" learning, that is, learning which is meaningful and which can be readily internalized, or related to one's own experience. Realization of this fact has led to the kinds of experimentation and institutional responses described in Chapter 3. In this area, there have been some particularly promising efforts to push back the boundaries of what we know about intelligence and learning. New conceptions are emerging which place greater emphasis on perception and emotion and which assign a more important role to experience and cultural influences.

2   Adults benefit by relating what they are studying to what they need to know. Since they are goal-oriented and feel the pressure of time more keenly than traditional students, they tend to be impatient with courses or routines that seem unrelated to their needs. Unfortunately, this principle is more neglected than any other in higher education. Here is what a professor of psychology, Arthur W. Combs, has to say on the subject: "In college, we select people who would learn whether we taught them or not. . . . a good example of

this is a course. A course is a package which you deliver to people whether they need it or not, and in an order that has, perhaps, nothing to do with the kinds of ways they see the problem."[14]

3 Adults are eager for new information and experience. Since they bring a certain amount of mental baggage with them, they do not react favorably to ideas that seem overly familiar and too stereotyped to provoke fresh thought. Professionals in continuing education are highly sensitive to this principle and are continually seeking new and stimulating subjects and methods of presenting courses and programs, as well as ways of discovering the deeper meaning of what is already known. This has led to increased experimentation with a variety of techniques—group discussions, value clarification, sensitivity training, encounter groups, role playing, and gaming—and to an increased use of audio-visual technology.

4 Adults learn best when they are active participants in the learning process. Taking their model from life rather than school, they see themselves as involved in a give-and-take of teaching and learning between themselves, the faculty, and other students. In this type of learning situation, it is just as blessed to give as to receive. The successful teacher of adult students functions as a facilitator, consultant, helper, and resource, rather than as the director of the process. The teacher–authority figure doling out knowledge from some Olympian height cannot meet the challenge of the mature student.

5 Adults require long and uninterrupted learning sessions, which means they will gain more from a two-hour seminar once a week than from three weekly fifty-minute sessions. This is a reflection of their need to learn by discovery rather than by rote. The traditional method of memorizing material in order to regurgitate it on exams may lend itself to brief, concentrated time periods, but integrating information with one's own judgment and experience requires a lengthier span of time.

6 Adults need to consolidate what they have learned before going on to new concepts or skills. This is known as "cumulative learning," in which there is a gradual absorption of what is learned; in effect, new learning is built on a solid base of previous learning. Again, this is a time-consuming process but one that provides more lasting results than the "instant" variety.

7 Adults require feedback during learning in order to avoid the difficulties of unlearning. For this reason, lectures alone are not satisfactory. The lecture-discussion format works better since it provides an opportunity to ask questions and explore ideas in depth.

8 A learning program for adult students should be structured so that they do not feel rushed or pressured by competition. Adult students are more concerned about how learning will benefit them as individuals than about coming out ahead of others. Although the evidence shows that adult students generally receive better-than-average grades, their concern is essentially with what the grades say about their individual performances; mature students tend to disapprove of grading on a curve, which assesses each student in relation to the other students.

The above eight points deserve a special place in the adult learner's survival kit, but they also apply more generally to higher education as it is being conducted in the United States today. Much of the criticism of traditional education that we hear today from younger college students and much of the mounting unease among faculty and administrators revolve around the learning requirements and conditions pinpointed in the mature student's manifesto. The intense competitiveness, the impersonality, the grading system under which grades become ends instead of means, the pressure-cooker environment, and the tendency to regard students as passive receptors rather than active participants—these are some of the problem areas in postsecondary education that are attracting increasing attention and concern.

The continuing and growing presence of mature and other nontraditional students on the campuses may serve as a catalyst for sweeping educational reforms in the years ahead; signs of this are already evident in such innovations as independent study, experiential and cooperative education, and credit for prior off-campus learning. As we shed the myths surrounding maturity and develop a deeper understanding of the needs, problems, and potentials of adults, we can expect not only our educational system but our other institutions as well to become increasingly humanized and enriched. As Erikson has suggested, we have had a century of the child and something like a century of youth; perhaps we are now ready for a century of the adult.

REFERENCES

1 Thomas Lathrop Stedman, *Medical Dictionary,* The Johns Hopkins Press, Baltimore, 1961.

2 William Shakespeare, *As You Like It,* Act II.

3 H. E. Jones and H. S. Conrad, "The Growth and Decline of Intelligence," *General Psychological Monographs,* vol. 13, 1933.

4 J. R. Kidd, *How Adults Learn,* Association Press, New York, 1959.

5   Simone de Beauvoir, *The Coming of Age,* Warner Books, Inc., New York, 1975.

6   Ibid.

7   J. E. Birren, *Age Changes in Skill and Learning,* 1955.

8   de Beauvoir, op cit.

9   H. A. Katchadourian, "Medical Perspectives on Adulthood," *Daedalus,* Spring 1976.

10   Erik Erikson, *Childhood and Society,* W. W. Norton & Company, Inc., New York, 1963.

11   Roger Gould, "Adult Life Stages: Growth Toward Self Tolerance," *Psychology Today,* February 1975.

12   Bernice L. Neugarten, *Middle Age and Aging,* The University of Chicago Press, Chicago, 1968.

13   "Adults and Part-Time Students in Higher Education," *Adults in Higher Education,* Mar. 28, 1972.

14   Arthur W. Combs, *Adults as Learners,* proceedings of a conference, Pennsylvania State University, 1974.

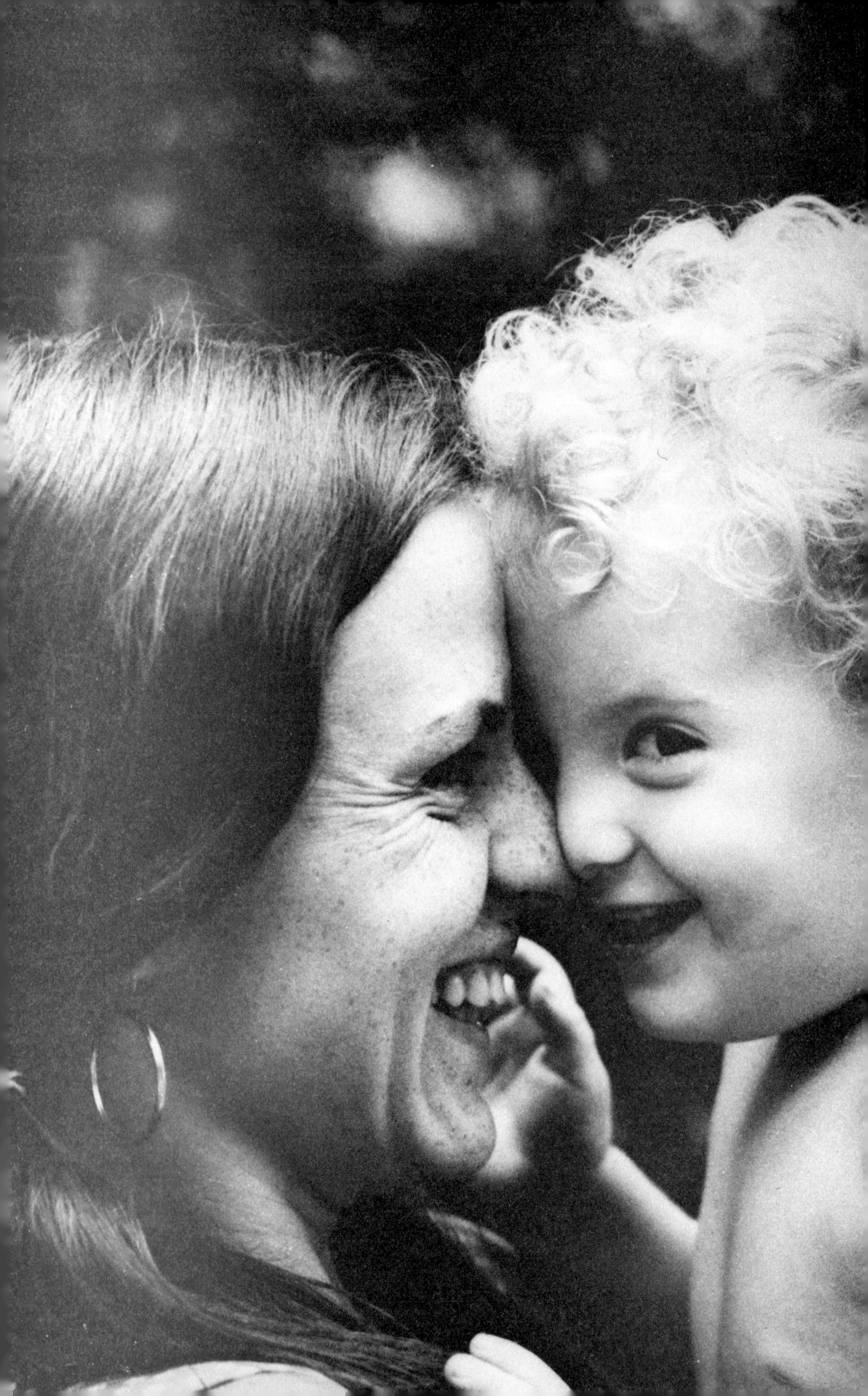

7 New and Former Relationships

It takes energy to grow, to examine your life, to change your habits and your interests while maintaining a healthy interaction with the people around you. Dr. Lee McEvoy, clinical psychologist, UCLA.

Being an adult means, among other things, that you are involved in an extensive and intricate web of personal relationships. In addition to parents, spouse, children, and even grandchildren, there are also friends and business associates and perhaps ex-husbands or ex-wives, stepchildren, in-laws, and so on. Your decision to return to school has important implications for all these people in your life. Becoming a student in adulthood means that you are taking on a new role in life, and this can have a profound effect upon both your former and your new relationships. Change, while essential to growth, is always risky, and even more so in today's social climate, in which familiar roles are being reexamined, revised, and often replaced.

Adult students frequently experience some degree of discomfort as they begin to change their roles and attempt to adjust to new environments. Yet this aspect of returning to school is rarely anticipated; as a result, not only are many adult students unprepared to deal with these problems, but they often become overwhelmed by unfamiliar pressures and tensions. As one student from the University of Michigan has said, "One of the difficulties in returning to school is the adjustment that one must make to various roles that have to be played *simultaneously*."[1] Another student from the same university added, "When you have many roles to play already and you add the student role to the others, I should think that you would have guilt feelings and fears that you may be placing your efforts in the wrong direction; that your family may suffer now even though you may be helping them in the long run."[2]

In addition, adult students have certain anxieties about how they will be accepted on campus. They worry about their competence and achievement, of course, but they also worry that they will be seen as "freaks" by faculty members and younger students—as helpless, doddering, and confused. Some adult students have even made efforts to move about the campus incognito, disguised behind dark glasses, baseball caps, or scarves.

All this points to the fact that adults going back to school experience *change*, and most people deal ambivalently with change. It is bittersweet, bringing both excitement and apprehension. Adult students experience excitement as they think about the new things that lie ahead—involvement, stimulation, and learning—but they also feel apprehensive about the possible dangers, such as disappointment, rejection, and demands that cannot be met. Change is unavoidable, and so is the ambivalence. The important issue is how the adult student deals with both.

What is all this talk about role change? Why is "role" something we should be concerned about in this book? To answer these questions, we need to look at part of what is occurring in our American culture. More and more people are questioning what the appropriate roles are for men and women. This questioning has evolved historically as a result of a number of forces. First, because of increasing technological advances (sometimes called the "continuing Industrial Revolution"), men and women are asking themselves how they want to spend their potentially freer hours. After all, life spans are increasing, birth control measures are making it possible to have fewer familial responsibilities than in the past, and household conveniences provide more leisure time. Second, the women's movement (and the emerging men's liberation movement) has awakened in people the idea that our society no longer needs to make sex-linked assignments of what individuals are supposed to do with their lives. Women are finding that they have options open to them other than the traditional wife-mother role. Men are beginning to feel less pressured to devote themselves single-mindedly to work. Finally, along with these two forces, a social revolution is occurring in which individuals, both men and women, are looking for meaning in their lives. It is almost as if we are experiencing a societal menopause in which individuals of all ages are asking, "What should I do with the rest of my life?" Consequently, men's and women's lives are converging "away from the extremes of a lifetime of domesticity for the one, and a lifetime of all-encompassing work for the other—the mainstream is becoming increasingly composed of men and women who share a common conviction. A serious career is essential to their lives, but time spent with their families and in a wide variety of leisure activities is equally important."[3]

Along with new freedoms, these societal changes are causing a great deal of confusion about men's and women's roles. As one Southern California woman has put it:

> Women of all ages are living through a period of great change. This is causing exhilaration and hope, but also confusion, fear, anger, and tensions—both in personal lives and in society. As a middle-aged woman with already-established "roles," I have felt a lot of confusion as these roles hit head on with the awareness of new possibilities. One wrestles with the questions of "supposed to be" and "want and am able to be." It's one thing to free yourself, and it's quite another to live in a free situation, especially if you have long-standing responsibilities and commitments. I have often had the feeling that the higher my consciousness has been raised, the deeper my predicament becomes.

In many cases, men are saying just about the same thing; only the circumstances of their lives are different.

As people begin to redefine their lives, one of the intermediary steps they often take is that of going back to school. This is, in itself, a change of role for many (or an addition), but it is also a means of reaching another role definition. One of the following is likely to describe a woman's return to school:

1 She returns on a part-time basis when her children are of preschool age so that she will be ready to return full time when they reach school age.

2 She returns part time or full time after her children are in school or have left home to go to work or attend college themselves.

3 Although working, she returns to upgrade her skills or become professionalized.

4 She returns to school as a result of separation or divorce, which makes it necessary for her to find a job.

5 She returns after the disablement or death of her husband, again to become job-prepared.

For a man, the return to school is likely to occur when:

1 He is laid off or fired.
2 He needs to upgrade or professionalize his skills.
3 He faces a midcareer crisis.
4 He retires from work or the military.

All this is to say that when contemplating a change in role, you should anticipate that a number of relationships will need to be renegotiated, ranging from those with your spouse, your children, and other significant people in your life to the less personal relationships you have with your hairdresser or your garage mechanic. There is tremendous variety in the way different people handle interpersonal relationships, particularly when change is involved. It is apparent that in many cases the issues for men and women are different, even though the changes they face are similar. We have also found that the return to school has differing impacts on specific categories of individuals including the family person, the single parent, the "older" adult, the person who is making a mid-career change.

RELATIONSHIPS WITH YOUR SPOUSE

Perhaps the most enlightening commentary on spousal relationships to appear in recent years is Jessie Bernard's *The Future of Marriage*.[4] Most appropriate to our discussion of changing roles is her comment that in speaking of marriage, one must "specify whose marriage he is talking about: the husband's or the wife's."[5] She says that "there is . . . a very considerable body of well-authenticated research to show that there are two marriages in every marital union, and that they do not always coincide."[6] For example, if a couple were asked to describe each other's typical day, there would probably be a great deal of distortion on both sides in the direction of the other's having a "better day." Husbands think that "housewives" have more free time; wives perceive their husbands' work situations as more glamorous and stimulating. The truth is that for both spouses, most days, whether at home or at the office, are filled with details, some boredom, and certainly frustration and that the moments of real interest are usually few and far between.

Bernard's insight has profound implications for anyone attempting to change roles. In essence she is saying that a wife's day-to-day reality is often perceived inaccurately by her husband and that a husband's day-to-day reality is likewise perceived wrongly by his wife. Both individuals bring to the marriage realities based on their own experiences, needs, values, and expectations. This often leads to misunderstanding between the spouses, particularly when one is changing his or her role definition in ways like going back to school.

Clinical research in male-female role and identity problems has demonstrated that this misperception between husbands and wives is at the root of many marital problems. In an extensive survey conducted in the United States and Europe, the women studied said that they wanted their men to be sensitive to their (the women's needs), to be family-centered, and at the same time to be strong and self-assertive. But the men, while they said they would like to be strong and aggressive, believed that this was not what their women really wanted. The women in this study indicated that they wanted to be more than wives and mothers; they said that they would like to become more self-sufficient, but they felt that this was not what their men wanted. The men, however, insisted that they would like to see their wives achieve greater personal fulfillment and independence.[7]

Our first suggestion is that you discuss with your husband or wife the realities of your return to school. Obviously, if you are going back to school for a single evening class, the realities for both of you may be changed little or not at all. On the other hand, if you are going back to school full time in a location other than your hometown, a whole range of very complicated issues must be discussed. We suggest that you involve your spouse in the initial stages of your return to school, including just thinking about what you want to do. Resistance to your additional workload is inevitable at some point down the line; however, we have found that it is much less acute in families where the returning student has involved his or her spouse in the planning stages. Often it is useful to set up a timetable of things that need to be done and issues that need to be resolved, with completion dates attached. One or two years before the actual return takes place is not too early to begin this process, particularly when there will be major changes such as moving or finding new jobs.

Increased fatigue and added demands on an already busy schedule are two other results of going back to school, and these, of course, affect one's spouse directly. Because a spouse's demands can usually be put off (at least when compared with a crying child, a homework assignment, or a car that won't start), wives and husbands of adult students often are neglected during the back-to-school phase. *This is a big mistake.* Anyone who is married knows that a husband and wife must have daily communication, certainly some sexual activity, and time to spend together alone. We strongly urge that when you go back to school, you carve out time for your husband or your wife—for even a few minutes on a daily basis, for vacations without the children or work demands, and for unplanned, mutually satisfying activities. Make this your first priority and arrange everything else around it. Your marriage may depend upon it.

The process of going back to school really demands that the adult student have a supportive spouse and family. Optimally, support from your spouse is expressed in concrete, practical acts of helping such as assuming more household responsibilities or working part time to support the family. Minimally, support is expressed by not complaining about the inconveniences caused by the return. One thing is certain: The support you get is likely to fluctuate a great deal throughout the back-to-school period. As one University of Michigan woman has expressed it:

> Certainly, you should discuss [going back to school] thoroughly before you go back . . . but, let me give you one word of advice. Don't think that it is all settled even when your family agrees initially. Their attitudes won't remain stable, they will oscillate back and forth from warm to very cold as the impact of your school responsibilities hits them. There are times when your husband will say, "I wish you'd quit school." If you realize that this is bound to happen, it isn't so hard to take.[8]

It would be wonderful if all of us had unlimited support from our husbands or wives during our return to school, but such is not the case. You can help both yourself and your spouse deal with the added stress by specifying, as far as possible, how long your schooling will last—two years, for example. One further suggestion is to let your spouse know that you are willing to reverse the situation once the school period for you is over. In other words, you can set up a "renewing" phase for your husband or wife after you have graduated, which could take the form of change of career or a return to school. If you can determine that now is your time to "renew" and that there will also be such a time in the future for your spouse, you are much more likely to receive the support you need.

A woman in her forties who was working toward her Ph.D. in education was concerned about the fact that most of her weekends were occupied with her studies, leaving her husband without companionship in his free time. They had been accustomed to spending weekends and holidays on their sailboat, and her husband had no interest in taking the boat out alone. She did some research, located a sailing club, and persuaded him to join. She reports that this has worked out very well and has dissolved her "weekend guilt."

It is this sense of mutuality between equal partners, each concerned for the other's autonomous growth, which is the basis of a healthy marriage or of any two-person relationship.

RELATIONSHIPS WITH YOUR CHILDREN

One of the causes of greatest anxiety for the returning student, particularly for the returning woman student, is the issue of child care. The demands of a spouse can be negotiated, and household maintenance can be placed low on the priority list, but children are a constant responsibility. As one woman student put it, "If the house gets dirty, it's just too bad. At some point down the line, it will get cleaned, or it won't. Anyway, it's not crucial. However, there is no point at which I will let my children suffer. That simply cannot occur." The degree to which this is a problem depends on several factors, such as the number and ages of your children, the scope of your school commitment, the children's health, the kinds of child care arrangements available, and the availability of finances for child care. (Obviously, child care is not an issue for everyone. Many couples at this point are choosing not to have children; in fact, there is evidence that childless marriages tend to be happier and more conducive to the wife's having a career. For more information about this topic refer to Jessie Bernard's *The Future of Marriage*[9] and *The Future of Motherhood*.[10])

Unless the father has been at home a great deal, his return to school will have little effect on the children. The effect of a mother's returning to school, particularly when she has spent most of her time at home, is the issue which causes the greatest concern for both parents. "How will they manage without me?" "No one can take care of my children as well as I can." "Will my leaving cause psychological damage to the children?" "Yes, your going back to school will hurt the children." Whatever concerns parents have about their children vis-à-vis a return to school are often fueled by the children's actual resistance to the idea. This is a very normal reaction. Resistance, it must be understood, is legitimate, especially where there is a strong and loving relationship between parents and children.

In a recent review of the research literature on the effects of maternal employment on children, Claire Etaugh concludes the following:

> Infants and Pre-schoolers: Although the greatest concern is expressed about the effects of a mother's employment on infants and young children, this group has been studied the least. However, from recent research it is becoming evident that (1) As long as the working mother interacts frequently with her child during the times they are together, young children can form as strong an attachment to a working mother as to a non-working mother; (2) For children of working mothers, a stable, stimulating substitute care arrangement is important for their normal personality and intellectual development.
>
> Elementary School Children: There is no evidence to indicate that elementary school children are adversely affected by their mothers' working.

From studies of black and white grammar school children, the best adjusted children appear to be those whose mothers are "satisfied" with their lives, *working or not working.*

Adolescent Children: Research studies involving adolescents of working mothers appear, once again, to indicate that there are no harmful effects on adolescent adjustment as a result of their mothers' working (although some studies showed that low income boys and girls may experience some difficulties in adjusting to a mother's full-time work schedule). Other studies indicated that, in fact, in comparison to adolescent children of non-working mothers, adolescents of working mothers tend to have more household responsibilities; about the same amount of leisure time activities; higher achievement orientations; higher educational aspirations; and daughters, in particular, have higher career aspirations.[11]

Here is what a woman student has to say about her experience:

Sure a mother's going back to school has an effect on her family and sometimes it produces problems. At one time, my daughter got lost. But, this could have happened no matter what I was doing. I think this kind of problem needs to be met with an awareness of our guilt and not by knocking ourselves, feeling, "Oh, no, if only I had been a good mother, she wouldn't have gotten lost." Well, this is nonsense. We give our kids a lot. They don't really suffer because we're not with them all the time. My children don't suffer because someone else gives them their lunch. Giving my children more responsibility has done them a lot of good, too. They are growing in independence. I can't find household help, so I paid them fifty cents an hour to scrub the kitchen floor.[12]

The crux of the problem associated with children obviously is not the fact that you are going back to school but what happens to them during your absences. Children in school require varying amounts of attention under different circumstances: before and after school, on weekends, during school vacations (including holidays and summers), at times when you must be out of town, when they are ill or have medical or dental appointments, and when they are engaged in certain kinds of school or leisure-time activities. Somehow, their needs must be met in a way that is satisfying both to you and to them. Younger children who are not in school must be cared for all the time. How do you find the best care? This is not an easy question to answer; in fact, finding good child care may be one of the most difficult tasks the returning student faces.

A useful guide for choosing child care is Auerbach and Freedman's *Choosing Child Care: A Guide for Parents.*[13] In this comprehensive, practical booklet the authors give step-by-step instructions for choosing child care. First, they stress the complicated nature of the process, indicating that it is almost as "stressful as finding a new place to live."[14] They also warn the reader against taking the first thing that comes along since "the problems of an unsuitable or unsatisfactory child care arrangement can become as great an emotional and energy drain as finding child care in the first place."[15] Finally, the authors give a detailed account of how to choose the best plan, which is summarized below:

1 Know your child and your child's needs, including his or her personality and his or her ability to adjust to different situations and new people.

2 Find out what your alternatives are. Your choice of child care will probably fall into one of three categories: an individual sitter in your home or in the sitter's home, a group family day care home, or a child care center.

3 First explore the options open to you by telephone. Then narrow down your choices to a few individuals or centers that you can actually visit and investigate thoroughly.

4 Match up the combination of your child's needs and your needs and goals with the alternatives you have explored. Then make a choice and also develop a secondary plan in case your first choice doesn't work out.

5 Prepare your child for the transition to the child care situation.[16]

As in dealing with your spouse, the key to handling your children during your back-to-school experience is consideration on your part and a good deal of preplanning. They need to know what you are thinking about, when changes will occur, and how all this will affect them. Given sufficient time and support, they will not only adapt but probably also thrive.

RELATIONSHIPS WITH FAMILY AND GOOD FRIENDS

"Last Sunday I was describing to my mother, with a great deal of enthusiasm, my latest term paper and she rather plaintively asked me, 'aren't you ever going to get through with school?'"[17] Parents may be less than enthusiastic when a grown son or daughter decides to go back to school. To them it seems, at the very least, out of character. Unless your parents are among the few enlightened ones, they will undoubtedly question you about your motivation, your maturity, and even your emotional stability. We suggest that you ride with this disapproval for a while; it usually diminishes with time (or maybe you just become less aware of it). In another vein, we suggest that if parents or other close relatives offer you their financial support or promise to provide child care, be sure that both you and the people offering the help know exactly what your expectations are so that future misunderstandings can be avoided.

Friends, too, are often unenthusiastic about your going back to school. After all, it means that you will be less available to them for things like tennis games and child care exchanges. In some cases friends feel threatened by this kind of move since it represents what in fact they have wanted to do for a long time but have been unable to. Similarly, colleagues at work may view your return to school as a competitive threat in terms of your increasing knowledge or skill advantage.

Occasionally the adult student is seen by family and friends as a pioneer in the little-known territory of education, paving the way for those who are waiting to follow. In these cases the student not only receives support but also gains a great deal of respect.

OTHER RELATIONSHIPS

Other relationships that will be affected by your return to school are, those people with whom you would classify as casual acquaintances. You will undoubtedly notice a rather rapid decline in such relationships. This is due to a number of reasons, the most salient of which is that there will be less time to maintain these contacts. In addition, you will find that new relationships will develop at the acquaintanceship level as you meet people in classes, in the university coffee shop, or in the college car pool. Some returning students feel guilty about replacing old relationships with new ones. However, it is important to view the taking on of new friends as a natural part of your growth process and adaptation to change, rather than as abandonment of friends. Like spouses, *good* friends are somehow able to withstand the rigors of one's going back to school. It is the "not-so-good" friends that tend to fall by the wayside. In all likelihood, your new student role will force you to reconsider many of your professional relationships as well.

Your relationships with people whom you see on a business or professional basis will also go through a period of redefinition. Keeping an appointment with a dentist across town may have been simple when your life was less complicated, but now the one-hour round trip may seem like more trouble than it is worth, and so you find a dentist closer to home. You may switch to a bank with a drive-up window so that you can save a precious fifteen minutes, and a repair service that is willing to show up at ten o'clock rather than "sometime in the morning" may become your choice, even though the cost is higher. Clarity, lack of complication, and convenience are the key to these kinds of relationships.

SPECIFIC LIFE SITUATIONS

The Family Woman

The person who has the primary responsibility for the care of the children and the house plays a pivotal role in the ongoing functioning of the family unit, and it is not until this person's role is changed that the centrality of it becomes clear. It is absolutely necessary for the family of the wife-mother-student to understand that if her return to school is a serious endeavor, it will make significant demands upon her time. As a consequence of the new demands, there will be a necessary shifting of the traditional housewife responsibilities either to other family members or to outside help, or perhaps there will be a reduction in what has been considered minimally acceptable standards. A part-time return to school sometimes allows the adaptation to occur on a slower, smoother basis. If the wife-mother returns full time, then restructuring needs to take place immediately.

Perhaps the most important fact for the husband of the adult student to understand is that the change in his wife's role will affect him. Unless they are living in isolation, anything she does has implications for him, and likewise anything he does has implications for her. More than verbal support is needed from the husband if the return to school is to occur with any degree of smoothness. It is very easy for him to say, "Sure, do your own thing, as long as my life is not affected." (Interpretation: "as long as dinner is ready at the usual time and the kids are taken care of.") But this, of course, presumes that the wife is a nonperson and that the husband's needs are the *only* concern. Talking with other couples who are in the back-to-school phase is often helpful since it gives you a perspective on the issues that you are dealing with. It is probably important for both the husband and the wife to know that the first six months are the most stressful and that things seem to smooth out after that.

The Midlife Career Change

What's it like to be a successful lawyer who goes back to the classroom after a twenty-year hiatus? What's it like to be a bookkeeper who decides it's time to get a degree in accounting? For the person who begins his or her education on a supplementary basis (that is, going back to school while maintaining a full-time job), the primary issue is one of time and fatigue. It seems as though there just is not enough time to go to work, perhaps have a family, and go to school too. For this person the family relationships are most likely to suffer. This is obviously accentuated in the case of a wife-mother-worker who is taking on the additional responsibility of going back to school. The best advice we can give is to set up priorities for yourself and then judiciously organize your time according to these priorities. It is absolutely essential that you map out time to spend with your spouse and your children, time for recreation, and time for physical fitness. Unless you plan for these things, they just won't happen.

The changes brought about by a decision to leave work and make a full-time commitment to the educational arena are, perhaps, more complicated though not necessarily more exhausting. The major thing that occurs is that all those relationships which have been associated with work become abruptly severed. Irrespective of the degree of dissatisfaction which initially motivates the move to school, the ongoing friendship patterns at work represent a significant part of the worker's identity. Suddenly with these relationships gone, the adult student finds that there are no new ones to replace them. This can be a rather depressing situation for the new student. In fact, what often happens is that he or she attempts to revive the old work relationships by dropping in at the office for a talk or meeting the "gang" for lunch. What inevitably occurs, however, is that the amount of mutual satisfaction derived from these relationships begins to decrease significantly. The not too obvious reason is that most work friendships are dependent upon shared work experiences; when these are changed or gone, the friendships begin to wane. This is not to say that a major consequence of a midcareer job change is that all previous work relationships necessarily dissipate. However, friendships which are dependent upon frequent contacts and conversation related entirely to the work situation are likely to fade.

New "Seniors" on Campus

A seventy-seven-year-old student at Columbia University has grown accustomed to people on campus assuming that he is a professor. He is one of the thousands of older students, in the postretirement-age bracket, who are entering higher education in ever-increasing numbers. As a result of early retirement and greater longevity, elderly men and women now make up a significant part of the adult enrollment. Many of them are making up for educational opportunities they missed in their youth, and their presence on campus is providing a refreshing addition to campus life. Dr. Aaron Warner, dean of the School of General Studies at Columbia University, describes these "seniors" as "good people to teach. We find them very highly motivated, very thoughtful people, and they are usually highly intelligent. Their life experience is rich."

Younger students are also registering their approval of elderly students on campus, seeing them as a force for bringing events and ideas into perspective. They ask: What better resource could an American history class have than a man who actually fought in World War I? What better practical insights could a developmental psychology class have than the experience of a retired teacher or a grandmother?

The relationships of the older student tend to be generally unaffected by the return to school. Since most people in this age group are retired, the addition of a student role does not take significant time away from spouse or friends, who may even become educational converts themselves.

Programs like the Institute for Continued Learning are encouraging the increase in older-student enrollments. University extension programs and community colleges have taken the lead in opening their doors to the elderly. These institutions are offering such programs as Planning Now for Retirement, with classes on social security, changing life styles, and health in the later years. In these courses, post retirement people who may have felt isolated and cut off from productive activity are developing new relationships with others who have the same interests and problems.

An education writer described this late-life education as "a bit like having sex for fun instead of for procreation. It's a sin, at least according to the Protestant ethic which says: get ahead, succeed, gain tangible results from hard work—not from leisurely contemplation."[18] Older adults are really getting "turned on" to education. They are finding that going back to school provides them not only with something to do but also with a community of like-minded, concerned friends. They are finding that they are enjoying subjects that they hated as twenty-year-olds; physically and psychologically, they are improving. As one senior citizen said, "If you don't use your mind, like any muscle, it will deteriorate. . . . We get together with many people, many of them bright. . . . We try to look into many things and widen our horizons. Just because we're retired doesn't mean we're dead yet."[19] And a fifty-four-year-old homemaker, when asked by a friend what she was "going into," replied: "Old age with confidence."[20]

The Single Parent

Of all the types of returning students mentioned thus far, the single parent faces some of the most difficult problems. Needless to say, going back to school is very complicated for the single parent. When substantial financial resources are available, the situation is somewhat better (but this is the exception rather than the rule). Where finances are concerned, the financial-aid office is probably the first campus contact the single parent should make. This office has information concerning both on-campus and off-campus resources available specifically to the single parent.

The most critical variable the single parent needs to deal with is that of providing adequate child care for his or her children. Without it, the single parent's ability to function will be severely hampered by anxiety and guilt.

The single parent also faces some unique problems with regard to new relationships. Not having a nuclear family for support, this person is much more dependent on good interpersonal relationships. There is a great need both to maintain current friendships that are satisfying and to develop new friendships that are supportive of the newly emerging student role.

Many single parents have found that university housing meets many of their needs and, more important, many of their children's needs. At the very least, it provides the children with a community of people who have similar life patterns. In addition, the single parent has an important support group nearby, as well as access to student co-ops for food, books, and child care. Financially, university housing is usually less expensive than other kinds of housing.

If, as a single mother, you are not aware of *Momma*, an organization and newspaper devoted specifically to your needs, this might be a good time to get acquainted with it.[21]

CAMPUS RELATIONSHIPS

We have found that sometimes adult students adapt to the college environment in rather unproductive ways. Because they lack confidence, some try to make themselves feel more comfortable by imitating younger students. We have called this particular behavior pattern the "jeans-and-workshirt" syndrome, adding to it the option, for men, of wearing a medallion and going barefoot and, for women, of going braless. Our experience has been that rather than aiding in the assimilation process, such behavior actually confuses everyone, including the student. What sometimes happens is that signals are given out that are wrongly interpreted. Women, in particular, seem to be both excited and distressed when they receive their first sexual advance from someone who is ten or fifteen years their junior. Men are both excited and disoriented by the frank sexual responses of younger women. Some of this, of course, is due to more permissive sexual attitudes on campus, but we also contend that a lot of it is of the adult student's own making.

On campus we strongly suggest that you try to strike a happy medium somewhere between the extremes of ultraconservative dress and the jeans-and-workshirt look. Your clothes should reflect your age and your role on campus. In other words, if you are forty years old, look and act like a forty-year-old.

Another important issue is the way adult students deal with questions they have. Some feel so out of place on campus that they spend enormous amounts of time bumbling around and making mistakes before they work up the courage to ask someone a very simple question. If you don't know what a professor means when he says he's putting some books on reserve, ask him!

You should also know that most instructors set aside a certain number of hours each week to meet and talk with students. If their scheduled times are inconvenient for you, at least ask whether you could meet at a better time. The worst that could happen would be to have an instructor say "no" to your request. We have found that in most cases, requests of this kind result in a mutual accommodation.

Remember that the policies of the college you choose to attend have been set up to meet the needs of the normal, younger student population. But we want to remind you that policies and rules are made by people, and therefore they can also be changed by people. The key to being an effective adult student is to be assertive, clear, persistent, and reasonable in your relationships. It is also useful to keep in mind that once you have paid your fees, you are a student, and you have rights and privileges as a member of the academic community as well as obligations.

REFERENCES

1 Jane Gibson Likert (ed.), *Conversations with Returning Women Students,* University of Michigan, Center for Continuing Education of Women, Ann Arbor, 1967, p. 1.

2 Ibid., p. 23.

3 Felice N. Schwartz, "Converging Work Roles of Men and Women," *Business and Society Review: Innovation,* Autumn 1973, p. 3.

4 Jessie Bernard, *The Future of Marriage,* The World Publishing Company, Cleveland, 1972.

5 Ibid., p. 4.

6 Ibid.

7 Steinmann and Lenz, *New Life Options: The Working Woman's Resource Book,* McGraw-Hill Book Company, New York, 1976. Chapter 17.

8 Likert, op. cit., p. 21.

9 Bernard, op. cit.

10 Jessie Bernard, *The Future of Motherhood,* The Dial Press, Inc., New York, 1974.

11 Claire Etaugh, "Effects of Maternal Employment on Children: A

Review of Recent Research," *Merrill Palmer Quarterly,* April 1974, pp. 71–98.

12 Likert, op. cit., p. 26.

13 Stevanne Auerbach and L. Freedman, *Choosing Child Care: A Guide for Parents,* Parents and Child Care Resources, San Francisco, 1976.

14 Ibid., p. 9.

15 Ibid., p. 8.

16 Ibid., pp. 34–70.

17 Likert, op. cit., p. 8.

18 Bill Schwartz, "Back to School at 65," *San Francisco* magazine, August 1976, p. 35.

19 Ibid., p. 91.

20 *The Third Century: Postsecondary Planning for the Nontraditional Learner,* Educational Testing Service, Princeton, N.J., 1976.

21 *Momma: The Newspaper for Single Mothers,* Box 567, Venice, Calif. 90291.

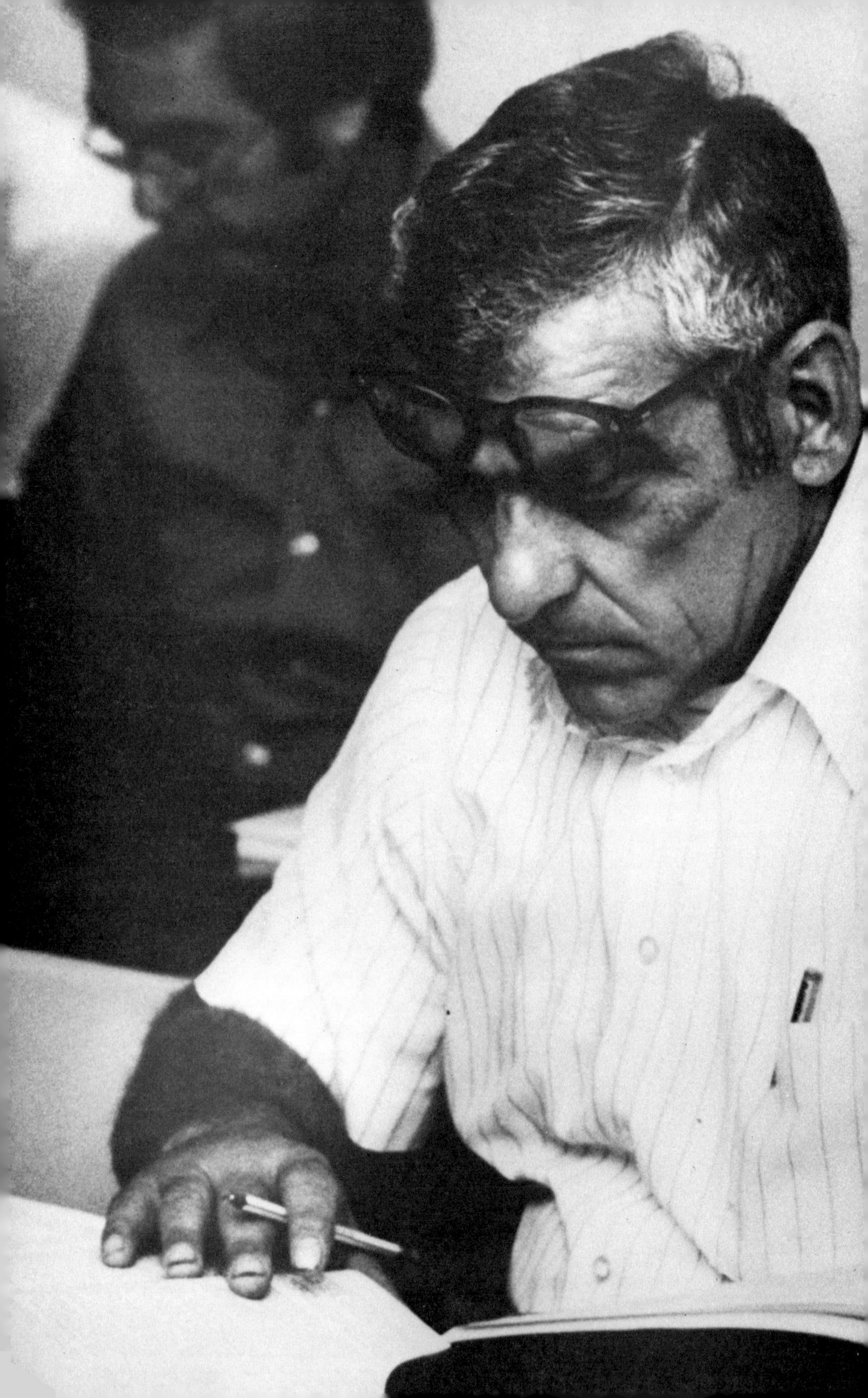

8 How to Study and Make the Grades

You can read and you can study, but it's only when you've got to take that exam that those cogs start moving. Fifty-year-old college freshman majoring in history, mother of two grown sons, and wife of a successful TV film writer.

Most adults who return to school are concerned about whether they are going to be able to "make it" academically. They tend to operate out of a fear of failure, to believe that they lack intellectual capacity, and to dread what they assume to be their inability to learn. As one woman who was returning to school put it, "I was afraid that I was going to flunk out and disappoint my husband, my children, and the whole United States of America." That this attitude is self-defeating is obvious; it is also mistaken. In the previous chapter we indicated that, in fact, adults are capable of performing equally as well as younger students, if not better.

But as an adult student, it is important for you to anticipate the skills you will need to use (and probably upgrade) after having been away from the classroom for a period of time. For example, you will probably have to polish up your methods of taking class notes, studying, taking exams, and writing papers. You will also have to become acquainted or reacquainted with how to make the best use of such resources as libraries and language labs. First, a number of excellent books are available on various techniques of studying, writing, exam taking, and so on, which you may want to consult (see Box 6 for a sample).

Box 6 Studying, Writing, and Exam-Taking Resources

> Millman, Jason, and Walter Pauk: *How to Take Tests*, McGraw-Hill Book Company, New York, 1969.
>
> Pauk, Walter: *How to Study in College*, Houghton Mifflin Company, Boston, 1974.
>
> Shroades, Caroline, et al.: *The Conscious Reader*, The Macmillan Company, New York, 1974.
>
> Strunk, William, Jr., and E. B. White: *The Elements of Style*, The Macmillan Company, New York, 1963.
>
> Thatcher, Rebecca: *Academic Skills: A Handbook for Working Adults Returning to School*, Cornell University, New York State School of Industrial and Labor Relations, Ithaca, N.Y., 1975.
>
> Turabian, Kate: *A Manual for Writers of Term Papers, Theses, and Dissertations*, The University of Chicago Press, Chicago, 1967.
>
> Yaggy, Elinor: *How to Write Your Term Paper*, Chandler Publishing Company, San Francisco, 1958.

WHAT IS STUDYING?

After working with adult students for a number of years, we have found that many panic at the thought of studying, particularly when they anticipate having to take examinations. In fact, many adults really do not know what studying is. For some people, it is simply reading the assigned textbook; for others, it is memorizing the material that seems essential. But although studying certainly involves both these processes, it encompasses more steps than simply reading or memorizing. *Webster's New World Dictionary of the American Language* defines study as follows: "the act or process of applying the mind so as to acquire knowledge or understanding, as by reading, investigating, etc." But even this definition doesn't tell one what to do in order to study. We suggest that *studying is a procedure an individual uses to comprehend, and then master, a given amount of material in such a way that he or she may be able to demonstrate competence with that material at a later time.* Studying is a process that involves (1) *gathering information* (through reading, listening, observing, and so on); (2) *categorizing information* (by organizing disparate pieces of information); (3) *summarizing information* (by forming concepts around the basic elements of the categorized information); and (4) *storing the information in such a way that it may be recalled at a later time.*

It is important to point out that there are good ways *and* poor ways of studying. Good study skills allow people to maximize both their time and their minds. Poor study skills usually lead to failure, frustration, or, at the very least, inefficient use of one's time and energy. One further point we want to make is best illustrated by this student's comment: "I just don't understand why I'm not doing well—I worked so hard." Needless to say, working hard and working constructively are not necessarily the same thing. Good study skills almost always involve some hard work (although some people would disagree even with this). What is important to know is that good study skills allow people not only to learn material thoroughly and permanently but also to be successful in the competitive world of education.

ORGANIZING YOURSELF TO DO EFFECTIVE SCHOOLWORK

Walter Pauk says, in *How to Study in College,* that one should approach college as systematically as one would approach any job or profession. A systematic approach means organization. You can begin the process of becoming a good student by organizing your life in specific, study-oriented ways.

A Place for You

Whether you are entering college for the first time or are beginning a Ph.D. program, the first thing you need to do is establish for yourself a place where you can study. Some people try to "make do" by studying one morning in the kitchen, the next day in the bedroom, and a few minutes here and there in the bathroom. This type of student usually ends up losing papers, misplacing books, and spilling spaghetti sauce all over tomorrow's assignment. The implication of such behavior is that the individual is not taking his or her studying seriously.

Although your study space can be a library "stall," a room at home, a neighbor's attic, or your office away from home, the following considerations are important:

1 It should be a well-lit place to which you have access during the hours you have established as your study times and where you can work undisturbed by the people around you.

2 It should contain a small bookshelf (certainly this can be a temporary bricks-and-board arrangement) where you can keep materials for reference, including dictionaries, a thesaurus, writing manuals, journals, books from the library, and textbooks.

3 There should be some kind of storage container for papers, notebooks, pens, erasers, typing paper, carbon paper, folders, index cards, and so on.

4 You should have a large, flat writing surface (a desk or table) for studying, reading, and writing and a comfortable straight-backed chair (mind you, not a chair that is too comfortable, like an easy chair—you don't want to fall asleep).

5 There should be a wall calendar on which to note semester assignments, exam schedules, and other important dates.

In order to maintain a "businesslike" atmosphere, you should keep your study place free from distractions (such as the noise of television, radio, or other people). Studying is best done in solitude and with a minimum of external interferences, including a view of the outside world through a window, pictures of loved ones on the desk, or bowls of candy and fruit nearby. Staking out a study space, however small, is the first step in setting up good conditions for study.

A Time for You

The second step in setting up good study conditions for yourself is to establish the times when you will be studying. According to an instructor of an adult "survival skills" course, "For adult students, one of the biggest problems is unknowingly overcommitting themselves—the lack of good time management." It is obvious that most older students are multifaceted people who have many responsibilities other than schoolwork. The addition of the student role to these responsibilities often overcrowds an already busy schedule. What usually happens is that older students try to "fit in" their studies between and after other obligations; this approach almost guarantees disaster.

We suggest that you develop a weekly schedule as soon as you know your class schedule (what classes you are taking and when). Sometimes it is difficult to remember that for everyone, good and bad students alike,

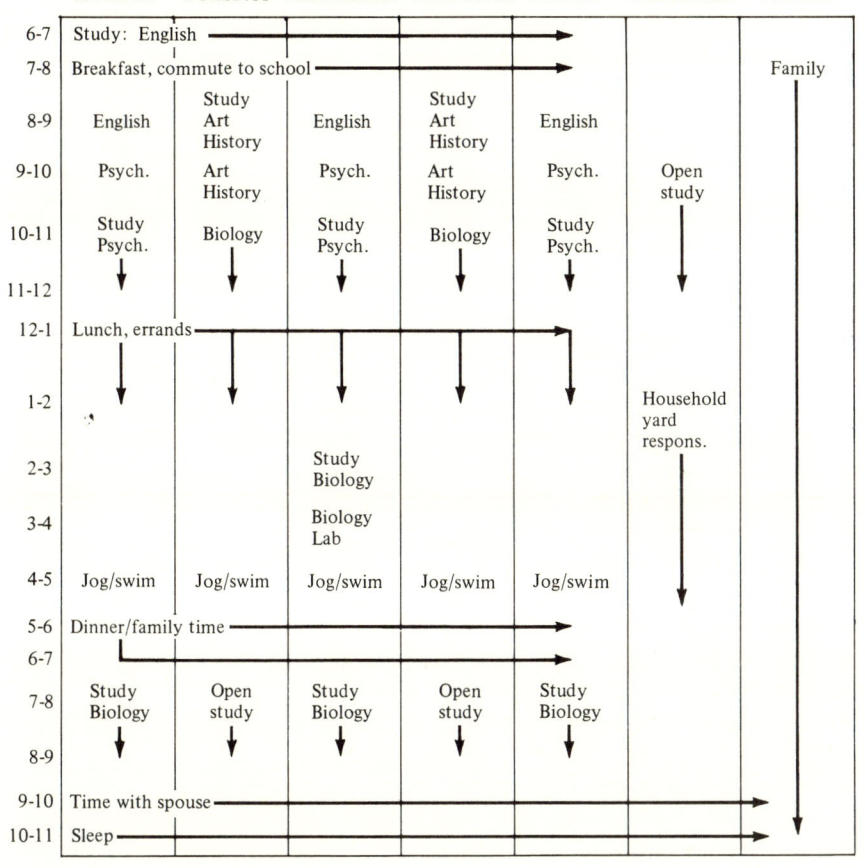

	MONDAY	TUESDAY	WEDNESDAY	THURSDAY	FRIDAY	SATURDAY	SUNDAY
6-7	Study: English →						
7-8	Breakfast, commute to school →						Family
8-9	English	Study Art History	English	Study Art History	English		
9-10	Psych.	Art History	Psych.	Art History	Psych.	Open study	
10-11	Study Psych.	Biology	Study Psych.	Biology	Study Psych.		
11-12	↓	↓	↓	↓	↓	↓	
12-1	Lunch, errands →						
1-2	↓	↓	↓	↓	↓	Household yard respons.	
2-3			Study Biology				
3-4			Biology Lab			↓	
4-5	Jog/swim	Jog/swim	Jog/swim	Jog/swim	Jog/swim		
5-6	Dinner/family time →						
6-7							
7-8	Study Biology	Open study	Study Biology	Open study	Study Biology		
8-9	↓	↓	↓	↓	↓		
9-10	Time with spouse →						↓
10-11	Sleep →						

Figure 4 A weekly study schedule

the day is only twenty-four hours long (and the week is 168 hours long). Good students, however, tend to gain control over their time by establishing definite study periods for themselves.

Obviously, each person would add to such a schedule times for medical or dental appointments, shopping, going out with friends, family gatherings, and so on. But the point we want to make is that you should decide what is important (time with spouse, studying, time with children, physical fitness) and translate those priorities into time slots on a schedule. Everything else is then planned around those assigned times. As one student said, "In my case, I had to be absolutely scheduled or I never would have gotten anywhere. When you have as many responsibilities as I do, you can't spend all day studying: you've got to get things in neat packages and you have to stay on a schedule or you simply don't get it all in."[1]

In planning a weekly schedule, there are some facts you should be aware of. First, research on work efficiency and fatigue has shown that people work most effectively when they "study intensively for about fifty minutes, and then rest for ten minutes."[2] Bear this in mind when you have one-hour slots before, between, or after classes (time that many students waste). Blocks of two- or three-hour study periods are more efficient for longer-term projects, such as writing papers, because they save precious time in "warming up," getting materials gathered, and organizing one's thoughts before plunging into the task.

Second, most people find that they are able to work or study at peak efficiency at certain times during the day or night. For some, the best time to study is early in the morning. For others, it is midevening. Do you know what your peak times are? Try to schedule at least some of your study hours during these times. You may not be able to do this religiously every day, but it is a psychological advantage to know that two or three times during the week you are studying at your best time.

One of the prime requisites for study is a lack of distractions. Thus a third factor that adult students must keep in mind when planning a study schedule is the need to isolate themselves from their families when they are studying at home. Early mornings are a good time to do this. One student suggests that you "go to bed early, about nine-thirty or so, and then wake up at five-thirty and work before the family gets up. Better to do your work the first thing in the morning when your mind is fresh and you're feeling energetic than at the end of the day [when you are] exhausted."[3] It is rather nice to have finished a good part of your studying early in the day; then you may have the rest of your day free for nonstudent activities. Obviously, the early-morning routine is not the answer for everyone, but many adult students have managed to adapt themselves to such a schedule.

Other considerations in setting up a weekly time schedule are:

1 Allow study time for each class you are taking. Although this varies from class to class, the general rule is to study two hours out of class for every hour you spend in class.

2 Set up your schedule so that you stagger daily assignments with longer-term assignments (such as papers or art projects). In this way you will avoid suddenly finding that a large assignment is due in a couple of days.

3 Talk to other older students about the ways they have found to save time.

GOING TO CLASS

As you think back on your previous school experience (high school or college), you may recall sitting in a classroom with your head nodding, feeling bored by the instructor's monotone delivery style. Boredom undoubtedly is still generated in college classrooms today, but the situation may be somewhat different for you as an adult going back to school. What was boring to you at eighteen may not be boring to you at twenty-eight or forty-two. Many adults come back to school with unbelievable energy for learning. Besides, education is not meant to be entertaining; it involves discipline and, like most activities, a certain amount of drudgery. The enjoyment comes not from being passively amused but from gaining a sense of active personal growth and achievement.

We suggest that you become a wise "consumer" of courses. That is, you should look for the classes and instructors that other students consider good. Aside from asking other students for their opinions, there are several other avenues to this information. Many campuses conduct student evaluations of courses and instructors (administered by the associated students' organization or possibly even the administration), which are published and made available to the student population. If such a guide is available, be sure to use it before you register for classes.

Different Types of Classes

What kinds of classroom experiences are you likely to have? By and large, students attend three kinds of classes: lectures, discussion groups or discussion sections, and laboratories. The most usual kind of classroom experience is the lecture. Fifty, one hundred, or even five hundred students may attend this kind of class. Typically, in a lecture, a professor speaks from lecture notes he or she has previously prepared; the students listen and take notes, but there is little or no interaction between them and the lecturer, except perhaps for a formal question-and-answer period at the end of the class. Discussion groups, on the other hand, are usually smaller classes, ranging in size from ten to thirty students. In this kind of class the professor usually takes the role of facilitator and encourages questions and interaction with and between students. Laboratories are classes that provide students with opportunities to deal with the more practical dimensions of a discipline. As with discussion groups, the enrollment is usually limited to ten to thirty students. Laboratory classes are designed for the biological and physical sciences, where such activities as dissecting animals or measuring sound transmissions become an important part of the learning process. Another type of laboratory is the language laboratory, which students of foreign languages attend in addition to their foreign-language classes. Here, with the use of tape recorders, students may individually listen to programmed tapes of the languages they are studying, record themselves while practicing pronunciation, listen to themselves, and then try to correct their accents on the spot. In addition to lectures, discussion classes, and laboratories, colleges and universities also have relatively small seminars for graduate students; performance classes in the arts and physical education; supervised instruction in the clinical fields of psychology, social work, and medicine; and field courses for sociology, public administration, and business.

How to Be an Effective Classroom Participant

The difference between passing into sleepy oblivion in a classroom and making full use of a classroom experience is preparation. In fact, the more you prepare for a particular class, the more you are likely to get from it. The following are guidelines for utilizing the classroom experience to the fullest:

1   Attend the first class meeting. It is at this time that many professors give an overview of the class, pass out reading assignments, indicate when exams will be given, and give clues as to their criteria for grading students' performances. The first class is also a time when instructors look around the classroom, try to connect names to faces, and generally acquaint themselves with the students they will be teaching for that term.

2   Sit toward the front of the classroom, where you can see and hear and where you can be recognized and heard.

3   Read textbook assignments or complete assigned problems before every class meeting. Not only will you be prepared to answer questions that the instructor asks of the class, but you will also avoid the anxiety of feeling unprepared for classroom discussion or the "pop quizzes" that sometimes occur. Completing assignments beforehand will also make you more efficient at taking notes during the class.

4   Be an active listener and a selective note taker. Rather than record each word uttered in the class, look for *key words, main points,* and *concepts that are being developed* by the professor. Write your notes clearly and legibly in your own words. If you need to improve your note taking, you should become familiar with the Cornell system, described in Pauk's *How to Study in College.* This is one of the best-developed techniques in existence.

5   Participate in the classroom experience silently or openly during class discussion. Learning takes place much more quickly when you

are actively engaged than when you are waiting around to "be taught." It is also useful to know that class participation is often a part of a professor's grading criteria.

6 Take a few minutes after a class to summarize the major points that the instructor covered and to organize the details of your note taking. This is also a good time to fill in the gaps that occurred when you participated in the class. According to an authority on study skills, summarization is very important because "forgetting takes place most rapidly immediately after learning. Going over the main points of a lecture for ten to fifteen minutes after class really reinforces this information in your memory and makes reviewing for exams later a quicker, simpler task."[4]

ESSENTIAL SKILLS FOR ACADEMIC STUDY

If you are going to be undertaking academic study of any sort, you ought to develop four essential skills: note taking, reading, taking examinations, and writing papers. It has already been suggested on the previous page that you use the Cornell System of note taking. The last three of these skills are discussed in the following sections.

Reading

If you do anything in college, it will be reading papers, textbooks, journal articles, and what seems like whole sections of the college library. People in college read many things for many different reasons. Some read for pleasure, and some read to keep up on the news. Generally speaking, however, the major reason people read in college is for study purposes. It is this kind of reading that concerns us here.

There are many ways of reading, even for study purposes. At times students may skim their reading assignments; at other times they may read slowly and carefully. On still other occasions they may read in such a way that they actually memorize what they are reading. All these reading techniques are appropriate, depending on what material is being read. If you are going to read for your classes effectively, there are some general guidelines you should follow:

1 Have a goal in mind for the reading you are going to do (for example, getting through a certain number of pages or gaining an understanding of a concept that you were having a great deal of difficulty comprehending).

2 Get an overview of the assignment. Look at the table of contents to see how the chapter or chapters you are going to read fit into the total context of the book and skim through the material to see what the main headings and the subheadings are.

3 Begin reading the assignment by asking yourself what you want to find out from your reading. Develop some questions that you want to have answered at the end of your reading assignment. Proceed as you would when taking good notes during a professor's lecture. Look for the *main points,* the *important definitions,* and the *concepts that are being developed.*

4 When you come to a word that you do not know, look to the sentence or paragraph for possible meanings. Then jot the word down so that you can look it up at the end of your study period.

5 Review your notes. Summarize them (just as you were advised to do with your lecture notes) in such a way that you reduce them down to key words, points, or concepts that will most efficiently trigger your memory. This summarization process in your reading is a very important step in your overall preparation for examinations.

6 At the end of your reading assignment, integrate what you have read with previous reading assignments and with notes you have taken in class.

7 Recitation is an important step in *remembering* what you have read. According to Mimi O'Hagan, in *How to Improve Your Reading Skills,* 85 percent of college work involves some kind of reading.[5] Therefore, a reading deficiency can significantly detract from your effectiveness as a student. Although a number of good books (most particularly refer to the SQ3R method in Pauk's *How to Study in College*) have been written for the individual who wants to learn to read better, this is one area where we suggest that you go to a campus professional for help. You will ultimately develop good reading habits on your own, but you will save yourself a lot of time if you get the help of a reading specialist in determining just what your deficiencies are.

8 Reward yourself for completing an assignment. Read something that is light and entertaining.

Taking Examinations

Professors often kiddingly refer to examinations as the student's "major occupational hazard." Indeed, in many courses, exams are the culmination of one's time and effort spent going to class, doing the reading assignments, and so on. And, depending on how much or how little you have prepared for exams, they *can* be hazardous to your life as a student.

There are no magical formulas for taking tests, but there are proved, effective study techniques for preparing for and taking exams. First we describe the various kinds of tests and examinations students are asked to take, and then we give some hints on how to take these exams more effectively.

Types of exams Basically there are two major types of examinations: objective and essay. Although there tends to be only one form of essay test, there are a number of forms of objective examinations. Box 7 lists the various major types of objective examinations and provides samples of typical questions.

Box 7   Objective-Examination Types

Examination	*Typical Questions*
Fill-in-the blank,	In _____, the United States of America celebrated its Bicentennial.
True-false	In 1976, the United States celebrated its Bicentennial. True or false?
Multiple-choice	The United States celebrated its Bicentennial in: ___1 1952 ___2 1938 ___3 1976 ___4 1943 Mark an X beside the correct answer.

Matching	Match the titles with the correct descriptions in the following:
	( )1 Year the United States established its independence from Britain.
	( )2 Slang term for a person from the northeastern part of the United States.
	( )3 Date each year when the United States celebrates its independence.
	( )4 Song sung by George M. Cohan.
	  a "Yankee Doodle Dandy"
	  b Yankee
	  c Fourth of July
	  d 1776

Objective examinations break down complex ideas into component parts and require students to deal with very specific pieces of information. These tests require students either to recognize a correct answer or to recall a detail about a subject. They are called "objective" because the same test can be corrected by a number of people and (assuming that the same answer code is used) will be scored the same in every case.

Essay examinations require students not only to recall data but also to organize and synthesize these data into written "essays," ranging in length from a couple of sentences to one or more pages. Box 8 gives three examples of essay questions.

Box 8 Essay-Examination Types

> Question: Would you say that the lyrics of the latter-day "Yankee Doodle Dandy" are more relevant to the Bicentennial celebration than the lyrics of the children's song "Yankee Doodle"?
> Give evidence to support your answer.
>
> Question: Trace the economic development of the United States from 1776 to 1976.
>
> Question: Discuss the relevance of the Bicentennial celebration for the black American from a current psychosociological perspective.

Preparing for examinations The best way to study for exams is to maintain, on a day-to-day basis, efficient classroom and reading-assignment procedures (such as have been mapped out in this chapter) and to continually review your study materials by organizing them into related units. Studying for exams actually begins as you enter the classroom for the first time, and it ends with your evaluating the results of the test you have taken. Specific steps we recommend for taking examinations are:

1 Long-term preparation
   a Study new materials as they are presented in class. Then organize and consolidate your information into summaries.

   b Almost daily, review your class summary notes, bearing in mind that one forgets most rapidly what one has *just* learned.

   c Find out about the details of the examination: What is the purpose of the test? Will the test be objective, essay, or both? How much material from the reading assignments and how much from the lecture or class discussions will be covered?

   d Once an examination date has been set, organize a study schedule for that exam that does not interfere with your ongoing weekly study schedule.

   e Try to predict what some of the exam questions might be.

   f Study first the material you feel least confident about. Once you have mastered this, move on to the easier, more familiar material.

Needless to say, it does no good to spend a great deal of time on something that you already know.

g At almost any cost, avoid cramming for examinations. At the very least, cramming is inconsistent with good learning techniques on two counts: First, forgetting occurs most rapidly right after learning, and, second, effective studying takes place during relatively short (fifty-minute-long) sessions over an extended period of time.

2   Preparing during the hours immediately before an examination

a Get plenty of sleep the night before. Before going to bed, spend an hour or so going over your accumulated summary notes.

b On the day of the test, get up early enough so that you do not have to rush. Take a shower, so that you feel refreshed, and eat high-energy breakfast food.

c Make sure that you have all the supplies you need for the exam before you leave (blue book, pens, pencils, a watch, erasers, slide rule, scratch paper, and so on).

d Arrive at the exam room with plenty of time to spare so that you can get a good seat, away from distractions. Do not sit near friends, especially if they have a tendency to distract you.

3   What to do during the examination

a Find out how long you have to take the exam.

b Look at the entire test before you begin working to get an overview of what you will be doing. Very quickly, on the basis of this perusal, allot yourself a certain amount of time for each of the various parts, noting the time allotted in the margin beside each exam question. Depending on the length of the test, save some time for review and improvements. Obviously, you should spend most of your time on the sections that will give you the most amount of points.

c Carefully read the instructions for the test. (Many students fail exams simply because they misunderstand or misread the directions.)

d Look for critical words in the directions or in the questions. Be wary of such words as "none," "most," "never," "always," "only," and "may."

e Concentrate on one question at a time. Do not think about one question while answering another.

f Answer the easy questions first. Skip over difficult questions or questions that stump you and go back to them after you have completed the easier sections.

g Take all the time you have been allotted to complete the test. If you finish before the time is up, go back to the questions you were uncertain of. Use this time for review and improvement.

In addition to following these general prescriptions for taking exams, also keep in mind the specific techniques for taking objective and essay exams listed below:

1 Special techniques for taking objective examinations

a Find out in advance whether there are penalties for guessing at answers.

(1) If there are no penalties, be sure to answer every question, whether you know it or not.

(2) If there are penalties for guessing, the general rule to follow is: "If you can eliminate just one option as unlikely to be correct, you will probably come out further ahead by guessing from among the others than if you had simply skipped the question."[6]

b Read a question and anticipate the answer in your own words. Then look for your answer among the options presented by the instructor. Be sure to read *all* a question's alternatives before marking your answer.

c If you have time to reread the examination and you want to change an answer, do not be hesitant. According to Millman and Pauk, "Research studies have shown that test takers generally increase their scores with changes."[7]

2 Special techniques for taking essay examinations

a After you have read the exam questions, take a minute to outline them on the back of the exam paper or on a separate piece of paper. This not only helps you to remember what you have learned but also gets a kind of momentum started for the exam-taking process.

b Note whether you are given a choice of questions to answer. Very often instructors will say something like, "Answer two out of three of the following questions."

c More than anything else, essay questions require that you be organized in your thinking. Be sure to answer an essay question immediately and directly in the first sentence or paragraph. You should definitely flesh out your answer by using some kind of outline form (with major points and supporting data). Do not make your answers difficult to read because of either sloppy handwriting or long, wordy, sentences.

d Even if you do not know the answer to a specific essay question, try to answer it with whatever partial information or fragments you may recall. This effort will probably give you some score, as opposed to no score at all. Also, starting to answer questions often triggers a mechanism which allows you to recall information that you might not have remembered initially.

e Become familiar with and know how to answer questions containing "key" words. Box 9 outlines these key words.

Box 9 Common Key Words Used in Essay Questions

Compare	When you are asked to compare, you should examine qualities or characteristics in order to discover *resemblances*. You are usually asked to "compare with," which implies that you are to emphasize similarities, although differences may be mentioned.
Contrast	When you are instructed to contrast, you should stress *dissimilarities* or *differences* between associated things, qualities, events, or problems.
Criticize	In a criticism you should express your *judgment* with respect to the correctness or merit of the factors under consideration. You are expected to give the results of your own analysis and to discuss both limitations and good points.
Define	Definitions call for concise, clear, authoritative *meanings*. In such statements, details are seldom required, but boundaries or limitations of the definition which should be briefly cited. You must keep in mind the class to which the item to be defined belongs and whatever differentiates it from all other classes.
Diagram	In a question which specifies a diagram, you should present a *drawing, chart, plan,* or other *graphic representation* in your answer. Generally you are also expected to label the diagram and, in some cases, to add a brief explanation or description of it.
Discuss	The term "discuss," which appears often in essay questions, directs you to *examine, analyze carefully,* and *present* considerations pro and con regarding the problems or items involved. This type of question calls for a complete and detailed answer.

Enumerate	The word "enumerate" specifies a *list* or *outline* form of reply. In such questions you should recount, one by one, in *concise* form, the points required.
Evaluate	In an evaluation question you are expected to present a careful *appraisal*, stressing both advantages and limitations. Evaluation implies *authoritative* and, to a lesser degree, personal appraisal.
Explain	In explanatory answers it is imperative that you *clarify*, *elucidate*, and *interpret* the material you present. In such an answer it is best to state the "how" and "why," reconcile any differences in opinion or experimental results, and, where possible, state causes. The aim is to make plain the conditions which give rise to whatever you are examining.
Illustrate	A question which asks you to illustrate usually requires you to explain or clarify your answer to the problem by presenting a figure, diagram, or *concrete example*.
Interpret	An interpretation question is similar to one requiring an explanation. You are expected to *translate, exemplify, solve,* or *comment upon* the subject and usually to give your judgment or reaction to the problem.
Justify	When you are instructed to justify your answer, you must prove, or show grounds for, decisions. In such an answer, *evidence* should be presented in convincing form.
List	Listing is similar to enumeration. You are expected in such questions to present an itemized series or a tabulation. Such answers should *always be concise*.
Outline	An outline answer is *organized description*. You should give main points and essential supplementary materials, omit minor details, and present the information in a systematic arrangement or classification.
Prove	A question which requires proof is one which demands *confirmation* or *verification*. In such discussions you should establish something with certainty, by using logical reasoning or by evaluating and citing experimental evidence, giving sufficient examples.
Relate	In a question which asks you to show the relationship or to relate, your answer should emphasize *connections* and *associations*, usually in descriptive form.
Review	A review usually specifies a *critical examination*. You should analyze and comment briefly on, in organized sequence, the

	major points of the problem. Sometimes, however, a review question asks simply for a list.
State	In questions which direct you to specify, give, state, or present, you are called upon to *express the high points* in brief, clear form. Details and examples may be omitted.
Summarize	When you are asked to summarize or present a summary you should give in condensed form the *main points* or *facts*. All details, illustration, and elaboration are to be omitted.
Trace	When a question asks you to trace a course of events, you are to give a description of *progress*, historical *sequence*, or *development* from the point of origin. Such questions may call for probing or for deductions.

Note: The word "analyze" is seldom used directly in essay questions, but the process of analysis is involved in answering most of the listed types. If you are asked to analyze, chances are that the question requires you to give reasons, interpret, compare, contrast, define, evaluate.

Box 10 Sample of Poor and Good Essay Answers

Question: The fifteenth- and sixteenth-century voyages of exploration produced lasting changes in the political and social structure of Western Europe. Would you say that these voyages tended to hasten or delay the growth of national states? Explain.

A POOR ESSAY ANSWER

Interesting, but what does this have to do with the question?	The "voyage of exploration" is a rather ambiguous term because actually there was no sudden burst of interest in exploring the world around them—they just were looking for easier trade routes to the Orient. This so-called age of exploration if it was indeed exploring, took place quite by accident.
But how does all this strengthen nationalism?	When the first countries colonized the New World, every other country wanted to get in on it. However, to make voyages in the first place, knowledge was needed in shipbuilding and navigation. Henry the Navigator bettered the conditions of European states by contributing to navigation, maps, etc. He also began a school for navigation. Countries put forth no great effort to build more and more ships or to go and colonize for themselves. For example, when Spain started some colonies

	in the New World, France, England, Holland, etc., started sending explorers and colonizers out.
No reasons given. Only a conclusion is being stated.	So the voyages of exploration didn't delay the growth of the national states. The voyages were all a part of the national states. The explorers who reached other lands claimed their finds for their countries. These many voyages induced the growth of the national states.
Competition, wealth, trade, and pride are all suggested, but their relation to the development of nationalism is hard to see.	I think these voyages of exploration bound a nation together, since anything a group of people do together—and these voyages were made by a whole country, not just its leaders—tends to unite them. Many times newly discovered lands brought great wealth to the mother country and new places for people to settle and raise families. Then when trading was carried out with the newly found places, this again helped to unite the nation. People were also united in a common cause, this being to beat other countries to these places, for trade and colonization. The lands that were claimed, and the prestige and trade that followed those voyages, affected all the people of the country and made it stronger and richer.

A GOOD ESSAY ANSWER

Starts with a direct answer to the question.	The exploration of the fifteen and sixteenth centuries *hastened* the growth of national states. The reasons have to do with danger, wealth, trade, and prestige or pride.
Preoutlines order of topics.	
Starts one of the reasons.	One of the prime ingredients in the beginning of national states was a common danger from the outside. Because countries went to war over the right to control certain colonies and trade routes, they had to unite within in order to fight off an aggressor.
Transition.	Other forms of competition between one country and another contributed to the growth of national states. Competition for land and wealth was fierce. The resources of the new lands, such as coffee, spices, and minerals, were considered valuable. Each country was eager to gain land because the products of the land meant more wealth, as when Cortez conquered the Aztecs. A united country could best succeed in this form of competition.
Specifics	
Specifics	
Phrase to show relevance to question.	

Afterthought to make sure relation of point to the question is clear.	These resources brought about by the new discoveries increased the power of mercantilism. With the opening of new trade routes, the Northern and Western European states were able to break the Venetian-Arab trade monopoly with the Indies. The colonization led to a system involving a state-controlled market between the colony and the mother country. This permitted the nations of Europe to become economically separate units, with no common market existing between them—a condition which fostered nationalism.
Amplifies with an example.	It is interesting to note that Italy, which did very little exploration, took longer to become a united nation than the other countries of Europe.
Transition. A new point which came to mind during the writing.	Another feature in producing national states was the national pride these voyages tended to produce. The voyages were financed by a national government. Any new discovery was associated with the sponsoring governments and added to the spirit of nationalism.

Compare this answer with the poor answer given to the same question.

The key to maximizing your college experience lies in your ability to develop good study habits and skills that lead to effective exam-taking techniques. Once you have familiarized yourself with these skills and have set up a schedule to practice them and polish them, you will not only feel less anxiety about going back to school but you also enjoy the experience of successful learning.

Writing Papers

In talking with college writing instructors we have learned that there are some major differences between teaching younger students to write and teaching older students. Younger students today seem to have difficulty with the technicalities of writing. (As one instructor put it, "It's obvious that they have been watching television rather than reading and absorbing grammar and spelling skills.") Older students do not appear to have these problems to such a degree (older students did not grow up watching as much television as their younger counterparts). Another difference is that whereas younger students do not have much to say because they lack experience, older students do not have much to say because they lack confidence in saying it or because they lack confidence in the validity of their experiences. Writing instructors are also struck by adults' tendency to generalize in their writing. For example, rather than saying "I believe in the freedom of speech," they say, "Everybody believes in the freedom of speech." Perhaps this tendency stems from what we have observed as the "modesty syndrome" in our culture. Many people seem to believe that it is immodest (or at the very least inappropriate) to venture an opinion, take a firm stand, or say something positive about themselves.

In a similar vein, once they have ventured an opinion, adult writers often drop the idea rather than develop it. Again, we suggest that their hesitancy stems from a certain lack of confidence, which becomes particularly apparent when they say, "I just can't write." We suggest that, rather than not being *able* to write, most people don't want to write or don't feel like writing or don't want to write at this particular time because they are unpracticed at writing. Almost no one "can't write."

Yet many adult students do have a great deal of difficulty *approaching* the task of writing papers. They remember isolated dictums from their old English teachers, such as, "Every paper should have an introduction, a body, and a conclusion!" and "Plagiarism is the gravest of all sins." Probably they also remember in great detail how they worked on papers—word by word, sentence by sentence, until they were *finished*! Writing techniques today are no different from what they were in the past; hard work is still involved. But, just as with studying, there are effective ways of approaching an assigned paper as well as ineffective ways. In the following section we describe the kinds of papers you are likely to be assigned; then we present some approaches to writing that might make more sense to you than the ones you used in the past.

Types of papers There are four types of papers that students are asked to write in college. The simplest to write, at least in terms of its form and style, is the *report*. This kind of paper is usually assigned in a science class and involves describing the factual results of your own experiment or research. Another type of paper is the *composition*, which is usually assigned in writing courses for the purpose of developing students' writing skills. In the composition, particular attention is paid to proper grammar, spelling, punctuation, and organization (or structure) and to the development of a writing style. A third type of paper is the *critical essay*, written mostly for literature or language classes. In this type of paper assignment, the student is asked to evaluate a book or another piece of writing. Finally, there is the *research paper*. This type of paper can be short or long; it is written on a subject of your choice or a subject assigned by the professor. The major feature of the research paper is that it requires extensive investigation of a subject area—that is, searching out relevant material and doing in-depth reading of this material—as well as sorting out the information you have collected and putting it into order (first on index cards, in bibliographies, into outline form, and so on, and then into the research paper itself). Most of the papers assigned in colleges and universities are of this type. Of course, there are overlaps in the emphases of all these types of papers. A beautifully written composition may be graded down if content is lacking; likewise, a carefully researched paper may be graded down if it is full of spelling and grammatical errors.

A general approach to paper writing What is a good general approach to writing any of these four types of papers? First, if you have a choice, write your paper on a subject that really interests you. Obviously, you will do a better job gathering research materials or writing a critical essay or composition if you are interested in your subject. The first few times you tackle an assignment, do not be overambitious—choose topics that you can work with. By the way, the easiest writing is often that which describes your own personal experiences. You might start with compositions that recount some of these. Second, whatever the subject is, start working on it early enough so that you are not in a last-minute panic situation. If you have research material to gather, do it over a period of time, which will allow the material to percolate in your head—and perhaps grow in scope and complexity—before you sit down to write. Third, when you begin your writing, do it freely. "Dump" whatever thoughts you have in your head onto the paper without regard to style, grammar, structure, and so on. First drafts are not meant to be handed in, so don't worry about what you say or how you say it. *This last suggestion is probably the most important advice we can give you because it is the attempt to write a final draft from the beginning that keeps most individuals from writing effectively.* Fourth, once you have a first draft, use the "cut-and-paste" method for reorganizing what you have written; then add to that; then rewrite and edit; then put in the footnotes; then polish your paper.

Although many fine writing manuals are available (refer to Box 6 on page 172), getting help from someone who is an experienced writer is essential for improving your writing skill. The ingredient missing from a book is personal feedback to you about how to improve your writing. You can get this type of help in writing courses, from university writing clinics, or from individual tutors. Many students make good use of editors, people who can give them objective help in rewriting, reorganizing, or correcting their papers.

What You Should Know about Grading

One of the most controversial issues on campuses today is "grade inflation," as it has come to be known. What this means is simply that more A's and B's and fewer C's and D's are being awarded, while the F is becoming an endangered species (see Appendix B for standard definitions of letter grades).

Two relative newcomers in the grading lexicon—the incomplete and the pass/fail—have come into increasing use as a means of avoiding the F and encouraging students to take courses without worrying about grades. "We don't fail anyone unless he's really dumb or insulting," a philosophy professor and former graduate dean has admitted.

A 1976 survey by *The New York Times* revealed how widespread the practice of inflating grades has become. The average grade at Kenyon College in Ohio, with a possible maximum of 4, has risen from 2.58 to 2.96. The University of Florida has a "grade forgiveness" policy which permits a student to take a course again rather than accept a low grade. Ohio State University has had more graduates with straight-A averages since 1971 than it did in its first 100 years, and at the University of Texas, where professors complain that "students can't write," 68 percent of the freshmen are receiving A's and B's in English.

Various reasons are being offered for this trend. Among them are that (1) it is a carryover from the Vietnam era, when some professors helped students maintain high-enough averages to stay in school and out of the war; (2) some professors believe that grades are essentially worthless which has contributed to the awarding of fewer low grades; (3) some faculty members feel that rigid grading standards should be relaxed for the benefit of increasing numbers of women and minority-group students; and (4) some professors are being pressured to give higher grades to help students gain entrance to medical and law schools and other graduate programs. The result of all this is a growing conviction in the academic world that higher grades are an indication of lower standards rather than of more able students.

If you are returning to school at this time, you may find grade inflation a welcome development. It is, after all, only human to wish to accomplish one's goals with the least amount of strain and sweat. But since, from all the available evidence, there is very little relation between grades and achievement beyond the walls of academe, the question of grade inflation becomes literally academic. As an adult student with well-defined goals, you should realize that value placed on grades may have little relation to your educational needs and the personal rewards you hope to gain from continuing your education.

What is more to the point is that you be graded fairly, not only as a matter of simple justice, but also so that you can accurately estimate your progress. Should you at any time feel that you have been given a grade which is less than you deserve, do not hesitate to make an appointment with the professor to discuss it. In large lecture classes, your papers and exams will be graded by graduate students serving as teaching assistants or readers, and their interpretation of your research paper or test answers may not accord with the professor's. If you do decide to challenge a grade, however, be sure you are on firm ground and have a clear, well-thought-out argument to support your challenge.[8]

WHEN YOU THINK YOU NEED HELP

We have not yet discussed the tutor, who is a resource available on most campuses. A tutor is a person knowledgeable in one or more subject areas whose role it is to explain academic material in a fashion that makes it comprehensible to you. Competent tutors are facilitators used by students for brief periods of time when they are becoming accustomed to new techniques or concepts. Many adult students fail to realize that when they don't understand something in a subject area, usually it is because their background is lacking, or perhaps the text or the professor has provided inadequate information. Under these circumstances the usual route of spending more time on the subject is not the answer; a tutor, someone who can impart his or her thorough understanding of the information to you, is the solution.

Obviously, there are good tutors and bad tutors. How do you go about finding a good tutor? First of all, many colleges and universities house tutorial services on their campuses, and competent people can be found there. Second, instructors and academic departments are often able to recommend individuals. Third, although the quality aspect is less assured, one can look for advertisements of tutorial aid in campus newspapers and public bulletin boards. One can also advertise *for* tutorial services.

Particularly when you are choosing a tutor who has not been recommended to you by someone you trust, there are some guidelines to follow. Obviously, the person must be competent in the discipline in which you are seeking help. Ask the prospective tutor for some proof of his or her competency. You should also be able to understand your tutor; after all, he or she is supposed to be helping you grasp academic material. Don't hesitate to change tutors if you find the tutor you hired explains things in a way that is incomprehensible to you. In addition, your tutor should be able to suggest study assignments for you to do in between tutoring sessions so that you get the maximum benefit from your time together. Your tutor should also help you prepare for examinations and papers and then review the results with you. (Perhaps it is unnecessary to say this, but your tutor should not be expected to write papers or take examinations *for you*.) Finally, your tutor should be pleasant, interested, and willing to help; in general, he or she should be someone whom you like as a person.

It is not unusual for a junior instructor or a graduate student to charge

$5 or $10 an hour for individual tutoring. An undergraduate might charge somewhat less, perhaps $2.50 or $3 an hour. If these prices seem a bit high to you, you might form a study group for the purpose of hiring a tutor. The advantage of a tutorial study group is that group members share the cost of the tutoring; also, they can help and support one another even when the tutor is not around.

Success and achievement in studying, as in any other endeavor, require hard work, motivation, determination, and a real commitment of time. Developing your study skills will help you to maximize your time and energy so that your return to school can be a truly rewarding and fulfilling experience.

REFERENCES

1   Jane Gibson Likert (ed.), *Conversations with Returning Women Students,* University of Michigan, Center for Continuing Education of Women, Ann Arbor, 1967, p. 17.

2   Gary E. Brown, *A Student's Guide to Academic Survival,* Harper & Row, Publishers, Incorporated, Perennial Library, New York, 1976, p. 7.

3   Likert, op. cit., p. 43.

4   Mimi O'Hagen, *How to Prepare for Examinations,* Association of American Publishers, New York, 1976.

5   Mimi O'Hagen, *How to Improve Your Reading Skills,* Association of American Publishers, New York, 1976.

6   Jason Millman and Walter Pauk, *How to Take Tests,* McGraw-Hill Book Company, New York, 1969, p. 65.

7   Ibid., p. 20.

8   Gene I. Maeroff, "College Keeping Most 60s Changes," *The New York Times,* Mar. 28, 1976.

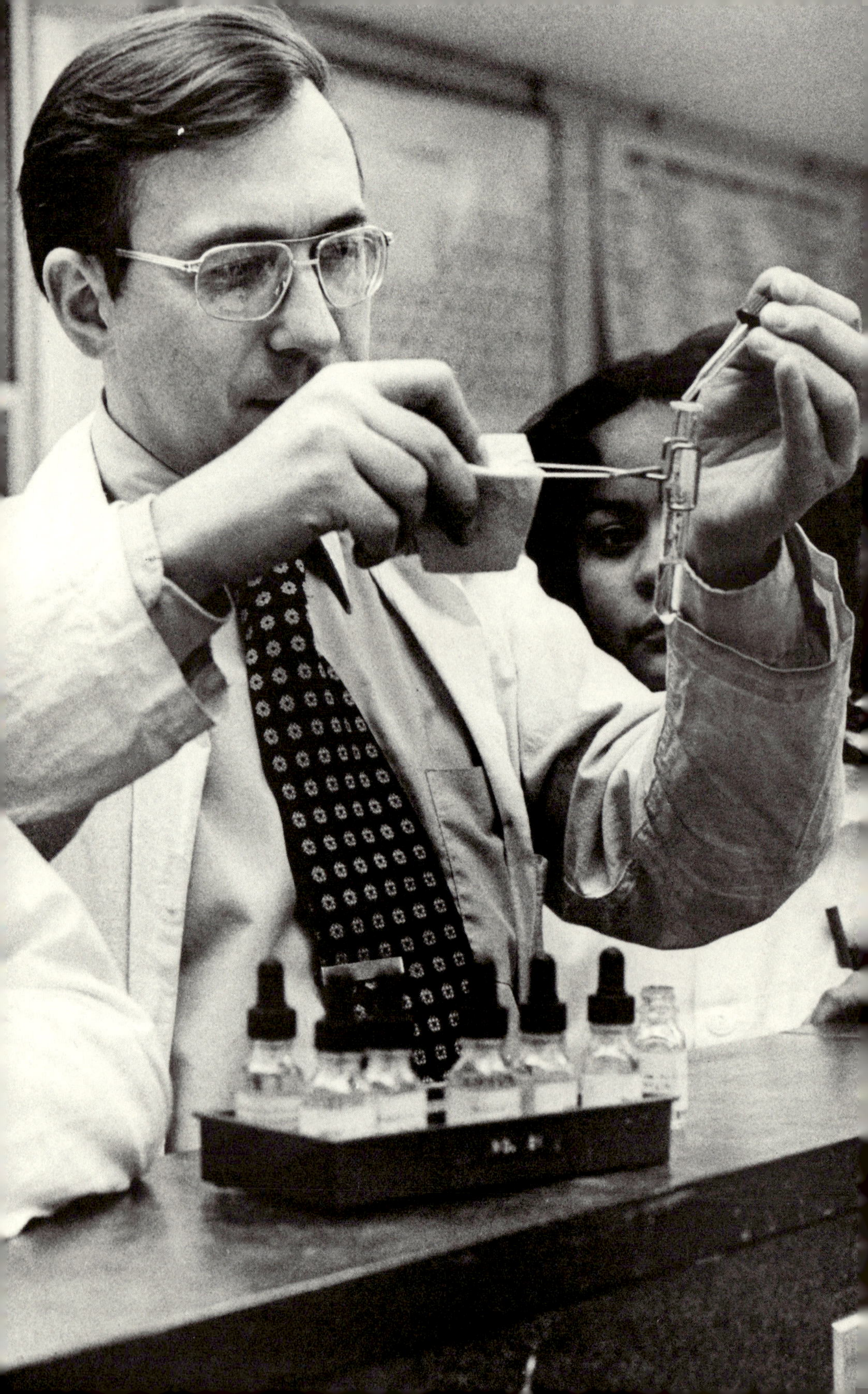

9 Avoiding the Traps and Traumas

Education can be a very dangerous thing. One never knows where it will lead to. Thirty-eight-year-old mother of two enrolled in a sociology doctoral program.

So here you are at the school of your choice. You've made it past the gatekeepers, chosen your courses for your first semester or quarter, and acquired a library card, a parking place, a packet of class cards (that, you are warned, are not to be "folded, spindled, or mutilated"), a collection of shiny new paperbacks from the student store, and an exhilarating sense of embarking on an open-ended adventure with unlimited possibilities. After years of housekeeping, typing letters, or directing a sales force, you have suddenly acquired a new status, a new role: occupation student. You may have college-age or married children; you may have been recently divorced or widowed. There are laugh lines around your mouth even when you're not laughing, and the fine print is becoming more difficult to read without your glasses. No matter—you're a student on your way to a B.A. or a graduate degree, and it's a good, satisfying feeling.

From here on, it should be smooth sailing—and that's the way it can be, with a reasonable amount of preparation. We're referring here to psychological preparation, frequently the most important factor for adult learners and all too often overlooked in adult and continuing education. As our exploration of myths about maturity revealed, adults are expected to be past the crises and disruptions of youth; the "growing pains" that are acceptable in a seventeen-year-old are considered inappropriate if not downright absurd in a man or woman in the midyears.

Since you, as a mature student, are not expected to have emotional problems, there may be inadequate provision for dealing with them if they arise. The counseling of adults has been described as "the most impoverished and depressed area in adult education."[1] Counselors in education have been trained to deal with the crises and difficulties confronting the young, and they are often ill equipped to advise on the problems of midlife students. But the situation is improving—again, in response to the increasing number of older students entering postsecondary education. Conferences on the counseling of adult students and a growing number of articles on the subject in the professional journals are indications that counselors are becoming more sensitive to the needs of adults and are recognizing that new approaches and perspectives are required to deal with adult learning problems.

From interviews with counselors, clinical psychologists, faculty members, administrators, and midlife students, we have identified the most common traps and traumas with which mature learners must cope, and we have come up with recommendations for dealing with these problems.

LACK OF CONFIDENCE

Women are more likely than men to experience anxiety arising from a sense of insecurity and inadequacy, particularly those who have been homemakers during the time they were away from school. In returning, a woman worries about whether she will be able to take notes, find her way around the library, write term papers, pass exams, and communicate with the other students and the professors. Doubts and questions multiply and nibble away at the resolve which took her out of her familiar domestic setting and placed her in this strange new world of the college campus.

The women's movement has helped somewhat in alleviating this problem, but it continues to plague women who have had little or no experience outside the home. Women who have taken this step against the advice of friends and family, as is frequently the case, require more than the availability of a women's resource center to shore up their fragile sense of security. The fact that college services are geared to younger students in very different life situations serves to aggravate the returning woman's self-doubts and uncertainties.

Men, though less susceptible, are certainly not immune to the lack-of-confidence syndrome. The male returning to school in midlife is often concerned that his decision will be construed as a sign of failure, the assumption being that if he'd been able to "make it" in his career, he wouldn't be returning to college at this time of his life. In our success-oriented culture, achievement at an early age is associated with masculinity. The more rigidly a man subscribes to the traditional masculine success stereotype, the more difficult it will be for him to adjust to his new life as a student, in which "success" or "failure" may not conform to his previous experience or self-concept. A retired business executive presently enrolled as a junior at a Western campus was dismayed to receive a barely passing grade on his first examination, on which was written the terse comment, "information accurate but poorly organized." He had always prided himself on his ability to communicate clearly and coherently, forgetting that his reports and speeches had been written for him by staff assistants.

To keep your confidence from sagging, allow yourself a period of transition between your former life situation and your return to school. This interval should serve as your retooling time. Most adults who have been away from school for any length of time need this opportunity for a refresher. They need to learn how to study efficiently and confidently; how to read with purpose, flexibility, and speed; and how to listen, take useful lecture and reading notes, write exams, and prepare research papers.

The retired executive mentioned above notes that even though he had been an avid reader all his life, he found it difficult at first to adapt to the reading style demanded by college-level studies. Formerly, his reading had consisted of either perusing business documents or settling down with a book or a magazine for pleasure and relaxation. In either case, retention was not required. "When you're reading a business report, you can skim and extract the key parts; but when you're reading history or philosophy, for example, you don't know what the key parts are unless you've been given some clues."

The most direct way to go about the retooling process is to enroll in an adult education program, either at a high school near your home or at a college or university extension division. The high school programs are good preparation for community college; the extension programs are recommended if you are planning to enter a four-year college or university.

Continuing education programs, especially for women, have been established around the country to serve as "halfway houses" for homemakers returning to school. The Group Counseling Program for Women at the UCLA extension, which was launched in the mid-1960s, is one of the pioneering efforts of this type; it has been highly successful in preparing women for a return either to school or to work. Similar programs are now offered at extension divisions in most colleges and universities. One of the most important benefits of such programs is that they provide a psychological boost to the woman who is venturing out of her home for the first time. She discovers that she is not alone, that she will be meeting and attending classes with women who share her interests and concerns.

The programs are also helpful in encouraging women to assess themselves realistically in a supportive atmosphere. The emphasis is on the individual's strengths, capabilities, values, and aptitudes and on past experience that can be useful in her new situation. The following worksheet is used in the UCLA extension program:

1   What is your educational background? List formal education toward a degree, certificate or other diploma and informal non-credit study. List on-the-job training courses, favorite courses, or major areas of study. Include names of institutions, locations and dates attended.

2   What is your work experience, both paid and volunteer? Describe each position briefly, e.g., library research assistant or orientation counselor. Tell what the duties and responsibilities of each position were in as few words as possible.

3   What other experience have you gained from the circumstances of your life that might prove valuable? e.g. You grew up with a mentally retarded sibling, you've been through a divorce, you've coped with unusual problems, or you're been fortunate enough to have unusual opportunities. How can these experiences be turned to your advantage now?

4   What specific skills and abilities do you have to offer a volunteer director or an employer? Don't just list "organization" as a skill; say who, what, or how you organized.

5   Which of your past experiences did you like best? Least? Of all "climates" you have been in (school, volunteer, hospital, fashion, business, etc.) which have you liked most? Least? Do you prefer working alone, with someone on a one-to-one basis, or with a group? Have you thought about standing all day on a job or availability during school vacations?

6   What would be your ideal job, either volunteer or paid? Would it require further training?

This self-inventory serves as a basis for a later assignment, which requires the writing of a job résumé. Assembling the information for such a self-assessment should give you a clearer picture of your capabilities. When you have completed the task, you are advised to discuss the results and their practical application with your husband, a friend, or a professional counselor.

Group counseling programs often make use of guest speakers who are graduates of the program and who share with the group their experience in successfully combining a return to school with family responsibilities. Representatives from the college or university come to discuss academic requirements, curriculum, and resources available to mature students. Representatives of companies in the area speak about employment opportunities and requirements.

Following the group counseling experience, the continuing education program offers the returning student a wide range of credit and noncredit classes. These are scheduled during the day and evening and may be held in churches, civic centers, and private homes throughout the city and suburbs, making them more accessible. Some of the courses offer tutorial assistance in brushing up on skills that have been lying fallow for some time—such as working out math problems, taking notes, writing papers, and extracting the meat from a book or article. Even one or two of these classes can be invaluable in familiarizing potential returning students with the college setting and helping them regain confidence in their ability to do academic work. There are also special reentry programs which provide an opportunity to take a semester of work before matriculating and have it credited if you decide to become a student and work toward a degree.

Once you're enrolled at your college or university, find out whether there is a learning-skills center on campus. These centers, which can usually be found on large metropolitan campuses, have been established within the past few years to assist students of all ages, since so many recent high school graduates have been found lacking in basic learning skills. An excellent resource for effective learning, they offer such services as:

> Study seminars dealing with approaches to studying and with methods of preparing for midterm and final exams and graduate entrance examinations
>
> Assistance with reading problems through diagnostic-instructional seminars
>
> Assistance with writing through individual and group sessions devoted to the thinking, organizing, writing, and evaluating processes involved in course-assigned papers, from freshman themes to graduate theses
>
> Assistance in math and science through individual counseling in sci-

ence, mathematics, statistics, and economics, with the emphasis on concept-grasping and problem-solving methods

Encouragement of speech awareness by providing the opportunity to develop ease in talking with and before groups and to examine individual speech behavior and habits through the use of video recording for self-appraisal

A mentor (see Chapter 4) can also be helpful in guiding you through the intricacies of registration, course selection, and requirements and in showing you how to locate the "what" and the "who" that you'll need. Just being able to find your way around campus can be a boost to your morale, which is why we suggested earlier that you take time to become acquainted with the physical layout of the school you have chosen to attend before enrolling. You can do this either on your own or by joining one of the regularly scheduled visitors' tours offered by most of the larger schools.

Tackling the lack-of-confidence successfully is essentially a matter of making the best use of the available resources both before and after entering college. Fortunately for the mature student, as Chapter 4 indicates, these resources are becoming more plentiful all the time.

THAT OUT-OF-PHASE FEELING

A woman in her late forties who returned to school after twenty-five years as a homemaker gave the following account of her first day on the campus of a Midwestern university: "It was the week before registration, and the campus was swarming with youthful scholars, sandaled and dungareed. In my navy knit suit and sensible shoes, with my short graying coif, I felt suddenly heavy and displaced. As I stood in a long line of registering students, my spirits sagged. What was I doing here, anyway, intruding into this private universe of the young?"

The "out-of-phase" feeling which this woman was experiencing is reported in varying degrees by nearly all adult students, according to counselors and psychologists. The sudden plunge into a youth culture can be disorienting to the midlife student. Dr. Lee McEvoy, a clinical psychologist at UCLA, finds that older students are "highly susceptible to the feeling that they can't keep up with the young." This is less likely to happen at the community college, of course, where adults make up a larger proportion of the student population. But at the four-year college or university which was designed to meet the educational needs of the young, anyone over thirty (or even, as some maintain, over twenty-five) can feel like a "deviant."

The returning housewife finds herself, Diane Rothbard Margolis writes, "not among that community of scholars she anticipated but in a bureaucracy geared to instruct and dispatch adolescents. Professors are her own age, or worse yet, not much older than her children. She doesn't know how to deal with them or they with her."[2]

The problem is a reflection of the age segregation of our society. "To the extent that youth has been removed from the labor market, the number of occasions on which they meet adults in working situations contracts," James Coleman has observed.[3] But even adults who have regular contacts with the young, within or outside the family, often find themselves feeling out of phase as they attempt to assume a role, that of college student, which has customarily been reserved for eighteen- to twenty-two-year-olds.

Adult students tend to react to this situation in one of two ways. Either they assume a low profile, reducing their visibility as much as possible and making contact only with those in their own peer group, or, at the other extreme, they attempt to join the youth culture by adopting its mannerisms, styles of dress, speech, food, and even values and opinions. Let's examine these two approaches and see what they have to offer.

During the early transitional period, which is often characterized by loneliness and a sense of alienation, the tendency to seek out one's peers and socialize with them is understandable—it is always comforting to congregate with those who have similar concerns and viewpoints. Recognizing this, one Midwestern school established an organization called the Comeback Club, consisting of people over thirty who have returned to college to earn their degrees. This organization sends a newsletter to adult applicants, who usually "overcome their anxieties about returning to college if they realize there are others in the same situation."[4]

There are important benefits to be gained from contacts with those who, like you, are entering college at a nontraditional age. Such contacts will help you lose the "deviant" feeling and provide you with the support and psychological sustenance necessary to ease the process of adjusting to your new situation. "Find yourself a group" is the suggestion offered most frequently by adult students who have been "through the mill," and with the average college age on the rise, this is becoming easier to do. You might even consider getting together with other mature students to start a Comeback Club on your campus if no such organization exists.

But there are also significant benefits to be derived from relationships between older and younger students. The opportunity to widen one's angle of vision is enhanced by youth-adult interaction—"The daily contact between youth and adults in common activities leads each to see the point of view of the other and reduces the explosive potential inherent in the isolation of youth."[5] The life experience that adults bring with them to the campus is a valuable resource for the younger students. And adults are less likely to develop a rigid "mindset" when they are exposed to the views and attitudes of the young. "I enjoy the association with another generation," says a retired manufacturer now majoring in history at UCLA. "I have found them more serious and conservative and also brighter and more aggressive than I had anticipated."

The other side of this coin is a style of behavior which we have identified as the jeans-and-workshirt syndrome, or "If you can't join 'em, imitate 'em." Because "student" has always been synonymous with "young" and because this is a youth-obsessed society, it is not surprising that adults attending college sometimes find themselves irresistibly attracted to the folkways of the younger students. As they pick up the fads and the jargon, they begin to identify with a generation ten or twenty years younger than they are, enthusiastically accepting the cults and causes of this generation. (Ironically, this may create a gulf between them and their own college-age children, who discover that while they may have gained a buddy, they have lost a parent.)

Adult students who fall into this trap are usually those who have an abnormal fear of growing old and who believe that all the good things in life belong to the young. In returning to college, they were probably motivated, at least in part, by a desire to regain something associated with their younger days, and they are likely to rationalize their behavior by perceiving it as a kind of growth, a reaching out toward a more attractive and, as they see it, more promising time of life.

This adoration of youth is underscored by the media, whose advertising messages are centered on the pleasures and appetites of healthy, vivacious youngsters who bear little resemblance to real-life human beings. "The 'young' of the TV hucksters are not even representative of these fascinating human beings, with their infinite variety of deeper needs and sorrows, but depict instead a succession of mindless, ever-grinning, synthetic mannequins ignorant of life's realities: the so-called Pepsi generation."[6] The message coming from the media is loud and clear: Only the young are attractive, healthy, and happy.

Resisting a constant barrage of such propaganda is not easy, particularly in the youth-oriented setting of the campus, but adult students are urged to do so at all costs. Emulating the young is a form of antigrowth, an attempt to reject one's own life cycle, with its special rhythms and challenges, in favor of an earlier cycle that has been outgrown. Whatever momentary exhilaration it may bring, the attempt to slip into the consciousness and the costumes of the youth culture is most unlikely to succeed, and since it comes across as phony, it tends to increase the distance between the older and younger age groups.

Avoiding this trap requires an acceptance of each age for what it offers and a readiness to communicate naturally with people of different ages without relinquishing the special attributes of one's own life stage. It also means expanding the image of the student to accommodate people who are past the traditional college age. As adults grow and develop, they should be able to assume new roles that do not conform to rigid age-role categories. It is a matter of balancing internal needs and drives against external codes and pressures, meanwhile retaining a firm sense of self. The college environment offers an ideal setting in which to achieve this balance.

YOUTH-AGE COMPETITION

The fear of not being able to keep up with the young that Dr. McEvoy identified is a variation of the out-of-phase feeling that deserves special mention because of its prevalence among adult students. The competitive atmosphere of higher education tends to foster this feeling, and it can become traumatic for adults who are already experiencing some anxiety over the disparity in age between themselves and the traditional students. As we've seen, adults generally do very well in their studies and have little reason to worry about not keeping up with the younger students.

To be sure, this drive to excel may have a certain compulsiveness about it—it has been described as an "odd feeling that somehow I'm an impostor, that I don't belong. Perhaps that is one reason that, like so many overage students, I cram for each examination as if my life depended on it."[7] Whatever the reasons, the "overage student" usually does better this time around than during his or her earlier experience.

Two suggestions for coping with the "can't-compete-with-the-young anxiety" are:

> 1 Keep reminding yourself that this is an irrational fear which does not hold up in the face of recent discoveries about adult intelligence and learning capability.
>
> 2 Turn the competitive drive to your advantage by competing with yourself—that is, by constantly upgrading your own goals and standards. This means that you are working not merely to earn good grades but also—on another, more basic level—to satisfy your personal drives. Remember that, as an adult, you have had a better opportunity than the younger students to clarify your needs and motivations and that you are therefore in a more favorable position to define your progress in your own terms.

THE GUILT-EDGED COMPLEX

A thirty-eight-year-old mother of three, now enrolled in her first year of medical school, said:

> There are so many things to feel guilty about: not having enough time for my family (sometimes weeks pass without our exchanging more than a few hasty words at meals); taking the place of a younger student who could repay society for the cost of his or her education by practicing for many more years than I can hope for; draining the family savings for my professional education when the children will soon be needing the money for college themselves.

Feeling guilty about returning to school is another trap that women fall into more often than men. When a man in his midyears decides to continue his education by returning to college or taking professional courses, his decision may not be problem-free, but he is usually not caught up in the kind of role conflict that is common to so many women. For one thing, men are more readily accepted as serious students than women are. The traditional concept of a woman as a wife and mother whose first duty is to her family makes it difficult for a conscientious woman to take on a time- and energy-consuming venture which is personally fulfilling but which may require some sacrifice on the part of her family. She begins to wonder whether she is being selfish to indulge her own whim, deny her family the care and attention they should have, and spend money which could be used for a vacation trip or the children's education.

Home-related Guilt

The guilt feelings that assail women when they begin seeking directions of their own emanate from deep-rooted cultural patterns that are being challenged by the women's movement and by changing social needs and values. The rising divorce rate and the increasing number of households headed by women who must work in order to support their families are altering traditional attitudes and role models. The images which have been held up for women to emulate are being discarded as it becomes apparent that they have no place in today's real world. "I'm sick of being guilty," says Barbara Howar's heroine, "because I'm not a love goddess . . . or a martyr or the girl-next-door."[8]

But even though outworn ideas are being stripped away, there are real dilemmas and difficulties involved in combining a busy domestic life which includes children still at home and a full-time commitment to higher education. Interviews with women in continuing education programs reveal the difficulty that some experience in adapting to nondomestic roles. One woman expressed a sense of guilt because she was no longer able to starch and iron her son's shirts. Another woman was concerned because she thought her middle daughter might resent the fact that she (the mother) no longer had the time to make clothes for her, as she had done for her older daughter. Several interviewees said that they tried to study at times when this would intefere least with the family's activities: at night when everyone else had gone to bed, for example.[9] It is not surprising that women with families who are continuing their education occasionally complain of fatigue and cite conflicting demands on their time as their number one problem.

Many of these women, in order to allay their feelings of guilt, are attempting to take on too much, to be all things to all the people in their lives, to play the part of Superwoman. The decision to become a student sets up the need for choosing and for assigning priorities. You will have to let certain things go. Some of your social life, some of your community activities, and some of your hobbies will have to be put aside while you are attending college. Long, leisurely lunches with friends may no longer be possible; gourmet dishes that take hours to prepare may have to be replaced by quick and easy meals. Domestic perfectionism may have to give way to a more casual life style—and this is true even for women without families. As one childless divorcée said, "It took me a long time before I was able to leave the house in the morning for a nine o'clock class without making the beds and tidying up, but I finally managed to do it."

In some cases the midlife woman should, in view of the pressures upon her, reconsider her decision to return to school at this time. A counselor has described a mother of four children, active in church and community work, who, while trying to finish her Ph.D., discovered that she was pregnant. She was so overpressured that she became clinically depressed, and the counselor urged her to drop out of school for the time being and return when the demands upon her had lessened.

The feeling of guilt may extend even to the use of space in the home. Some women feel that they have no right to encroach upon the family's living space—to set aside the children's playroom, for instance, as a quiet, private place for studying. The "room of her own" that Virginia Woolf regarded as essential for a woman who wishes to accomplish something on her own is not always readily available (although in middle-class homes, a study or "den" for the husband who regularly brings work home from the office is often cited as a necessity). In lower-income homes, lack of space rivals lack of time as a problem for the woman who is trying to continue her education. Interestingly, when this problem was brought up in the study mentioned above, the interviewees admitted that if it were not for their own guilt feelings, they could probably find adequate space and facilities.

The question that suggests itself is: How much do a woman's guilt feelings contribute to the very real problems of balancing home and study? From all that we can gather, it would appear that these feelings are often exaggerated and that they are nourished by the woman's attempt to live up to some arbitrary standards imposed upon her by her upbringing and her social conditioning. In individual and group counseling sessions, women often discover that at least part of their problems are self-created and that the facts about their home and family life do not support their fears and anxieties. The core of the problem very often turns out to be inadequate communication within the family.

Communication breakdowns within families are cited by counselors and therapists as the cause for much domestic conflict and tension. There are some women in continuing education programs who hesitate to discuss their new interests with their families for fear of stirring up resentments; accustomed to a more self-effacing role, they are reluctant to call attention to their newfound self-determination. The unintended result is that they shut their families out, thus contributing to the very situation they wish to avoid. It is entirely possible that, by discussing their interests and concerns with their families in an open and sympathetic manner, they could considerably lighten their burden of guilt and at the same time enrich their family relationships.

School-Related Guilt

So far we have been talking about feelings of guilt that are home-related and found mainly among women. But there is another kind of guilt feeling among adult students that is school-related and arises from considerations of age rather than gender. Many returning students of both sexes, at the undergraduate as well as the graduate level, share the concern of the thirty-eight-year-old medical student quoted earlier that they may be taking the place of younger students who have a greater need for, and perhaps a greater "right" to, higher education. How valid is this argument?

It is true that our educational institutions do not have unlimited accommodations and that if large numbers of adults, along with most of the traditional college-age population, were to pursue higher education, we would need to build many more colleges and universities. But the younger student population has been declining along with the birthrate, and the prognosis is that this decline will continue into the foreseeable future.

As a result, colleges and universities are beginning to look to adults to take the places of the eighteen- to twenty-two-year-olds. "It is true that as long as we concentrate on traditional college-age students," says a leading educator, "the picture is one of decreasing numbers, the need for retrenchment, consolidation and curtailment. However, with the wider view that includes postsecondary education students of all ages past compulsory school age and with increasing emphasis on lifelong learning, the picture may not be so bleak."[10]

There is also the developing recognition, fostered by increased longevity among the population as a whole, that adults have the same "right" to education as the young and that, with today's rapid pace of change, it is absolutely necessary that education be made available on the basis of need and ability rather than accordingly to the strict criteria of age.

As a mature student, you have no reason to feel any guilt about occupying a place in a college or university; on the contrary, you should realize that you are helping to support our system of higher education and are preparing yourself to make a fuller and more valuable contribution to your family and community.

UNREAL EXPECTATIONS

In Chapter 2, "What Can You Expect?" we unrolled for you a tapestry of today's college scene so that you would have some idea of what awaits you when you return to school. But what about your personal expectations? What kind of payoffs are you looking for in your own life? Do you hope that this experience will change you and alter your life in certain basic ways? And if so, how?

We have suggested that, before you embark on this venture, you examine your motivation very carefully and be clear about the reasons that are bringing you, an adult with an established life style, into this new situation. But motivations and expectations are not always identical. You may be motivated purely and simply by the need to retool in order to qualify for a more satisfying, more lucrative career. At the same time, you may be expecting any number of fringe benefits, such as a more interesting social life, an enlarged world vision, an ability to converse knowledgeably on a variety of subjects, improved personal competency, a widening of options, or a gain in self-esteem.

These are the kinds of expectations that adult students bring with them, and in a substantial number of cases they are realized. In working with adults, it is gratifying to note how many are finding that their return to school is making their dreams come true. Repeatedly, one hears such expressions as: "It's been mind-expanding." "I feel stronger inside, as if I could push boulders." "So many new worlds have opened up for me." Adults, on the whole, have a better chance of realizing their expectations than younger students since they usually have learned through experience to trim these down to realistic size.

But it is also possible to experience disappointment even though your goal in resuming your education may seem to you to be entirely realistic.

Why shouldn't you expect, for example, that after achieving that cherished degree, particularly if it's a graduate degree, doors will open to you and interesting, well-paying jobs will be there for the taking? Despite the fact that the relation between degrees and jobs is no longer being taken for granted, there is still strongly implanted in the American ethic the idea that education is the sure route to bigger and better careers. And there are those for whom this conviction can lead to a severe letdown.

Consider, for example, the case of a fifty-four-year-old former dean of women at the University of Tulsa who gave up her job in order to upgrade herself professionally. She entered a Ph.D. program, and five years and several thousand dollars later she was awarded a doctorate in educational administration. She has been unable in the three years since then to find employment; with her Ph. D., she is overqualified for the jobs that are available, and she is beginning to wonder whether she will ever find the kind of position for which she has been trained. "Most of us who get this much education are some years along. You can't be nineteen and have this many years of schooling. We're not as young as the most marketable people."

With the benefit of hindsight, this woman believes she should have kept her job and continued her education through extension and other part-time programs, even if this would have meant forgoing the Ph.D. As her case illustrates, the uncertainties of the economy make job expectations the riskiest of all, which is why adult students are advised to cultivate as much flexibility and versatility as possible and to consider carefully whether they can afford to spend the time and money necessary to train for a highly specialized career.

On the personal side, the adult student's chances of finding social and intellectual enrichment are, as we've observed, fairly good. But here, too, there can be dashed hopes. To say that what you get out of an experience will be roughly proportionate to what you put into it may sound trite, but there's no getting around this truism. The more time, thought, and energy you are able to invest in social and academic activities, the greater the dividends you will receive. And this can pose a problem for the returning adult whose time and energies must be expended in many directions.

For example, adult students, most of whom have family and other responsibilities, rarely take part in extracurricular activities. We know of no forty-year-old mother of three, for example, enrolled as a sophomore, who has tried out for the volley-ball team or been on the college newspaper staff or entered the freshman-sophomore Frisbee match. It is here that one can find a clear line of separation between the younger and older students.

As most adults discover sooner or later, college for them is "only half a loaf."[11] However, perhaps through the workings of some law of compensation, returning students are generally satisfied with, and even grateful for, that half. In any case, it would be highly impractical and even a bit absurd for adults to attempt to take part in the typical round of college sports and social events (another form of overidentification with the young). There are, however, any number of activities going on around a campus that can add immeasurably to the adult's school experience without making outsize demands on time and energy. These can range all the way from inviting foreign students home for dinner to help ease them through their orientation period to spending an hour every other week with the campus yoga group. Associations of every kind abound on campuses: Shakespeare societies; groups of madrigal singers; Chicano-, Jewish-, and Asian-American study groups; history clubs; chemistry clubs; and clubs organized around every political persuasion and religious denomination. Some of these associations can benefit from the adult's experience, such as a service group which assists with a campus problem and which requires people who have the kind of tact and judgment usually found among the more mature. It is easy to get carried away by all these tempting opportunities, and you should rely on moderation, together with a firm sense of priorities, to guide you safely past the perils of overcommitment.

In short, if you have a fairly realistic idea of what lies ahead of you and if you can be flexible enough to adjust to changing circumstances, there is a very good chance that your expectations will be realized.

THE DRAG OF THE PAST

It may be almost heretical to suggest this, in view of a common tendency to romanticize the college experience, but not everyone's earlier encounter with higher education was a happy one. On the contrary, there are adults whose painful memories of their youthful college days make them fearful and hesitant about resuming their education. These memories, as they emerge in interviews with adult students, usually are tinged with a sense of personal failure. A typical recollection would be something like this:

> Our family was middle-class, but there never seemed to be enough money. My parents were very ambitious for their children. As the only son, I pushed hard to succeed. Financial sacrifices were required for my college education, and I had constant reminders of this. When I was accepted by a prestigious university, we had a big family celebration. My parents wanted me to study law or medicine or, at the very least, go into engineering or college teaching.
>
> I disliked college from the start; I felt lost, confused, like a nonentity. I had a feeling of being pushed toward meaningless goals; I couldn't find my own sense of direction, and the constant competition for grades, honors, and places in graduate school didn't seem to have anything to do with me. I felt

more and more like a misfit and became too self-involved and unhappy to make friends. My first-semester grades were a disaster—the family went into mourning. No improvement second semester—panic on the home front. I found a job that summer; just routine work, but earning my own money restored some confidence, and I made a few friends. When fall came around, I decided not to return to college. The family sadly accepted my decision, resigned to the fact that this offspring of theirs was not college material. Though I accomplished much to be proud of during the years that followed, I lived with a sense of failure hanging over me like a cloud. I have sound reasons now for going back, but I can't forget what it was like the first time.

Living with a memory of the first time—of dropping out because of bad grades or poor relationships with other students or with professors, because of an unhappy college love affair, or for any number or combination of reasons—can turn into a serious obstacle for the adult student. Even if he or she can overcome the initial hesitancy about making the return trip, the drag of the past may prove too strong to permit success on this new venture. And if the adult is coming back to school with the idea of remaking the past, the prospects for disappointment are very good.

Since human experience never repeats itself, whatever happened to you in college the first time has no relation at all to your present plans and purposes (which is why assessing adult applicants by their dated transcripts is such a meaningless practice). This is a completely new experience to which you are bringing a new self. Unlike your decision the first time, made when you were under the influence of your elders, this one is yours and yours alone, and it has grown out of your needs, interests, and self-knowledge.

It takes careful self-assessment to arrive at this discovery and to make this realization work for you in your new student role. Let's assume, for example, that in your earlier school days you disliked a certain subject—math, perhaps—and that now you are planning to major in sociology in preparation for a career in social welfare. But the prerequisite for sociology at the school of your choice is at least one course in statistics, which, as described in the catalog, deals with "interpretation of statistical measures, tables, and graphs of the types most frequently encountered in sociological literature."

Your first inclination is to forget sociology and try for another major. Before you do that, however, you should enroll in a math course at an adult education center or extension division and bring with you a fresh perspective on the subject, approaching it as if it were new territory which is yours to explore. In fact, there is an excellent chance that it will be new and different from what you remember, since most fields of study are continually changing in both content and methodology. Even more important are the changes that have taken place in you since the time of your former student experience. You may discover to your surprise that you don't dislike math after all, and you may even wonder why it caused you so much trouble way back then.

Once you internalize the fact that in going "back" to school you are actually going forward, you can overcome much of your initial resistance, and the drag of the past can be replaced by the pull of the present and the future. When this happens, you'll find that your inner resources have been strengthened and that you are more than able to deal with the traps and traumas discussed in this chapter.

REFERENCES

1 Stanley M. Grabowski, "Educational Counseling of Adults," *Adult Leadership,* March 1976.

2 Diane Rothbard Margolis, *Women on Campus, Change* magazine, New Rochelle, N.Y., 1975 in the chapter "A Fair Return."

3 James Coleman, *Youth: Transition to Adulthood,* report of the Panel on Youth of the President's Science Advisory Committee, The University of Chicago Press, Chicago, 1974.

4 Elinor Waters, "The Other Generation Gap: Admissions Procedures for Adult Students," *Journal of College Student Personnel,* November 1971, p. 466.

5 Coleman, op. cit.

6 John A. B. McLeish, *The Ulyssean Adult,* McGraw-Hill Ryerson Ltd., Toronto, Canada, 1976, p. 5.

7 Margolis, op. cit.

8 Barbara Howar, *Making Ends Meet,* Random House, New York, 1976.

9 Joseph Katz, "Home Life of Women in Continuing Education," in Helen Astin, et al. (eds.), *Some Action of Her Own,* D. C. Heath and Company, Boston, 1976, Chap. 5, p. 16.

10 Richard Millard, director of Higher Education Services for the Education Commission of the States, speech at the American College Testing Program, 1975.

11 Margolis, op. cit.

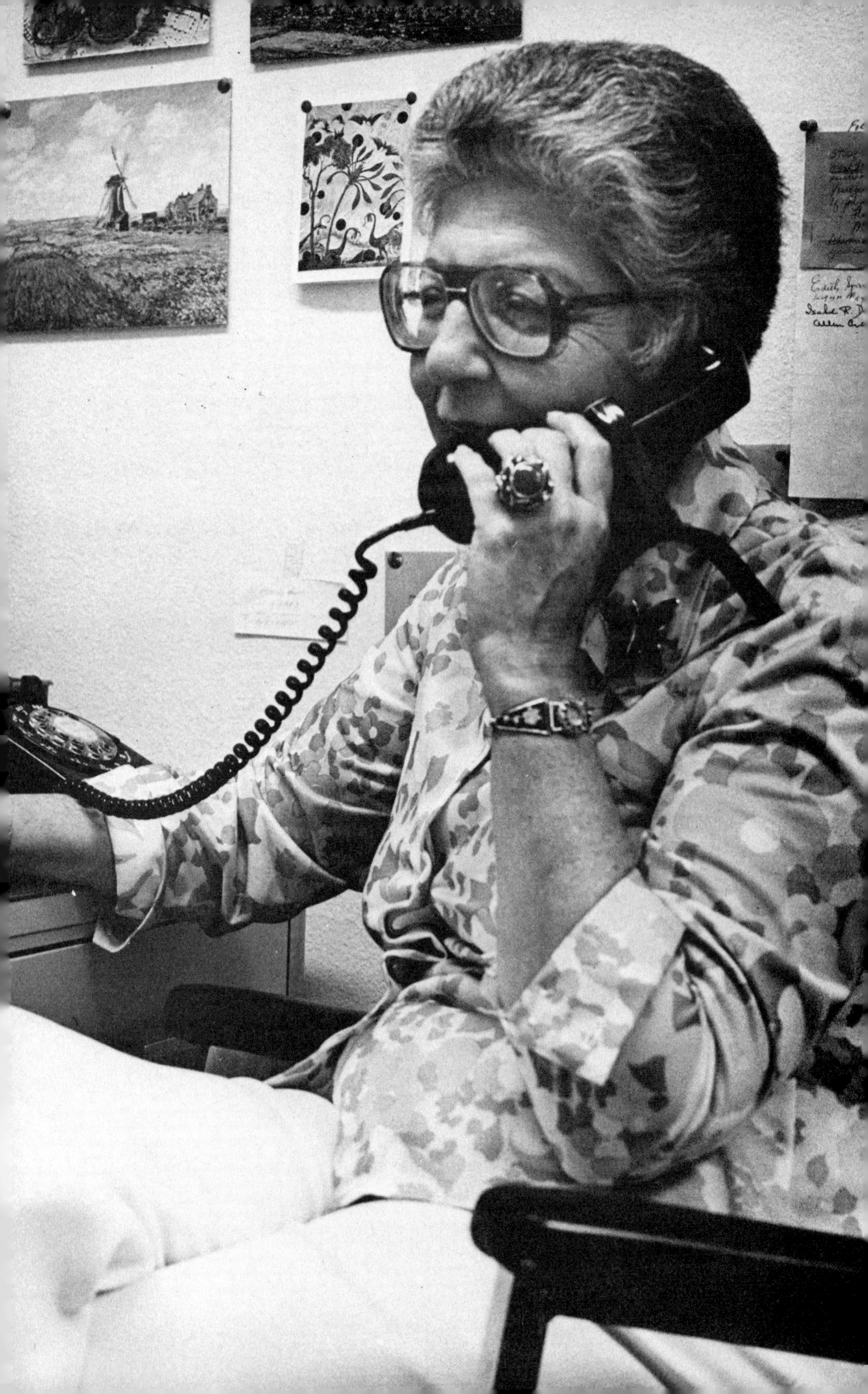

10 Making It Happen

The important thing is to structure the situation so that everything is running in your favor.
Forty-two-year-old widower, father of two, attending law school in the evening.

If at this point you can say to yourself, "Well, all right, now I know how to go back to school," but you are not yet enrolled in a school, what should your next step be? How can you put yourself into action so that returning to school can be translated from fantasy into reality?

Getting started is the most difficult task in making something happen, especially a complicated endeavor like going back to school. People often become so overwhelmed by the details of the process that they end up procrastinating, sometimes forever. How easy it is to say that you are not skilled enough, that you do not have enough time, or that you do not know how to begin the process. All these excuses, taken singly or together, usually mean that you have not worked out a plan for going back to school. Planning is the first step in making it happen.

THE PURPOSE OF PLANNING

Interestingly enough, we have found that many people balk at the idea of planning. They say that it is restrictive, that it makes them feel "locked in." Actually, at least some planning is involved in anything we do; our lives would be chaotic if this were not true. Probably, when people say they do not want to plan, they are referring to making plans that are inflexible—compulsive "overplanning." But there is no need to be inflexible in making plans. As a matter of fact, if you are sane about planning, it can be a freeing experience: Planning enables you to gain control not only over the present but also over the future. Rather than allowing your time to be controlled by default (for example, by fate or by others), you are able to make use of your time in order to do what you want to do. Of course, any plans you make must be flexible enough to be adjusted if the circumstances of your life change.

Let us say that you have decided that you need to draw up a plan for going back to school. What is involved? First, gather some planning materials—a calendar, some paper, and a pen or pencil. As your planning progresses, you most probably will also want to consult with certain other people (your spouse, your children, and so on) who will be affected by your plans. All these ingredients suggest that planning is more than thinking, talking, or daydreaming about something: Good planning involves *writing down* and organizing what it is you want to do.

STEPS IN PLANNING

Now we shall take you step by step through the planning process required for going back to school. First we shall indicate what each step is, and then we shall illustrate it by following a fictitious student through the process. Let us imagine that the student is a woman, Mrs. X. She is thirty-three years old and has a husband and two children (ages two and eight). Mrs. X completed about a year and a half of college thirteen years ago.

In developing a plan to go back to school, the first step is to *list your long-term educational and vocational goals,* no matter how "far out" or incredible they may seem.

Box 11 Long-Term Educational and Vocational Goals

> This is January, and Mrs. X has found, as a result of volunteer work she has just done, that she really likes helping people with their problems. She decides that she wants to go back to school so that she can work professionally in the field of either social work or psychology; therefore, her long-term educational and vocational goals are:
>
> 1 To get a master's degree in social work or a master's or doctoral degree in psychology.
>
> 2 To be licensed as a clinical psychiatric social worker or as a clinical psychologist.

The second step in planning your return to school is to *indicate in chronological order what your intermediate educational goals are.* In this step, you should list what you must accomplish before you can start working on your long-term goals. This is a useful procedure; not only do you lay out visually what must occur, but you are also often encouraged when you see that, in fact, some of your goals are not too far from completion. Setting intermediate goals is also useful for the individual who is unsure of what his or her long-term goals are.

Box 12 Intermediate Educational Goals in Chronological Order

> Mrs. X knows that she will have to complete her lower-division work before she can go on to take upper-division classes. She also knows that she must earn a bachelor's degree before she can begin her graduate work; therefore, she writes down as her intermediate educational goals:
>
> 1 To complete lower-division and then upper-division courses, which entitle me to do graduate work in either social work or psychology.
>
> 2 To earn a bachelor's degree.

Third, *indicate what your closest short-term educational goal is.* As you have probably noticed, we are asking you to be more specific and to deal with time periods that are closer to the present in each progressive step of your plan.

Box 13 Closest Short-Term Educational Goal

> Because Mrs. X has already completed about a year and a half of college, it appears that her closest short-term goal would be to complete her lower-division requirements. Of course, this will depend on how much credit she receives for her past schoolwork and on whether she receives credit for CLEP or other exams (see Chapter 4 for information about these exams). Let us assume that she chooses not to take any credit-giving exams and that, in consulting with several advisers, she finds that she has about two semesters' worth of classes to take in order to gain upper-division status. Mrs. X then lists her closest short-term educational goal as:
>
> 1 To complete these lower-division courses which are required in order to go on with upper-division work.

When you can name your short-term goal, the fourth step in your planning is to *be very specific in describing the various elements of your short-term goal, including what, where, when, and how much.*

Box 14 Short-Term Goal, Specified

> Mrs. X goes through the section in Chapter 3 on how to choose a college, and finally decides.
>
> 1 Beginning spring quarter, I will take lower-division classes on a part-time basis at Johnson Community College, which will enable me to pursue at a transfer college, a major that is appropriate for graduate work in either social work or psychology.

At this point, you have established a short-term goal to work toward. Now your task is to spell out all the different activities you will need to undertake in order to reach this goal. As we have indicated in previous chapters, going back to school will probably mean some role changes for you, and changes of this kind almost always necessitate some reworking of schedules, talking things out with the people who may be affected by the changes, and so on. The fifth step in "making it happen," then, is to *list everything you must get done in order to begin working to accomplish your short-term goal, without regard at this point to when it should be done.*

Box 15 Things to Be Done before Working on Short-Term Goal

Mrs. X sits down and begins writing out all the things she needs to take care of before she can actually go back to school. She quickly sees that she probably will not be able to think of everything in one sitting, and so she completes her list over the period of a week. Her final list looks like this:

1 Talk to Ray [her husband] and other family members about my schedule.

2 Find out deadlines for admissions and registration.

3 Find all-day child care for the two-year-old and after-school care for the eight-year-old [who will be in school until three o'clock in the afternoon].

4 Develop a study schedule.

5 Get help with the housekeeping (make arrangements for getting additional cooperation from the family and hire teen-age neighbor for a few hours a week).

6 Talk to Mother [who is an invalid] about the changes in my schedule that are likely to occur.

7 Get some help in improving writing skills.

8 Set up a study space for myself.

9 Get a school parking sticker for the car.

10 Talk to Janis [a friend who has already gone back to Johnson Community College] about what to do and whom to see.

11 Find out who a good faculty adviser is in psychology and make an appointment with this person to discuss my class schedule.

12 Get the car serviced and new tires put on before commuting begins.

13 Buy textbooks.

14 See whether there is an orientation program for older students or an office where older students meet together.

15 Get my hair cut, to lessen the hassle of getting ready mornings.

The sixth step in this planning process is to organize your list of things to be done according to three criteria: (1) *what needs to be done (including some details)*, (2) *by whom it must be done*, and (3) *by what time it needs to be accomplished*. This last element is very critical. Too often, people try to reach goals by starting in the present and working forward, which may result in their running out of time. We have found that doing just the opposite is more effective. In working toward a goal, determine the date by which it should be accomplished and work backward. For example, if you know that you must have made your child care arrangements two weeks before you go back to school (in order to allow some transition time for your children), then you can see that you need to allow at least a month for the process of looking for a sitter, visiting child care centers, or putting ads in the paper. Before that month is up, you will have had to sit down with your spouse to discuss what your needs are, what your children's needs are, and so on. If at this time there are two months left before school starts, by working backward from the date you want to have your child care arrangements taken care of, you can see that you need to start the process of finding child care *now* in order to do an effective job. (By the way, this working backward in time is also a very useful way of scheduling your work for papers and examinations.)

Box 16 Things to Be Done, When, and by Whom

Things to Be Done	Time Schedule	By Whom
1 Get car fixed	By two weeks before school	Mr. X
2 Talk to husband and family about schedule	Now, when I have class schedule, and later after having been on schedule a week	Mrs. X
3 Find out deadlines for admissions and get a registration schedule	Now	Mrs. X

4 Find child care:
  a Determine alternatives:
    At school
    Around neighborhood
    With mother-in-law
	Now	Mr. and Mrs. X

b Have choice made	Two weeks before school begins	
c Begin talking with two-year-old about Mommy going to school, having baby-sitters, and so on		
5 And so on, down the list		

The seventh step in your back-to-school plan is to *note on your calendar the dates on which tasks must be completed.* Look at your list of things to be done and the time by which they must be accomplished. Some things can be lumped together, like making a series of phone calls in one day or going out to the campus to take care of a number of details. The deadlines you have already set will provide you with a means of assigning priorities to what needs to be done. As you begin working on the actual tasks, it may be that you will delete some of the less important items and add to the list important things that had not occurred to you earlier—these additions and deletions will be a natural part of your flexible planning process.

And finally, the last step in "making it happen" is to *act now*! This is the most important step of all. You can know all about how to go back to school, and you can plan until you are blue in the face, but until you begin acting on your plans, it will never happen. Don't wait for tomorrow to call the admissions office. Don't wait until next week to go out to the campus of the school you are considering (even if you don't know where to park, if it seems confusing, or if you are afraid the younger students will wonder why you are there). Do one thing today. Do another tomorrow. In fact, no matter how small it is, until you are actually in school, do something every day.

We hope that your return to school will be satisfying in every respect and that the experience will become part of a continuing process in your life as you discover that living and learning are inseparable.

A Planning Schedule for Making It Happen

1 List your long-term educational and vocational goals.

a _____ *d* _____

b _____ *e* _____

c _____ *f* _____

2 Indicate in chronological order what your intermediate educational goals are.

a _____

b _____

c _____

d _____

3 Indicate what your closest short-term educational goal is.

_____

_____

_____

4 Describe specifically the various elements of your short-term goal, including what, where, when, and how much.

_____

_____

_____

5 List what you must do in order for your short-term goal to be realized, without regard to when it should be done.

a _____ *f* _____

b _____ *g* _____

c _____ *h* _____

d _____ *i* _____

e _____ *j* _____

6 Organize your list of things to be done in the following manner:

Things to Be Done	*Time Schedule*	*By Whom*

7 Note the tasks to be done on your own personal calendar.

8 Don't hesitate; act now.

APPENDIX A: Financing Your College Education

FINANCIAL AID

Most financial aid is not available to students whose family income is above $15,000 a year for the year that the student is in school. Also, part-time students usually are less eligible for financial aid than full-time students, although this situation is now changing somewhat.

1 Scholarships and grants. One can best learn about this kind of financial-aid source, already described in Chapter 5, by inquiring at the financial-aid offices of colleges or consulting one of the references listed at the end of this appendix. Scholarships and grants can come from individual colleges, states, the federal government, organized groups (religious groups, fraternal organizations, labor unions, commercial companies, military organizations), or racial or ethnic groups, or they can be won in national or state competitions. Certain moneys are available to students studying or writing dissertations in specific fields, such as nursing, vocational rehabilitation, and physical education, and to certain disadvantaged or handicapped students. One can apply to a scholarship computer bank such as the Scholarship Search (7 West 51st Street, New York, New York

10019) and, for a fee of $39, receive information on money sources available. The $39 is refundable to an individual if the Search cannot come up with either five or more money sources or at least $5,000 in potentially available moneys. Two types of special federally sponsored grants are:

   a Supplementary Economic Opportunity Grant (SEOG). Open to individuals with exceptional financial need, this federal government program offers moneys ranging from $200 to $1,500 a year as a supplement to and matching other types of financial aid. The money need not be repaid.

   b Basic Educational Opportunity Grant (BEOG). This grant, too, does not have to be repaid; like the SEOG moneys, it is awarded on the basis of having matching amounts available through other forms of financial aid. BEOG can be used to supplement SEOG but is open to more than the lowest-income-level student. Grants range from $50 to $1,400 a school year. These grants are open to part-time students but are restricted to individuals at the freshman, sophomore, and junior levels.

2 Loans

   a Federal loans

     (1) National Direct Student Loans (NDSL). Intended to serve low-income students, these loans are available to undergraduates (not to exceed $5,000) and graduate students (not to exceed $10,000, including amounts borrowed as an undergraduate) who are carrying at least a half-time academic workload. The loans are processed by the school. The rate of interest on these loans is 3 percent; both interest accrual and payments on the loan do not begin until nine months after graduation or after withdrawal as a student. The maximum repayment period is ten years; minimum repayments are $30 per month.

     (2) Federally Guaranteed Student Loans (FGSL). Formerly called Federally Insured Student Loans, these are available to undergraduates (not to exceed $7,500) and graduate students (not to exceed $10,000, including amounts borrowed as an undergraduate) who are at least half-time students. These loans are actually given out by banks, savings and loan associations, and credit unions, but individual schools must certify that the applying student has financial need and is in good academic standing. The rate of interest is 7 percent, and, as with the NDSLs, repayment does not have to begin until nine months after graduation or after leaving school. One may take as long as ten years to repay these loans too. Some lending institutions will give this type of loan only

to individuals who have had some kind of savings or checking account with them.

b State loans. Each state has loans available to students attending schools in its territory. In some cases, residency must be established for one year before one is eligible to receive state funds.

3 Work-study (see Chapter 5).

4 Emergency loans (see Chapter 5).

5 College-related moneys. Colleges and universities often award their own funds in the form of grants, loans, work-study, and scholarships, particularly the larger, private universities. Sometimes schools are willing to "defer" tuition or other payments for students who are experiencing short-term financial problems. It is important for students to know, too, that as they experience personal changes that affect their financial status (for example, divorce, pregnancy, or losing a job), financial-aid offices are sometimes able to help them adapt to the changes by providing financial aid.

OTHER WAYS OF FINANCING YOUR COLLEGE EDUCATION

1 Part-time jobs during the school year and summer jobs. Student employment offices on campus have listings of jobs available to students both on and off campus. More than minimum-wage jobs are available for those students who have specific skills to offer. One can also consult local newspaper want ads, visit no-fee employment agencies, or make personal job contacts.

2 Food stamps. Food stamps may be available for low-income people who have their meals at home. Check with your local Health, Education, and Welfare office to determine your eligibility.

3 Veterans' cold-war benefits. Veterans, widows and children of veterans, wives and children of disabled veterans, and other individuals often are eligible for moneys related to going to school. Specific information can be obtained at campus veterans' offices, from nearby VA hospitals or regional offices, or from the Veterans Administration Office, Washington, D.C. 20420.

4 Under current tax regulations, educational expenses that are job-related (such as enrollment fees, costs of books and supplies, parking and related travel costs, and living costs) may be deducted from taxes. Students should consult a lawyer, an accountant, or the appropriate state or federal tax agency for information specific to their own tax situation.

5   Personal or spouse's savings, trust funds, or inheritances.

6   Loans or gifts from parents, other family members, or friends.

7   Personal loans from banks, savings and loan associations, or credit unions.

8   Child care. Much has been written about the various child care resources in other sections of this book. We need only reiterate here some of the lower-cost ways of handling this problem: having members of one's family baby-sit; setting up a play-group exchange with friends or neighbors; forming or joining a student child care cooperative off campus; using public local day care centers or campus child care facilities; and providing room and board for other students in return for child care. In some states, funds are available through the financial-aid offices specifically to cover child care costs for low-income parents. Students who are on welfare can also apply for federal day care funds from their assigned social worker.

9   Government service agencies. For certain individuals, moneys may be available for going back to school under the auspices of such agencies as Aid for Families with Dependent Children, state vocational rehabilitation offices (for mentally or physically disabled persons), Social Security Administration offices, county or state welfare programs, and state employment offices (for unemployed or underemployed persons).

10   Assistantships and internships on campus. Many campuses have regularly funded positions in various departments that exchange your work for tuition, room and board, or other going-to-school expenses. These positions can be within academic departments (teaching assistantships), in residence halls (resident assistantships), or in nonacademic offices (internships in a dean's office).

11   Tuition-reimbursement plans. Some government agencies and many companies will reimburse employees for fees and other associated expenses for education that is job-related.

SPECIAL FINANCIAL RESOURCES

For Ethnic Minorities

Aspira (296 Fifth Avenue, New York, New York 10001, or 161 Remsen

Avenue, Brooklyn, New York 11212). Assistance for Puerto Rican and Spanish-speaking students.

Assistance for American Indians (Bureau of Indian Affairs, Lawrence, Kansas 66044, or Washington, D.C. 20242).

Bureau of Indian Affairs (Department of Interior, Higher Education Program, 123 Fourth Street, P.O. Box 1788, Albuquerque, New Mexico 87103). Administers grants to students who are one-fourth or more Indian, Eskimo, or Aleut of a tribal group served by the Bureau.

Catholic Scholarships for Negroes (254 Union Street, Springfield, Massachusetts 01105).

Drummond, Carl E.: *Going Right On: Information and Advice for Minority Students Who Want to Continue Their Education after High School* (College Board Publication Orders, Box 2815, Princeton, New Jersey 08540).

Ford Foundation (320 East 42d Street, New York, New York 10017). Graduate fellowships for American Indians, Mexican Americans, and Puerto Ricans. Middle Western and African field research fellowships for Afro-Americans.

Johnson, Willis L. (ed.): *Directory of Special Programs for Minority Group Members* (Garrett Park Press, Garrett Park, Maine 20766).

National Fellowship Fund (795 Peachtree Street, N.E., Suite 484, Atlanta, Georgia 30308). Graduate fellowships for black Americans.

National Scholarship Service and Fund for Negro Students (1776 Broadway, New York, New York 10019). Counseling and referral service for black and other minority students.

Student Opportunity Scholarships (475 Riverside Drive, New York, New York 10027). Scholarships for minority students who have extreme financial need.

The United Negro College Fund (55 East 52d Street, New York, New York 10022).

Youth Opportunities Foundation (8820 Sepulveda Boulevard, Los Angeles, California 90054). Financial aid and services for Mexican-American students.

For Women

Altrusa International Foundation, Inc. (332 South Michigan Avenue,

Chicago, Illinois 60604). Stipends, averaging $350 a year, for women training or retraining for employment, particularly in vocational areas.

American Association of University Women (Fellowships Programs, 2401 Virginia Avenue, N.W., Washington, D.C. 20037). Fellowships available for dissertation completion.

Business and Professional Women's Foundation (2012 Massachusetts Avenue, N.W., Washington, D.C. 20036). Scholarships, averaging $350 a year, for women going back to school for vocational training or undergraduate or graduate work. Graduate fellowships are available for doctoral candidates.

Center for Research on Women in Higher Education and the Professions (Wellesley College, Cheever House, 828 Washington Street, Wellesley, Massachusetts 02181). Grants of $500 to $1,000 for research on women.

Clairol Loving Care Scholarship Program (c/o Business and Professional Women's Foundation, 2012 Massachusetts Avenue, N.W., Washington, D.C. 20036). Scholarships for women thirty years and over, up to $1,000 for vocational training, undergraduate and graduate work.

Danforth Foundation (Director, Graduate Fellowships for Women, 222 South Central Avenue, St. Louis, Missouri 63105). Fellowships up to $2,450 per year for graduate work in secondary or college teaching or administration.

Diuguid Fellowship Program (Executive Director, Council of Southern Universities, Inc., 795 Peachtree Street, N.E., Suite 484, Atlanta, Georgia 30308). Grants from $3,000 to $6,000 for women wanting to attend school in the South for one year of study, internship, or independent study leading to a career.

Helena Rubinstein Foundation (261 Madison Avenue, New York, New York 10016). Grants awarded to colleges and universities for scholarships, mostly for women.

Nies, Judith: *Women and Fellowships, 1976* (Women's Equity Action League, Washington, D.C. 1976.)

Sears-Roebuck Foundation (Business and Professional Women's Foundation, 2012 Massachusetts Avenue, N.W., Washington, D.C. 20036). Loan funds available to women attending graduate schools of business.

A Selected List of Professional Training Programs and Internships (American Association of University Women, 2401 Virginia Way, N.W., Washington, D.C. 20037).

Soroptimist Awards (1616 Walnut Street, Philadelphia, Pennsylvania

19103). Fifteen awards of $2,000 each, given each year to women for training or retraining in vocational and technical fields.

GENERAL RESOURCES AND BIBLIOGRAPHY

Annual Register of Grant Support, Academic Media, Orange, N.J., 1975.

Brewer, Jack: *Fellowships from A to Z,* Doubleday & Company, Inc., Garden City, N.Y., 1968.

Federal Benefits for Veterans and Dependents, Superintendent of Documents, Government Printing Office, Washington. (75 cents)

Feingold, Norman: *Scholarships, Fellowships, and Loans,* Bellman Publishing Company, Arlington, Mass., 1972. ($17)

Five Federal Financial Aid Programs, U.S. Office of Education. (Free)

Freede, S. Robert: *Cash for College,* Prentice-Hall, Inc., Englewood Cliffs, N.J., 1975.

Getting It All Together: A No-Sweat Guide to a Better Deal for Ex-G.I.'s, National League of Cities, Veteran's Education and Training Service, Washington. ($1)

Human Resources Network: *How to Get Money for: Education, Fellowships, and Scholarships,* Chilton Book Company, Radnor, Pa., 1975.

Johnson, Amy Edith (ed.): *Making It: A Guide to Student Finances,* Harvard Student Agencies, Cambridge, Mass., 1973. ($4.95)

Kesslar, Oreon: *National Catalogue of Financial Aids for Higer Education,* Wm. C. Brown Company Publishers, Dubuque, Iowa. ($13.95)

Meeting College Costs: A Guide for Parents and Students, College Entrance Examination Board, New York, 1975.

Need a Lift? The American Legion Education and Scholarship Program, Indianapolis, Ind., published annually. (50 cents)

Nielson, Waldemar A.: *The Big Foundations,* The Twentieth Century Fund, New York, 1972.

Scaringi, Louis T., and Joyce W. Scaringi: *Student Financial Help: A Guide to Money for College,* Doubleday & Company, Inc., Garden City, N.Y., 1974. ($2.95)

A Selected List of Major Fellowship Opportunities and Aids to Advanced Education for U.S. Citizens, National Academy of Sciences, National Research Council, Washington. (Free)

Social Security Programs in the U.S., Superintendent of Documents, Government Printing Office, Washington. ($1.20)

Student Aid Annual, Chronicle Guidance Publications, Inc., Moravia, N.Y. ($7.50)

Suchar, Elizabeth W., et al.: *The Official College Entrance Examination Board Guide to Financial Aid for Students and Parents,* Simon and Schuster, New York, 1975.

APPENDIX B

College Terminology

Academic Adviser, Academic Counselor, Program Adviser: A member of the college or university administration or a faculty member whose responsibility it is to (1) help the student follow or design a particular course of study, (2) help the student choose courses, (3) and act as a sounding board for dealing with problems or issues relating to attendance in the institution.

Accreditation: Approval granted to a college by one or more professional accrediting associations if the college meets predetermined standards set up for such factors as academic program, faculty and administration, library facilities, physical plant, and extent and suitability of curriculum.

Auditor: A student who attends a class on a noncredit basis for reasons of listening and taking notes. Although he or she may choose to, the student is under no obligation to write papers, complete assignments, or take tests.

Baccalaureate or Bachelor's Degree (B.A., A.B., B.S., etc.): A degree received after satisfactorily completing a four-year, full-time course of study at a university or college.

Blue Book: A lined composition pad with a light blue cover (hence the name "blue book") in which students write the answers to exam questions.

Calendar: Although there is an infinite number of calendar arrangements in existence, particularly with the advent of nontraditional programs, the systems most widely used are the following:

Quarter System: A calendar year which is divided into four terms: fall, winter, spring, and summer.

Semester System: A calendar year which is divided into two terms between September and June: fall semester and spring semester. (Summer session is an additional option not included as a part of the regular calendar.)

Trimester System: A calendar year which is divided into three terms, sometimes offered between September and June, not including summer, and sometimes including summer as the third session.

Carrel: A small alcove in the stack room of the library designed for individual research and study. Students using carrels, which are usually assigned upon request, may keep books and other materials in them for a stipulated period of time.

Class Load: The number of units or classes a student takes during one term.

College Catalog: A booklet issued annually by a college giving information concerning such matters as requirements for admission, tuition and fees, degrees and majors, faculty roster, and courses of study. It is usually different and separate from a schedule of classes.

Colloquium: A meeting at which a preselected topic is discussed in depth. Colloquiums may take place occasionally or on a regularly scheduled basis.

Cooperative Education: Sometimes called "work-study," a college or university program which combines study with work that relates to the student's academic interests.

Credit Courses: Courses for which the student receives credit or units of hours toward a degree. College credits are determined by the number of class hours a student spends in class per week. For example, a student who spends four hours a week in class would usually receive four hours or units of credit at the completion of the class.

Degree: A title earned by a student after attending a college for several years and meeting its requirements. The following are various types of degrees offered:

Associate of Arts (A.A., A.Sc.): A degree granted by a community or junior college after two years of study.

Baccalaureate Degree or Bachelor's Degree (B.A., A.B., B.S., etc.): A degree received after completing a four-year, full-time course of study.

Doctor's Degree (Ph.D., M.D., Ed.D., D.D.S., etc.): A doctorate is offered minimally for three years of study beyond the bachelor's degree and sometimes after as many as seven years beyond the bachelor's.

Master's Degree (M.A., M.S., M.S.W., etc.): The degree granted for one or two years of full-time study beyond the bachelor's degree.

Abbreviations

A.A.	Associate of arts
A.S.	Associate of science
B.A.	Bachelor of arts
B.B.A.	Bachelor of business administration
B.M.	Bachelor of music
B.S.	Bachelor of science
D.D.S.	Doctor of dental surgery
D.M.A.	Doctor of musical arts
D.N.S.	Doctor of nursing science
Ed.D.	Doctor of education
J.D.	Doctor of law
J.S.D.	Doctor of the science of law
J.S.M.	Master of the science of law
LL.B.	Bachelor of laws
LL.D.	Doctor of laws
LL.M.	Master of laws
M.A.	Master of arts
M.A.Ed.	Master of arts in education
M.A.T.	Master of arts in teaching

M.B.A.	Master of business administration
M.D.	Doctor of medicine
M.E.	Master of engineering
M.F.A.	Master of fine arts
M.M.	Master of music
M.P.A.	Master of public administration
M.S.	Master of science
M.S.W.	Master of social work
M.U.P.	Master of urban planning
Pharm.D.	Doctor of pharmacy
Ph.D.	Doctor of philosophy

Divisions of Higher Education

University: An institution composed of several colleges and schools. In addition to undergraduate studies, it usually offers graduate and professional training and doctorates in more than one field of study.

College: Usually a four-year undergraduate institution, sometimes offering graduate work leading to a master's degree.

Department: A small group of professors organized to offer teaching in a specific field such as history, sociology, or philosophy.

Division: A group of related fields, such as the humanities or the social sciences.

School: Usually a professional training area within a university, for example, a school of social work, a graduate school of business, a school of education, or a school of law.

Early Admission: A procedure by which an individual is admitted to a university or college or to a specific program before the regularly scheduled admission dates.

E.S.L., or English as a Second Language: English-language courses for students from non-English-speaking countries.

Essay Examination: A form of test in which students are asked to write an essay or composition about a certain topic. This type of examination is in contrast to objective-type examinations (which include multiple-choice and true-false exams), but both types are often used at the same time.

Fees: Sums of money which must be paid for such things as an application for admission, a student activity card, registration, the use of laboratory or physical education equipment, and housing. Fees are usually assessed in addition to tuition charges.

Fieldwork: A learning situation in which a student learns by participating in actual work situations under the supervision of either professionals in that situation or an assigned faculty supervisor. Examples of fieldwork situations include a student teacher working in a school and a student social worker working in a social service agency. Fieldwork may be offered on a credit or a noncredit basis.

Final Examination: A test given at the end of a specific course offering.

Full-Time Student: A student taking what is considered by a college or university to be a "full load" of classes, usually twelve quarter or semester units. Colleges have varying fee structures, services, and policies set up for students, depending upon whether they are full-time or part-time students.

GPA, or Grade-Point Average: The average of grades a student receives for courses at college, computed at the end of each term (for that term) and as an average for all terms. Most colleges and universities use a system whereby a number value of 4 is assigned to an A grade; 3, to a B grade; 2, to a C grade; 1, to a D grade; and 0, to an F grade.

Grading: College *grades* usually include the following:

A	Excellent
B	Good
C	Fair
D	Barely passing
F	Failure
P	Pass (awarded for C work or better)
NP	No pass (awarded for D or F work)
I	Incomplete (usually requires that a student complete necessary work by the end of a specific period, or grade becomes F or NP)
W	Withdrawn (awarded when a student *formally* leaves a course before the last class meeting)

Graduation Requirements: Specified requirements set by an educational institution for graduation. They can include minimum grade-point average, minimum number of course units, certain courses, residency, and thesis.

Independent Study; Directed Study: A form of study, outside a formal classroom structure, in which a student studies "individually" under the supervision of an instructor.

Interdisciplinary: Refers to departments, programs or courses which cross academic lines, utilizing the knowledge from a number of academic disciplines (e.g., urban studies might utilize knowledge from sociology, business, psychology, engineering, and anthropology).

Liberal Arts: Generally, a course of study which allows for a broad education in the humanities, social sciences, or sciences.

Lower-Division Courses: Courses taken during the freshman and sophomore years of college; also, introductory courses taken during the first two years of college. In the college numbering system for courses, usually those numbered 1 to 99. All community college courses are assumed to be lower-division courses.

Major: A concentration in a specific field of study. A student may be required to take one-third to one-half of his or her total college courses in that field. One can have a history major or a premedical major for example.

Midterm Examination: An examination in a course given around the middle of the term.

Minor: Required by some colleges and universities and by some departments, a specific number of units in a field of study other than the student's major. It is designed to ensure that the student leaves college with a breadth of experience.

Objective Test: A test in which there are specific, correct answers to the questions asked. The most frequently used forms of objective tests are multiple-choice, true-false, and matching tests.

Open Admissions, Open Enrollment: Admissions policies involving few if any requirements.

Part-Time Student: A student taking what is considered to be less than a full load of courses, usually fewer than twelve quarter or semester units.

Prerequisite: A specific requirement (a competence, a degree, or a previous course) which must be met before one is eligible to take a particular course.

Residency Requirements: Requirements regarding residency in the state in which a school is located or amount of time spent on campus. Most public universities (state-controlled) require a student to have been a resident of that state for at least a year in order to be eligible for in-state tuition. (Out-of-state tuition is often double or more the amount of in-state tuition.) Also, most universities require that a student spend a minimum amount of terms taking courses on campus (as opposed to independent study, fieldwork, or courses in other colleges) to be eligible for graduation.

Schedule of Classes: A schedule published before each academic term listing individual classes, faculty members teaching the classes, when and where the classes are taught, etc. The schedule of classes can usually be purchased at the college bookstore.

Study Abroad, Year Abroad, Overseas Program: An arrangement sponsored by an educational institution under which a student spends at least one term, or even a year, studying at a university in a foreign country or taking part in a program on another campus operated by the student's home campus.

Transcript: An official record of courses taken by an individual student at an educational institution and of grades and credits earned.

Tuition: A sum of money which must be paid for taking courses at an educational institution. In some cases this is a flat rate; in others the rate is based on the number of units a student takes.

Upper-Division Courses: Courses taken during the junior and senior years of college; also, more advanced courses taken during the last two years. In the college numbering system for courses, usually courses numbered 100 to 199.

APPENDIX C: Regional Associations and Professional Agencies

Regional Associations

The following associations are responsible for institutional accreditation of colleges and universities in the states and territories listed:

Middle States Association of Colleges and Secondary Schools: Delaware, District of Columbia, Maryland, New Jersey, New York, Pennsylvania, Canal Zone, Puerto Rico, Virgin Islands.

New England Association of Schools and Colleges: Connecticut, Maine, Massachusetts, New Hampshire, Rhode Island, Vermont.

North Central Association of Colleges and Secondary Schools: Arizona, Arkansas, Colorado, Illinois, Indiana, Iowa, Kansas, Michigan, Minnesota, Missouri, Nebraska, New Mexico, North Dakota, Ohio, Oklahoma, South Dakota, West Virginia, Wisconsin, Wyoming.

Northwest Association of Secondary and Higher Schools: Alaska, Idaho, Montana, Nevada, Oregon, Utah, Washington.

Southern Association of Colleges and Schools: Alabama, Florida, Georgia, Kentucky, Louisiana, Mississippi, North Carolina, South Carolina, Tennessee, Texas, Virginia.

Western Association of Schools and Colleges: California, Hawaii, American Samoa, Guam, Trust Territory of the Pacific.

Professional Agencies

The following agencies are recognized by the U.S. Office of Education to grant accreditation for professional and specialized programs:

Architecture: National Architectural Accrediting Board, Inc.—five-year professional programs.

Art: National Association of Schools of Art—professional schools and programs.

Assistant to the Primary Care Physician: American Medical Association, in cooperation with the Joint Review Committee on Educational Programs for the Assistant to the Primary Care Physician—programs for the assistant to the primary care physician.

Bible College Education: American Association of Bible Colleges—three-year institutes and four- and five-year colleges.

Blind and Visually Handicapped Education: National Accreditation Council for Agencies Serving the Blind and Visually Handicapped—residential schools for the blind.

Blood Bank Technology: American Medical Association, in cooperation with the National Accrediting Agency for Clinical Laboratory Sciences—programs for the specialist in blood bank technology.

Business: American Assembly of Collegiate Schools of Business—baccalaureate and graduate degree programs. Association of Independent Colleges and Schools—private junior and senior colleges of business and private business schools.

Certified Laboratory Assistant Education: American Medical Association, in cooperation with the National Accrediting Agency for Clinical Laboratory Sciences—programs for the certified laboratory assistant.

Chiropractic: Council on Chiropractic Education—programs leading to the D.C. degree.

Clinical Pastoral Education: Association for Clinical Pastoral Education—professional training centers.

Cosmetology: Cosmetology Accrediting Commission—cosmetology schools and programs.

Cytotechnology: American Medical Association, in cooperation with the

National Accrediting Agency for Clinical Laboratory Sciences—programs for the cytotechnologist.

Dentistry: American Dental Association—programs leading to the D.D.S. or D.M.D. degree; advanced specialty and general practice residency programs; programs in dental hygiene, dental assisting, and dental technology.

Dietetics: American Dietetic Association—coordinated undergraduate programs in dietetics and dietetic internships.

Engineering: Engineers' Council for Professional Development—first professional degree programs in engineering; graduate programs; associate and baccalaureate degree programs in engineering technology.

Forestry: Society of American Foresters—professional schools.

Funeral Service Education: American Board of Funeral Service Education—independent schools and college departments.

Histologic Technology: American Medical Association, in cooperation with the National Accrediting Agency for Clinical Laboratory Sciences—programs for the histologic technician.

Home Study Education: National Home Study Council, Private Home Study Council—private home study schools.

Hospital Administration: Accrediting Commission on Graduate Education for Hospital Administration—graduate programs.

Journalism: American Council on Education for Journalism—baccalaureate professional programs.

Landscape Architecture: American Society of Landscape Architects—first professional degree programs.

Law: American Bar Association—professional schools.

Librarianship: American Library Association—five-year master's degree programs.

Medical Assistant: Accrediting Bureau of Medical Laboratory Schools—private medical assistant programs and institutions. American Medical Association, in cooperation with the American Association of Medical Assistants—one- and two-year medical assistant programs.

Medical Laboratory Technician Education: Accrediting Bureau of Medical Laboratory Schools—technical schools and programs. American Medical Association, in cooperation with the National Accrediting Agency for Clinical Laboratory Sciences—technical programs.

Medical Record Education: American Medical Association, in cooperation with the American Medical Record Association—programs for medical record administrators and technicians.

Medical Technology: American Medical Association, in cooperation with the National Accrediting Agency for Clinical Laboratory Sciences—professional programs.

Medicine: Liaison Committee on Medical Education representing the American Medical Association and the Association of American Medical Colleges—programs leading to the M.D. degree.

Music: National Association of Schools of Music—baccalaureate and graduate degree programs.

Nuclear Medicine Technology: American Medical Association, in cooperation with the Joint Review Committee on Educational Programs in Nuclear Medicine Technology—programs for the nuclear medicine technologist and technician.

Nursing: American Association of Nurse Anesthetists—professional schools of nurse anesthesia. National Association for Practical Nurse Education and Service—practical nurse programs. National League for Nursing—professional, technical, and practical nurse programs.

Occupational Therapy: American Medical Association, in cooperation with the American Occupational Therapy Association—professional programs.

Occupation, Trade, and Technical Education: National Association of Trade and Technical Schools—private trade and technical schools.

Optometry: American Optometric Association—professional programs.

Osteopathic Medicine: American Osteopathic Association—programs leading to the D.O. degree.

Pharmacy: American Council on Pharmaceutical Education—professional schools.

Physical Therapy: American Medical Association, in cooperation with the American Physical Therapy Association—professional programs.

Podiatry: American Podiatry Association—professional and graduate programs; programs for podiatric assistants.

Psychology: American Psychological Association—doctoral and internship programs in clinical and counseling psychology; doctoral programs in school psychology.

Public Health: Council on Education for Public Health—graduate professional schools of public health.

Rabbinical and Talmudic Education: Association of Advanced Rabbinical and Talmudic Schools—rabbinical and talmudic schools.

Radiologic Technology: American Medical Association, in cooperation with the Joint Review Committee on Education in Radiologic Technology—two-year programs for technologists in radiology and radiation therapy.

Respiratory Therapy: American Medical Association, in cooperation with the Joint Review Committee for Respiratory Therapy Education—programs for respiratory therapists and respiratory therapy technicians.

Social Work: Council on Social Work Education—baccalaureate and master's programs.

Speech Pathology and Audiology: American Speech and Hearing Association—master's degree programs.

Teacher Education: National Council for Accreditation of Teacher Education—baccalaureate and graduate programs.

Theology: Association of Theological Schools in the United States and Canada—graduate professional schools.

Veterinary Medicine: American Veterinary Medical Association—programs leading to the D.V.M. or V.M.D. degree.

The following organizations are members of the Council on Postsecondary Accreditation but are not on the U.S. Office of Education's list of recognized agencies.

Chemistry: American Chemical Society—undergraduate professional programs.

Home Economics: American Home Economics Association—baccalaureate programs.

Industrial Technology: National Association for Industrial Technology—baccalaureate programs.

Law: Association of American Law Schools—professional schools.

Public Health: American Public Health Association—master's degree programs; community health education.

Rehabilitation Counseling: Council on Rehabilitation Education—master's degree programs.

Index

Index

Academic adviser, 117–118
Academic fields of study, 75–76
Academic services, 117–120
   academic adviser, 117–118
   faculty adviser, 118
   mathematical-skills programs, 120
   reading programs, 119
   study-skills programs, 119–120
   writing-skills programs, 120
Academic-transfer programs, 55
Accreditation, 56–57
   for professional schools, 59–60
Admission to college, 79–108
   College-Level Examination Program, 88–90
   College Proficiency Examination Program, 90
   credit for: life experience, 102–103
     military experience, 103–104
     volunteer and homemaking competencies, 104–106
   General Education Degree test, 83–85

Admission to college:
   graduate school (*see* Graduate schools, admissions process)
   merit criteria and, 80–81
   the obstacle course, 81–83
     overcoming, 91–93
   planning for, 106–107
   Regents External Degree Examinations, 90
   rejection of application, 93
   requirements, 91–92
   Scholastic Aptitude Test, 85–88
   special programs for adults (*see* Special programs for adults)
Admission Test for Graduate Study in Business (ATGSB), 96
Adult education programs, 199
Adulthood, 131–133
Adults, special programs for (*see* Special programs for adults)
Affirmative action, 98–99
Aging (*see* Maturity, myths about)

Allen, Robert, 125
American Association of Retired Persons (AARP), 10
American College Testing (ACT) programs, 92
 decline in scores on, 98
 financial aid and, 115
 timetable for taking, 107
American Council on Education, 36
 Commission on Accreditation of Service Experience, 103–104
 Office on Educational Credit, 104
Antioch College, 102
"Athlete's exception," 99
Auerbach, Stevanne, 160–161

Bachelor of general studies, 101
Backup career plans, 18–20
Basic Educational Opportunity Grant (BEOG), 224
Bernard, Jessie, 156–157
Birren, James E., 137–138
Black liberation, x, 14
Blacks (see Minority group returnees)
Board of Governors bachelor of arts (BOG/BA) degree, 100
Bowdoin College, 98

Campus community, 9
Campus life, transition to, 27–51
  curriculum, 33–35
  educational supermarket, 29–33
  experiential education, 39–40
  faculty, 46–50
  government grants, 35–38
  from Gutenberg to McLuhan, 43–46
  instructional methods, 38–39
  mechanical aids, 46
  personalized instructions, 40–41
  prejudice: against part-time students, 58–59
   against returnees, 49
  reality gap, 27–29
   closing the, 50
  relationships and, 166–167
  responsibility for your education, 49
  returning student services, 128
  technological involvement, 41–43
  (See also Traps and traumas, avoiding)

Canadian Broadcasting Corporation, 44
Career analysis, 16–17
Career analysis worksheet, 21–24
Career change, midlife, 13–16, 163–164
Career-planning services, 123–124
Chicago State University, 100
Child care, 226
 facilities for, 126–127
 relationships with children and, 159–161
 single parent and, 165–166
Choosing Child Care: A Guide for Parents (Auerbach and Freedman), 160–161
Civil rights movement, x
 curriculum growth and, 34
Classes, 177–179
 participation in, 178–179
 types of, 177–178
Coleman, James, 203
"College boards," 85
College dropouts, 2
College Entrance Examination Board, 88–90
 Advanced Placement Program, 65
 sample tests from, 91
College-Level Examination Programs (CLEP), 88–90
College Placement Council, 11
College Proficiency Examination Program (CPEP), 90
College Scholarship Service, 115
College terminology, 231–242
Columbia University, 164
Combs, Arthur W., 148–149
Comeback Club, 203
Commission on Accreditation of Service Experience, 103–104
Community colleges (*see* Two-year colleges)
Competence, degree based on demonstrated, 101
Competition, youth-age, 205
Conference on Accrediting the Competencies Women Acquire from Domestic and Volunteer Work, 104
Confidence, lack of, 198–202
 adult education programs and, 199–200
 group counseling programs and, 200–201
 learning-skills centers and, 201–202
Conrad, Herbert S., 133, 134
"Continuing education," x, 62–63
 as college preparation, 200, 201
"Cooperative" education, 39–40

Correspondence study, 67–68
Council of National Organizations for Adult Education, 104
Counseling services, 121–124
  career-planning, 123–124
  placement, 123–124
  psychological, 121–122
    how to use, 122–123
Curriculum, growth of, 33–35

Daily Bruin, The, 29
De Beauvoir, Simone, 137, 147
De Funis v. Odegaard and the University of Washington, 99
Dental Admissions Test (DAT), 96
Divorced students, 3
  economic factors and, xi, 9
  midlife identity crisis and, 14

Eastern Illinois University, 100
Economic impetus for returning to school, 9–10
  divorced women and, 9
  earning capacity and, 10–13
    reduction in, 11–12
  inflation and, 10
Education:
  history of, ix–x
  merit criteria and, 80–81
  recent trends in, x–xi
"Educational inflation," 11–12
Educational opportunities (*see* Nontraditional educational opportunities; Traditional educational opportunities)
Educational supermarket, 29–33
  encouraging signs in, 33
  freedom and autonomy, 32
  massification, 32
  multiversities, 30
  paperwork, 31
Educational Testing Service, 85–88
  credit for life experiences and, 104
  minority students and, 94–95
  sample tests from, 91
  student survey of, 3–4
Emotional problems (*see* Traps and traumas, avoiding)
Empire State College, 101–102
Erikson, Erik, 140–142, 145, 147, 150
Etaugh, Claire, 159–160

Evening students, 20
Examinations, 180–193
  essay answers, 187–189
  grading, 191–193
  preparing for, 182–187
  tips for, 242
  tutoring, 193–194
  types of, 181–182
  writing papers, 189–191
Expectations, unreal, 209–211
  (*See also* Campus life, transition to)
Experiential education, 39–40
Experimental programs, 64–65
Extension courses, 62–63
External Degree, The (Houle), 65–66
External-degree programs, 65–67
Extracurricular activities, 210–211

Faculty, 46–50
  at four-year institutions, 58
Faculty adviser, 118
"Fear of success" syndrome, 17
Federally Guaranteed Student Loans (FGSL), 224–225
Finances:
  financial aid, 113–116, 223–225
    applying for, 115–116
    loans, 224–225
    scholarships and grants, 223–224
    types of, 114–115
  general resources and bibliography, 229–230
  graduate education and, 93
    decline in support for, 94
  sources of assistance, 225–226
  special financial resources: for ethnic minorities, 226–227
    for women, 227–229
Food stamps, 225
Four-year colleges and universities, 57–59
  admission process at, 82–83
  extension programs and, 199
  fields of study at: academic, 75–76
    vocational, 74–75
  out-of-phase feeling at, 202
  private, 59
  public, 58–59
Freedman, L., 160–161
Friends, relationships with, 161–162
Future of Marriage, The (Bernard), 156

General Education Degree (GED) test, 83–85
   sample tests and, 91, 96
   timetable for taking, 107
General Education Development (G.Ed.D.), 65
GI Bill, 10–11, 114
Goals, planning, 216–221
Goddard College, 102
Gould, Roger, 140, 143, 147
Government grants, 35–38, 223–224
   faculty and, 48–49
Governors State University, 100
Grades, 95
   transfer students and, 58, 92
   what you should know about, 191–193
Graduate Record Examination (GRE), 61, 95
Graduate schools, 60–61, 93–95
   admissions process, 95–99
      affirmative action and, 98–99
      grades, 95
      institutional response, 98
      letters of recommendation, 97–98
      qualifying exams, 95–96
      statement of purpose, 96–97
   part-time enrollment and, 19
   searching for the past and, 8
   time requirements for, 19
Grants, 114, 223–224
   era of government, 35–38
   faculty and, 48–49
"Growth and Decline of Intelligence, The," 133
Guilt-edged complex, 206–209
   home-related, 206–208
   school-related, 208–209

Handicapped student services, 128
Harvard University, 112
Health services, 124–126
High School Equivalency Examination, 83–85
"Hole-in-the-head" theory of learning, 135, 146
Homemaking competencies, credit for, 104–106
Horner, Matina, 17
Houle, Cyril, x, 7–8, 65–66
Housing services, 127

How to Improve Your Reading Skills (O'Hagan), 180
How to Study in College (Pauk), 173, 178

Identity crisis, midlife, 4–6
   career change and, 14
Independent study, 40
Inflation, 10
Instructional methods, 38–39
   audio-visual, 43–46
   mechanical aids and, 46
   personalized, 40–41
   technological, 41–43

Jarvik, Lissy, 136–137, 143
Jones, Harold E., 133, 134
Julliard School of Music, 63
Jung, Carl C., 139–140
Junior colleges (*see* Two-year colleges)

Keller, Fred S., 40
Kenyon College, 192
Kerr, Clark, 30, 48

Law School Admissions Test (LSAT), 95–96
Learning-skills center, 201–202
"Learning society," x
Legal services, 127
Letters of recommendation, 97–98
Lewis, Caleb A., 69
Life experiences, credit for, 102–103
"Lifelong learning," x
Lincoln, Abraham, 10
Loans, 115, 224–225
Locke, John, 146

McEvoy, Lee, 153, 202, 205
McLuhan, Marshall, 43–46
Margolis, Diane Rothbard, 203
Marvel, William, 28
Maslow, Abraham, 4
"Massification" of learning, 32
Mathematical-skills programs, 120
Maturity, myths about, 131–151

Maturity, myths about: biological and
    cultural clocks, 138–139
  learning revolution, 135–138
  limits to growth, 133–135
  making the most of maturity, 146–147
  manifesto for mature learners, 147–150
  milestones of maturity, 139–143
  self-awareness in maturity, 143–146
    male-female differences and, 144–146
Mead, Margaret, xi
Medical College Admission Test (MCAT), 96
Men:
  admission practices and middle-aged, 82
  cultural conditioning of, 16–17
  dropping out of college, 2
  guilt feelings of, 208–209
  lack of confidence syndrome, 198, 199
  life expectancy of, 133
  male-female differences, 144–146
  maturity myths about, 132
  midlife identity crisis and, 6
  reasons for returning to school, 156
  relationships with spouse, 156–158
  role change and, 154–155
  as school returnees, 3
Middle-aged students (see Maturity, myths about)
Military experience, credit for, 103–104
Millers Analogies Test (MAT), 95
Minority group returnees, 10
  affirmative action and, 98–99
  financial resources for, 226–227
  graduate education and, 94–95
  SAT's and, 91
Morrill Act, 10
"Multiversities," 30

National Board on Graduate Education, 94
National Direct Student Loans (NDSL), 224
National Institute of Education, 11–12
Need to know, the, 6–8
"New majority" of students, x
New York Times, The, 192
Nontraditional educational opportunities, 63–69
  correspondence study, 67–68
  development of, 63–64

Nontraditional educational opportunities:
  through educational technology, 68–69
  experimental programs, 64–65
  external-degree programs, 65–67
  nonclassroom activities, 65
Northeastern Illinois University, 100
Northeastern University, 95

Oakland Community College, 33
Obsolescence, combating, 17–19
Occupational trends, 17–18
Office on Educational Credit, American Council on Education, 104
O'Hagan, Mimi, 180
Ohio State University, 192
Open-admissions policy, 81
  at two-year colleges, 55
Ornstein, Robert, 28

Pace University, 101
Parents, relationships with, 161–162
Part-time students:
  graduate and professional programs and, 19
  prejudice against, 58–59
  time requirements and, 19
Pauk, Walter, 173, 178
Peace Corps, 34
Personalized Instruction System (PSI), 40–41
Placement services, 123–124
Plans for returning to school, 215–222
  purpose of, 216
  schedule, 221–222
  steps in, 216–221
"Prefigurative learning," xi
Professional schools, 61
  accreditation for, 59–60
  part-time enrollment and, 19
  time requirements for, 19
"Professional" students, 9
Programmed instruction, 40–41
Proust, Marcel, 8–9
Psychological counseling services, 121–122
  how to use, 122–123
Psychological preparation (see Traps and trauma, avoiding)

Radcliffe College, 30
Reading, 179–180
Reading programs, 119
    at Harvard University, 112
Reality gap, 27–29
Recommendation, letters of, 97–98
Regents External Degree Examinations (REDE), 90
Relationships, 153–168
    campus relationships, 166–167
    with children, 159–161
    with family and friends, 161–162
    other, 162
    specific life situations: the family woman, 163
        midlife career change, 163–164
        new "seniors" on campus, 164–165
        single parent, 165–166
    with spouse, 156–158
Remedial programs, 91
Retirement, 10–11
Retraining for professionals, 6–7
Returning to school, 1–25
    background of students, 1–4
    campus community and, 8–9
    career analysis, 16–17
        worksheet, 21–24
    economic impetus for, 9–10
    does learning equal earning? 10–13
    midlife career change, 13–16, 163–164
    obsolescence and, 17–19
    planning for, 215–222
        purpose of, 216
        schedule, 221–222
        steps in, 216–221
    psychological reasons for, 4–9
        midlife identity crisis, 4–6
        need to know, 6–8
        searching for the past, 8–9
    time requirements, 19–20
Ries, John C., 27, 49

Sarah Lawrence College, 30
Scholarships, 114, 223–224
Scholastic Aptitude Test (SAT), 85–88
    ACT programs and, 92
    admission procedures and, 93
    decline in scores on, 98
    timetable for taking, 107
School of your choice, 53–76

School of your choice:
    choosing a school, 69–74
        academic program, 71–72
        facilities and services, 72–73
        nontraditional program, 73
        physical characteristics, 70–71
    fields of study: academic, 75–76
        vocational or technical, 74–75
    nontraditional educational resources (see Nontraditional educational opportunities)
    options available, 53–54
    traditional educational resources (see Traditional educational opportunities)
Searching for the past, 8–9
"Self-actualization" concept, 4
Services for students (see Student services)
Sinclair, Upton, 34
Single parent, 165–166
Social security outlook, 10
Special-interest groups, 128
Special programs for adults, 99–106
    bachelor of general studies, 101
    Board of Governors bachelor of arts degree, 100
    credit for: homemaking competencies, 104–106
        life experiences, 102–103
        military experience, 103–104
        volunteer work, 104–106
    degree based on demonstrated competence, 101
    new directions, 101
    University without Walls, 101–102
Specialized schools, 63
Stanford University, 112
State University of New York:
    students at, x
    University Without Walls program at, 101–102
Statement of purpose, 96–97
Student services:
    academic services (see Academic services)
    child care, 126–127
    counseling services (see Counseling services)
    financial aid, 113–116
        applying for, 115–116
        types of, 114–115
        (See also Finances)

Student services:
  handicapped student services, 128
  health services, 124–126
  housing services, 127
  legal services, 127
  returning student services, 128
  services of the college, 112–113
  special-interest groups, 128
  veterans' affairs and services, 127
  youth orientation of, 199
Students returning to school, profile of, 1–4
Study-skills programs, 119–120
Studying, 171–194
  defining, 172–173
  essential skills, 179–191
    reading, 179–180
    taking examinations, 180–189
    writing papers, 189–191
  going to class, 177–179
    effective classroom participation, 178–179
    types of classes, 177–178
  grading, 191–193
  organizing yourself, 173–176
    physical location, 173–174, 207
    time, 174–176, 207
  tutoring, 193–194
Summer school, 62
Supplementary Economic Opportunity Grant (SEOG), 224

Tax regulations, 225–226
Teaching methods (*see* Instructional methods)
Terminology, college, 231–242
Test of English as a Foreign Language (TOEFL), 96
Tests, admission: College-Level Examination Program, 88–90
  College Proficiency Examination Program, 90
  General Education Degree, 83–85
  graduate school qualifying, 95–96
  Regents External Degree Examinations, 90
  Scholastic Aptitude Test, 85–88
  (*See also* Examinations)
Thoreau, Henry David, ix
Thorndike, E. L., 133–135
Time requirements of returning to school, 19–20

Traditional educational opportunities:
  extension courses, 62–63
  four-year colleges and universities, 57–59
    private, 59
    public, 58–59
  graduate study, 60–61, 93–95
  professional programs, 61
  specialized schools, 63
  summer school, 62
  two-year colleges, 54–57
    accreditation, 56–57
    private, 56
    public, 54–56
Transfer students:
  academic-transfer programs, 55
  private schools and, 59
  requirements for, 58, 92
Traps and traumas, avoiding, 197–213
  the drag of the past, 211–213
  guilt-edged complex, 206–209
    home-related, 206–208
    school-related, 208–209
  lack of confidence, 198–202
  out-of-phase feeling, 202–205
  unreal expectations, 209–211
  youth-age competition, 205
Tuition:
  at four-year institutions: private, 59
    public, 58
  at two-year colleges, 56
  (*See also* Finances)
Tuition-reimbursement plans, 226
Tutoring, 193–194
Two-year colleges, 54–57
  academic fields of study at, 75–76
  accreditation, 56–57
  adult education programs and, 199
  adults at, 202
  limitations of, 82
  private, 56
  public, 54–56
  tuition at, 56

U.S. Office of Education, 39
U.S. Supreme Court, 99
University of California:
  admission tests and, 83
  Center for Research and Development in Higher Education, 103, 105
  described, 30

University of California:
  Group Counseling Program for Women, 200–201
  at Los Angeles, 200
  at San Diego, 59, 69
  at Santa Cruz, 33
University of Florida, 192
University of Illinois, 100
University of Missouri, 90
University of the Pacific, 33
University of South Carolina, 101
University of Texas, 192
University of Toronto, 44
University of Washington, 99
University of Wisconsin:
  catalog of, 32
  described, 30
  miniworlds in, 33
University Without Walls (UWW) program, 101–102
  grades and, 95
  as nontraditional education, 65–67

Veterans' affairs, 127
  cold-war benefits, 225
  GI Bill, 10–11, 114
Vocational training, 11–12
  fields of study, 74–75
  at two-year colleges, 55
Volunteer work, credit for, 104–106

Warner, Aaron, 164
Western Illinois University, 100
Widowed students, 3
  economic factors and, xi
  midlife indentity crisis and, 14
Wilms, Welford, 11–12
Women:
  admission requirements and, 92–93
  affirmative action and, 98–99
  career-motivation of, 35–36
  child care facilities and, 126–127
  CLEP test and, 90

Women:
  credit for life experiences and, 104–106
  cultural conditioning of, 16–17
  divorced, 3
    economic factors and, 9
  equal educational opportunities, 114
  the family woman, 163
  fear of being out of touch, 7
  "fear of success" syndrome, 17
  financial resources for, 227–229
  Group Counseling Program at UCLA, 200–201
  guilt feelings of: home-related, 206–208
    school-related, 208–209
  lack of confidence syndrome, 198–202
  life expectancy of, 133
  male-female differences, 144–146
  maturity myths about, 132
  menopause and, 132, 139, 145
  midlife identity crisis and, 4–6
  new directions program and, 101
  out-of-phase feeling and, 202
  reasons for returning to school, 155–156
    psychological, 4–6
  recent trends in education and, x–xi, 35–36
  relationships with spouse, 156–158
  role change and, 154–155
  as school returnees, 3
  sex discrimination and, 14
  special programs for, 30
  statement of purpose and, 96–97
  supporting husbands through school, 2, 6
  underemployment of, 11
Women's liberation, x, 14
  curriculum growth and, 34
  lack of confidence and, 198
  nontraditional education and, 64
  role change and, 154
Worcester Polytechnic Institute, 101
Work-study programs, 115
Writing-skills programs, 120

Youth culture, 203, 204